THE AMAZING EMPEROR HELIOGABALUS

Published by Palatine Press

New York City, NY

First published 1911

Copyright © Palatine Press, 2015

ABOUT PALATINE PRESS

Ancient Rome forged one of the greatest and most influential empires in history, and books written by and about them continue to be popular all over the world over 1500 years after its collapse. Palatine Press is a digital publishing company that has reproduced the greatest works ever written by Romans, from the poetry of Virgil to the philosophy of Marcus Aurelius, as well as histories of Rome written by historians like Edward Gibbon.

PREFACE

The life of the Emperor Marcus Aurelius Antoninus, generally known to the world as Heliogabalus, is as yet shrouded in impenetrable mystery. The picture we have of the reign is that of an imperial orgy—sacrilegious, necromantic, and obscene. The boy Emperor, who reigned from his fourteenth to his eighteenth year, is depicted amongst that crowd of tyrants who held the throne of Imperial Rome, by the help of the praetorian army, as one of the most tyrannical, certainly as the most debased.

Few people have made any study of the documents which relate to this particular period, and fewer still have taken the trouble to inquire whether the accounts of the Scriptores are trustworthy or consonant with the known facts.

To this present time no account of the life of this Emperor has been published. Histories of the decline and fall of Imperial Rome there are in plenty ; other reigns have been examined in detail ; German critics have sifted the trustworthiness of the documents, few in number and all late in date, which refer to other reigns; so far nothing has been done on the life of Elagabalus.

The present writer started this study with the view that the Syrian boy-Emperor was, in all probability, what his biographers have painted him, and what all other writers have accepted as being a substantially correct account of the absence of mind, will, policy, and authority which he was supposed to have betrayed, along with other even more repre-hensible characteristics.

The first reason to doubt this estimate came from the continually recurring mention of a per-petual struggle between the Emperor and his female relatives ; a fight in which the boy was always worsting able and resolute women, carrying his point with consummate tact and ability, while allowing the women a certain show of dignity and position, where it in no way diminished the imperial authority or his own prerogative.

This circumstance alone was scarcely consonant with Lampridius' account of a mere youthful debauchee, who had neither inclination nor will for anything, save a low desire to wallow in vice and unspeakable horrors as the be-all and end-all of his existence.

On further inquiry, another circumstance obtruded itself, namely, that the boy had a vast religious scheme or policy, which he was bent on imposing on his subjects in Rome, and indeed throughout the world. This policy was the unification of churches in one great monotheistic ideal.

Religion may be neurotic in itself, but the scheme of Elagabalus was not essentially so. Certainly the course of action by which he purposed to effect his ideal was not that of a mere sensualist. It showed understanding, persistency, and dogged determination ; it was not popular, because in the general incredulity, the earlier deities had lost even the immortality of mummies.

Yet another reason which forced one to disagree with the usual summary of the character under discussion was that, despite (i) the awful accounts of the imperial orgies; (2) the accusations brought against the cruelty and incompetency of the government ; (3) the announcement that all good men were exterminated in the general lust for destruction of such worthies; (4) the account of the class and calibre of the men employed in all state offices; (despite all this) the authors inform us that the state did not suffer from the effects of the reign. This was obviously an impossibility at the outset, and the terminological inexactitude became even more ap-parent when all the known good men were mentioned as peaceably holding office, not only during the reign in question, but in that of Elagabalus' successor; either they had been resurrected or had never been exterminated.

Again, the account given of the military policy is not that which would be the work of a weakling.

The fiscal policy may have been unchanged, but the edict which enforced the payment of Vectigalia in gold, showed a considerable amount of sense, in demanding the payment of taxes in the one coin whose standard had been maintained when all others had been debased by preceding Emperors, and no one had been worse than the great financier Septimius Severus in this debasing of the currency.

In legal matters alone we are told that the period was sterile, because only five decrees of the reign are recorded by the editors of the *Prosopographia*. This may be true, but it is quite possible, in fact more than probable, that in later redactions much of the work which Papinian, Paul, Ulpian, and other such produced during this reign has been embodied in later decrees or codifications, and one can scarcely imagine that these men were entirely sterile for four years in the zenith of their authority.

Again, it is most noticeable that in the mass of abuse and obvious animus which the "life " exhibits, there is not one definite act of cruelty reported ; no wanton murder is cited; no hint given that the people were discontented with the appointments made, or that they suffered from any of the misrule which had been so prevalent for years past. On the other hand, we are told that the people considered Elagabalus a worthy Emperor, despite all that could be said to his discredit.

Chiefly it was this too obvious animus, shown on each page of the documents, which led the writer to examine the opinions of German and Italian critics on the measure of credibility which could safely be attached to the Scriptores Historiae Augustae. It was an agreeable surprise to find that their estimates of the Scriptores ranged from those of men who stigmatised the whole collection as an impudent and unenlightened forgery to men who, like Mommsen, contended that, though originally the lives might have had some real historical value, they had been so edited and enlarged as to lack the essential weight of historical evidence, and contained, as they stood, but a modicum of consecutive and unvarnished fact.

Authorities being so far in accord, the present writer set to work to sift the accounts which were obviously quite unnaturally biased, and to separate what was merely stupidly contradictory from what was mutually exclusive.

This method has been applied merely to the first seventeen sections of Lampridius' work, the portion which professes to contain a more or less historical account of the events from Elagabalus' entry into Rome to his disappearance into the main drain of the city.

In the latter portion of the life there is a wealth of biographical detail, which, in plain English, means an account *in extenso* of what has been already described too luridly in the foregoing sections. It is written in Latin, and has never been translated into English, to the writer's knowledge, nor has he any intention of undertaking the work at this present or any other time, as he has no desire to land himself, with the printers and publishers, in the dock at the Old Bailey, in an unenviable, if not an invidious and notorious position.

Those, however, who are capable of reading the Latin tongue, and therefore inured against further corruption, will find an excellent edition published in Paris by M. Panckoucke in 1847. The last three chapters in the present volume are an attempt to bring together all the material capable of publication in these seventeen sections, and take the form of three essays on the main figures of the Emperor's psychological imagination. They are in no way an endeavour to expurgate the sections referred to, as any such attempt would leave one with the numerals as headings and the word " Finis" half-way down a sheet of notepaper. It is better for the sapient to read the chapters for themselves, and so all men will be satisfied.

It has also been impossible, on the same grounds, to criticise the statements here made; the greater part are, like those in the biographical portion, frankly impossible, when not mutually exclusive. It is needless to say that the author accepts the whole with all the Attic salt at his disposal.

Another anomaly that may strike the reader is the fact that various names are used to designate the Emperor. Tristran remarks that " they are as many as the hydra has heads." The present idea is to use the titles which the boy bore at the different stages of his life, rather than apply to him on all occasions the nickname which was attached to him after his death.

In the earlier part of the work I have referred to the youth as Varius and Bassianus, the two names which appear most frequently, in reference to his reputed fathers, but have neglected Avitus, by which title he is occasionally known, in reference to his grandfather, as also that of Lupus, which is sometimes found in Dion, because, as Dr. Wotton remarks, there is no means of finding out whether he was so called (if ever he was given the name at all) on account of some ancestry, by reason of a false reading, or on account of some other matter now long laid to rest.

After the Proclamation, I have preferred to call the Emperor by his official name, Marcus Aurelius Antoninus, or Antonine for short, as this is the only manner in which the coins, inscriptions, and documents describe him. After his death, it seems allowable to give him the nickname which his relations and later biographers have applied to him, namely, the latinised form of the name of his God. I have nowhere adopted the later Greek spelling or adaptation, Heliogabalus, either when referring to the God of the Emesans or to the Emperor himself. The only form in which the name occurs in inscriptions is in describing the Emperor as " Priest of Elagabal" or the Sun. Lampridius certainly Hellenised its form a century later, on what grounds is by no means clear, when one realises that neither the boy nor his God had any trace of Greek blood, tradition, or philosophy about them, and that the identification of a particular Syrian monotheism with Mithraism or general Sun worship is not universally admitted as a necessary consequence, either in the case of Elagabal, Jehovah, or indeed in that of any of the other " El" claimants to exclusiveness, though the balance of probability may lie on the side of the identification. It is further unnecessary to drag in the Hellenised form of the Emperor's name in order to pander to a popular and erroneous conception of the reign, which conception this book is designed to combat and generally offend. Heliogabalus is nevertheless the sole title by which this Emperor is known to the world at large, in consequence of which I have allowed the name to stand on the title-page, chiefly in order that Mrs. Grundy's prurient mind may know, before she buys or borrows this volume, that it is the record of a life at which she may expect to be shocked, though she will in all probability find herself yawning before the middle of the introductory chapter.

As I understand the reign, the main object on the part of the boy's murderers in nicknaming him Elagabalus after his death, was to throw discredit on his memory by depriving him of the venerated title Antonine, and substituting therefor the name of a Syrian monotheistic deity, who by his exclusiveness was an offence and a byword in the eyes of the virile, pantheistic philosophy which then held sway.

A word must also be said as to the attitude in leaving untouched much of the scandal attaching to this Emperor's name. I have only been able to deal with the public side of his character, as there are no coins or inscriptions which refer to his private life, and have in consequence been forced to quote what the tradition, gained from his traducers' writings, states was his unfortunate abnormality.

These traditions may be true wholly or in part, they certainly could only be disproved by the actual persons implicated, who have written neither for nor against the Emperor's psychological condition. The traditions, however, as far as they treat of the public position and reputation of the Emperor, have been shown to be grossly unfair where they are not horribly untruthful, and may be—in all probability are—of an equal value, when they discuss private practices about which no one can have had any particular knowledge except his actual accom-plices. Suffice it to say, that any stick is good enough to beat a dog with once he is incapable of defending himself, and in this case it has been laid about Antonine's shoulders with almost diabolical ingenuity.

I much regret that I have been unable to find any portraits of the Emperor for whose authenticity Bernouilli will vouch. Alone of the whole family-there remain authentic busts of Julia Mamaea and Julia Paula, neither of whom are important enough to be included, since we are unable to give a portrait of Elagabalus himself. I have therefore confined myself to the use of coins, whose veracity is un-doubted, hoping that the reader will supply from his imagination that charm and beauty which the biographers have been unwillingly forced to allow both to the Emperor and his mother.

In the preparation of this work I have had much valuable and kindly assistance, for which I desire to acknowledge my deep indebtedness here. First, to Professor Bury of Cambridge, for his unwearying and sage advice on my whole manuscript; also to Dr. Bussell, Vice-Principal of Brasenose College, Oxford, for his interest and kindly corrections; to the authorities in the Bodleian Library; to the assistants in the British Museum, especially to Mr. Philip Wilson and Mr. A. J. Ellis for their continued help in my work there, and to Mr. Allen for the time and care he has spent in helping me find the coins that explain the text.

I have also to acknowledge with sincere thanks the permission of Mr. E. E. Saltus of Harvard University to quote his vivid and beautiful studies on the Roman Empire and her Customs. I am deeply indebted to Mr. Walter Pater, Mr. J. A. Symonds, and Mr. Saltus for many a *tournure de phrase* and picturesque rendering of Tacitus, Suetonius, Lampridius, and the rest. I also desire to thank Dr. Counsell of New College, Oxford, and Dr. Bailey of the Warneford Asylum, not only for their help in correcting my proofs, but also for their assistance in the preparation of my chapter on Psychology.

To all these gentlemen I owe a great debt, which, I hope, the general public will repay by an appreciation of their work. We have endeavoured to right a wrong; if our efforts are in any way successful, the reader will acknowledge that this *mauvais quart d'heure*, which has been stigmatised as full of impossible situations and intolerable surprises, is in reality a very human life which, like our own, has its exquisite moments of which we would as soon deprive ourselves as Elagabalus.

INTRODUCTION

The Emperor who is studied in this volume has commonly been treated as if his reign had no signi-ficance, unless it were to show to what deep places the Roman Empire had sunk when such a monster of lubricity could wield the supreme power. If the chronicle of his naughty life has been exploited to illustrate the legend that the pagan society of the Empire was desperately wicked and infamously corrupt, he has not been taken seriously as a ruler. Yet Elagabalus appeared under too ominous a constellation to justify us in dismissing his brief attempt to govern the world as unworthy of more than a superficial description and a facile condemnation. His reign lasted less than four years; but those years fell in a period which was critical for the future of European civilisation, and he was brought up in a circle intensely alive to the religious problems which were then moving the souls of men. Mr. Hay has broken new ground, and he has done history a service, in making Elagabalus the subject of a serious and systematic study.

The third century, so obscurely lit by poor and meagre records, saw the Empire of Rome shaken to its foundations. There was a manifest decline in its strength and efficiency, marked by the insolent domination of the common soldier, and luridly illustrated by the statistical facts that from Septimius Severus to Diocletian the average reign of an Emperor was about three years and that there were only two or three sovereigns who were not the victims of a mutiny or a conspiracy. As one of the efficacious causes of this decline has often been suggested (most recently by M. Bouché-Leclercq) the detachment of men's interest from the public weal by the attraction and influence of individualistic oriental religions, which did not aim at securing the stability of the state, like the old religions of Rome and Greece, but undertook to save the individual and ensure his happiness in a life beyond the tomb. It is undoubtedly true that in this period religious currents were stirring society to its depths, and several rival worships were engaged in a competition of which the issue was decided in the following century. And if the state was really weakened by a cleavage which had become sensible between the private spiritual interests of the individual citizen and the public interests of society, if its cohesion was endangered by the tendency to place the former interests above the latter, we can understand the statesmanship of Constantine the Great, who, by closely connecting the state with one of those individualistic religions, conciliated and identified the two interests. I do not suggest that Constantine formulated the problem in the general terms in which we may formulate it now; he was pushed to his far-reaching decision by a variety of particular social facts, which involved the general problem, while they forced upon him a particular solution. But the problem which he solved had long been there, and a hundred years before Constantine established Christianity, another Emperor had attempted to solve it. That Emperor was

Elagabalus.

The religious currents of the age of the Severi did not escape the notice, or fail to engage the interest, of the Court. Julia Domna, Julia Mamaea, Alexander Severus, were all under the influence of the spirit of the time. These were the days in which Julia Domna and Philostratus discovered for the world a new saviour in the person of Apollonius of Tyana. But the religious zeal of Elagabalus was more passionate than the intellectual interest of any of his house. He conceived a universal religion for the Empire, and his abortive attempt to establish it is examined by Mr. Hay with a full sense of its significance and an unprejudiced desire to understand it.

With all his unashamed enthusiasm, Elagabalus was not the man to establish a religion; he had not the qualities of a Constantine or yet of a Julian ; and his enterprise would perhaps have met with little success even if his authority had not been annulled by his idiosyncrasies. The Invincible Sun, if he was to be worshipped as a sun of right-eousness, was not happily recommended by the acts of his Invincible Priest. I have said "idiosyncrasies"; should I not have said "infamies"? But it is unprofitable as well as unscientific simply to brand Elagabalus as an abominable wretch. His life is a document in which there is something demanding to be comprehended. If all men and women are really bisexual, this Syrian boy was of that abnormal type in which the recessive is inor-dinately strong at the expense of the dominant sex; he was a remarkable example of *psychopathia sexualis*; but in his age there were no Krafft-Ebings to submit his case to scientific observation. From this point of view, which Mr. Hay has taken, Elagabalus becomes an intelligible morbid human being. And the young man, though so highly abnormal and spoiled by the possession of supreme power before he had reached maturity, was far from being repulsive. A salient feature of his character was good nature ; he appears to have wished to make everyone happy. His pleasures were not stained by the cruelties of Nero. It amused him to shock people, but he was always good-humoured. He is said to have genially inquired of some grave and decorous old gentlemen who were his guests at a vintage festival, whether they were inclined for the pleasures of Venus. The anecdote, if not true to fact, seems to be character-istic. It is told in the *chronique scandaleuse* of Lampridius, one of the writers of that Augustan History round which a forest of critical literature has grown up in recent times. The outcome of all the criticism is generally to the discredit of these authors, and Mr. Hay has the merit of having strictly applied this unfavourable result to the Life of Elagabalus.

But though the religious enterprise of this eccen-tric Emperor was doomed to fail, it was not by any means the wild project of a madman, which those who judge *post eventum*—after the triumph of Christianity—or who, like Domaszewski, see in it merely *eine Vergöttlichung der Unzuckt*, are apt to take for granted that it was. In those days, it was not in the least certain, as yet, that Christianity would be chosen and its rivals left; this religion was not, as its apologists would have us believe, the only light in a dark world. To a disinterested mind it would appear that Mithra or Isis might have become the divinity of western civilisation. They were certainly well in the running. We may guess what circumstances aided the worship of Christ to rise above competing cults, but for inquirers, like Mr. Hay and myself, who hold no brief, and do not accept the easy axiom that what happens is best, it is unproven that Christianity was decidedly the best alternative. Perhaps it was. Yet we may suspect that, if the religion which was founded by Paul of Tarsus had, " by the dispensation of Providence," disappeared, giving place to one of those homogeneous oriental faiths which are now dead, we should be to-day very much where we are. However this may be, it seems that in the third century the Christians were far from commending their doctrine to the rest of the world by any signal moral superiority in their own conduct. The bad opinion which pagans held of their morals in the time of Tertullian cannot be explained as a mere wilful prejudice, and Tertullian's reply that the charge is only true of some but not of all nor even of the greater number *(Ad nationes,* 5) is a significant admission that, taking them all round, the Christians were not then conspicuous as a sect of extraordinary virtue. Moreover, there was nothing in the ethics of their system which had not been independently reached by the reason of Greek and Roman teachers, and they are entitled to boast that the success of their religion depended not on any superiority in its moral ideals to those of pagan enlightenment, but on its supernatural foundations.

Slander, with ecclesiastical authority behind it, dies so hard, that I may take leave to add a remark which to well-informed students of antiquity is now a platitude. The offensive performances of Elagabalus prove nothing as to the prevailing morality of his time, just as the debauches of Nero prove nothing for his. To judge the private morals of the pagan subjects of the Empire from the descriptions of Suetonius and Lampridius is even more absurd than it would be to portray the domestic life of Christian England from the reports of the Divorce Court. The notion that the poor Greeks and Romans were sunk in wickedness and vice is a calumnious legend which has been assiduously propagated in the interest of ecclesiastical history, and is at the present day a commonplace of pulpit learning. If pagans, in ignorance or malice, slan-dered the assemblies and love-feasts of the early Christians, it will be allowed that Christian divines of later ages have, by their fable of pagan corruption, wreaked a more than ample revenge.

Among readers of Gibbon, the very name of " Heliogabalus" will always "force a smile from the young and a blush from the fair." But it may be expected that, after Mr. Hay's investigation, it will be recognised that this Emperor made, according to his lights, a perfectly sincere attempt to benefit mankind, which must be judged independently of his own moral or physiological perversities.

J. B. BURY.

THE SCOPE OF THIS BOOK

The age of the Antonines is an age little under-stood amongst the present generation. The documents relating thereto are few in number, and for the most part the work of very second-rate scandal-mongers. Like the Senate of the time, these writers had so far lost their sense of personal responsibility that they were quite willing to record anything that their " God and Master" ordered. The pleasures and vices of the age were lurid and extravagant. The menace of official Christianity, with its destruction of literature and philosophy, was almost at the gates of the city. All which facts serve to render this most magnificent period of Roman history unreal and fantastic to men of our more practical and rationalistic age.

The reign of Elagabalus is not a record of great deeds. It shows no advance in science or in military conquest. Save in the realm of jurisprudence, it is not an age of great men, because these are born in the struggles of nations. It is not an age of poverty or distress. It is rather a record of enormous wealth and excessive prodigality, luxury and aestheticism, carried to their ultimate extreme, and sensuality in all the refinements of its Eastern habit. Such were the forces that swayed the minds of these eager, living men, made idle by force of circumstances.

It was a wonderful and a beautiful age, full of colour, full of the joy of living ; and yet, as we look back upon its enervating excitements, who can wonder at the greatness of the decline which followed the triumph of so much magnificence ? Rome was at the apex of her power; the Empire was consolidated ; the temple of Janus was closed; the Pax Romana reigned supreme, and with it order and government in the remotest corner of that vast dominion. What mattered the extravagances of a foolish boy to the merchants of Lyons or to the traders of Alexandria, so long as they were undis-turbed and taxation was at a minimum ? What mattered the blatant outburst of a Semitic mono-theism, when men's minds—amongst the super-stitious—were already attuned to the kindred mysteries of Mithra and the spiritual chicanery of Isis ? The harm had been done both to reason and to ancient belief by the secret dissemination of other superstitions, whose effete neuroticism, whose enervating and softening influences had done almost more to ruin the glorious fighting strength of the Empire than all the luxury and effeminacy of the bygone world.

It was a pitiful exhibition, the powers of ignor-ance and mystery undermining the strength of knowledge and virility, till the barbarians, whom the very name of Rome had conquered and held entranced, overthrew a greatness which, in the age of reason, the world had found irresistible. It is pitiful, but it is true, and the record of merely a part will be found in the Augustan Histories.

The difficulties presented to the student of the Scriptores Historiae Augustae are manifold and ever increasing. Not the least of them lies in the variation of standard by which this collection has been judged, and in the diametrically opposing theories which eminent scholars have drawn from the same passages.

The criticism owes its origin to the confusions which are bound to exist in any series of lives covering a period of 167 years and purporting to be the work of several—though none of them con-temporary—writers.

The Biographies which have survived are nomin-ally the work of six authors, to wit, Aelius Spartianus, Julius Capitolinus, Vulcacius Gallicanus, Aelius Lampridius, Trebellius Pollio, and Flavius Vopiscus. The author of the Life of Elagabalus in this series is Aelius Lampridius, of whom personally nothing is known. Peter[1] postulates that he was not a plebeian, as he wrote at Constantine's bidding, and presumably, from the virulence of his attacks, with some ulterior object in view. This was probably an attack on the Imperial author of that species of Mithraic worship which Constantine desired to extirpate, as the most formidable opponent of his own new religion.

Lampridius dedicates his Life of Elagabalus to this Emperor, which at once shows us that at least 100 years had passed since the events recorded had taken place, and calls for an inquiry into the sources of Lampridius' information. The text as it stands to - day is at times incomprehensible, largely through the efforts of scholars of the Bonus Accursius and Casaubon type,[2] while Dodwell in 1677 played his part in corrupting, according to his lights, what must always have been a document whose need of further mutilation was highly un-necessary. The first attempt at modern criticism of the texts began in 1838, when Becker[3] of Breslau endeavoured to reassign the various lives to their respective authors, without very much success. In 1842 Dirksen[4] of Leipzig attempted to ascertain the sources employed by the various Scriptores, and their use or misuse of the material to their hands. He founded his criticism mainly on the recorded speeches and messages of the Emperors, which, unfortunately for the theories then put for-ward, were discovered by Czwalina,[5] in 1870, to be largely spurious.

The next work of any importance was done by Richter[6] and Peter,[7] when the former tried to date the Scriptores themselves from internal evidence; the latter threw light on the time when the actual lives were written, and, amongst others, assigns Lampridius'

---

[1] *Die S.H.A. Sechs litterar-geschichtlicht Untersuchungen,* Leipzig, 1892.

[2] See Peter, *Hist. Crit.* cap. ii. ; Bernhardy, *Proemii de S.H.A.*

[3] *Observationum S.H.A.,* Breslau, 1838.

[4] *Andentungen zur Texteskritik,* 1842.

[5] Czwalina, *De epistularum auctorumque quae a S.H.A. proferuntur,* Bonn, 1870

[6] " Über die S.H.A.," *Rhein. Mus.* vol. vii.

[7] Peter, *Hist. Crit. S.H.A.,* Leipzig, 1860.

Life of Elagabalus to a period in or about the year a.d. 324. In 1865 the same author[8] placed the study of the Scriptores on a firmer basis altogether, by introducing the system of textual criticism as applied to the sources, both Latin and Greek, from which the writers had drawn their facts.

Amongst Latin sources the chief name mentioned was Marius Maximus, of whose works nothing now remains. He was Consul under Alexander Severus and a devoted servant to that Emperor, at whose direction he attempted to complete Suetonius [9] by a popular and scandal-mongering edition of recent events. Mueller,[10] in 1870, after a careful investigation of all the references to this author, concluded that his work was the compilation of a volume styled *De vitis imperatorum,* which contained the lives of Nerva, Trajan, Hadrian, Antoninus Pius, Marcus, Commodus, Pertinax, Julianus, Severus, Caracalla, and Elagabalus. That the last of these lives should have been written by the friend and servant of Elagabalus' murderers is in itself unfortunate, as one immediately suspects that some attempt will be made to justify the crime, or at any rate that veiled malignancy rather than a true historical portrait will be the result. It is easily discovered from the shortest perusal of the wealth of mere abuse which it contains that no veil was considered either necessary or expedient, and that if Lampridius drew his information of the Emperor Elagabalus from Maximus, as a sole source, his work was, historically speaking, as worthless a caricature as that with which Maximus had bolstered up Alexander's government. Mueller, therefore, propounded the theory that though Maximus was the main Latin source, other authors were used by the Scriptores in a supplemental way. In this theory he was supported by Ruebel, Dreinhoefer, and Plew,[11] who cite, amongst other names, that of Aelius Junius Cordus, an author who is quoted with considerable frequency throughout the lives. This theory of one main Latin source—Maximus— held ground until quite recently, when the work of Heer, Schulz, and Kornemann, as we shall see, put a somewhat different, if less satisfactory, complexion on the matter. It may be remarked, in passing, that Niehues,[12] in 1885, attributes the earliest life of Macrinus and his son Diadumenianus—amongst other

---

[8] *Peter, Jahresbericht,* 1865-82, " S.H.A."

[9] *Ibid.*

[10] " Der Geschichtschreiber Marius Maximus," *Untersuch.* vol. iii., Leipzig, 1870.

[11] Ruebel, *De fontibus quatuor priotum S.H.A.,* Bonn, 1872; Dreinhoefer, *De auctoribus vitarum quae feruntur Spartiani,* etc., Halle, 1873; Plew, *Marius Maximus, als direkt undindirekt Quelle der S.H.A.,* 1873.

[12] *De Aelio Cordo reruvi Augustanwi scriptore commentatio,* Muenster, 1885.

Emperors whose period does not concern us in this present inquiry—to Cordus rather than Maximus, which may account for a certain amount of impartiality about Macrinus' life, there being no special end to serve either way.

The Greek sources used by the Scriptores are more easily fixed, for, though most of the authors have perished, the work of Herodian is preserved, and the abbreviation of Cassius Dio, which was made by Xiphilinus of Trebizond for ecclesiastical purposes, is still readable. It is perhaps necessary to state Haupt's[13] opinion that the Scriptores did not actually transcribe the Greek sources, and that these can only give one a certain idea as to how the writers used their materials. Unfortunately for the reign in question, neither of these two authors can be considered as unprejudiced authorities. Indeed, circumstances have conspired to obscure the history of Elagabalus at every point. Cassius Dio is by unanimous consent the best historian of the third century, infinitely superior to Maximus as a man of literary ability and historical insight; he is not highly exciting, and has an annoying habit of mistaking sententious platitudes for speculative - philosophy. His impartiality is certainly very questionable, and his obviously superstitious credulity notable. But these defects are easily overlooked by the student, because his work does embody a vast store of information on the workings of the Imperial system. In all probability he was absent from Rome during the reign of Elagabalus, since he tells us (79-7) that Macrinus appointed him Curator of Smyrna and Pergamum in the year 218, from which posts he was not removed by Elagabalus.[14] When next he appears it is as the friend and servant of Maesa, at the beginning of Alexander's reign. He was then—successively— twice Consul, Proconsul of Africa, Governor of Dalmatia and Pannonia Superior, and presumably died under Alexander at 80 years of age, as we have no work from him after that date. As servant of the dominant faction, Dio's history must have been compiled to support Maesa's action in causing the murder of Elagabalus, and to justify the succession of Alexander, when once the women had cleared the headstrong boy and his mother from their path. Dio advances his information as that of an eye-witness, and as such it was presumably derived from the same source as that of Maximus— so much so, that Giambelli[15] in 1881 tried to prove that Dio's main source for his history was Maximus throughout and none other.

The other Greek contemporary is Herodian, the facts of whose life are by no means certain. Kreutzer[16] thinks that he came to Rome about the beginning of the third century,

---

[13] **Haupt, *phiologus*, xliv. 575**

[14] **Dio, lxxx. 1.**

[15] **Gli Scrittori della Storia Augusta, 1881.**

[16] **De Herodiano rer. Rom. scriptore, 1881.**

and subsequently held some minor administrative posts in the government. He stands on a different plane from Dio, as he possessed very small qualifications as a historian. He narrates, it is true, salient features of court life and current foreign affairs, though he has small conception of their bearing and less regard for their chronology. In this matter it is only fair to remember that the ignorant emendations of Bonus Accursius and a tribe of mediaeval scholars may account for much that now looks so outrageous.

As regards the sources from which Dio and Herodian took their facts, much has been written, though the attempts[17] made since 1881 to show that both used Maximus are at best poor and inconclusive. Mueller[18] in 1870 pointed out with some considerable weight that the similarities which exist between the parallel accounts found in Herodian and the Scriptores were probably due to the fact that both had used Maximus. This line of argument was developed by Giambelli and Plew[19] on the basis of a supposition that Herodian had been worked over before he was used by the Scriptores, thus endeavouring to account for the discrepancies between Herodian and Maximus, and supporting the Maximus-as-root-base theory of both authors. Boehme[20] in 1882 introduced the name of Dexippus as the probable intermediate writer, and pointed out that the references made by certain Scriptores to Herodian, under the name of Arrianus, are hard to understand if the scriptor had the correct name before him. Certain passages can however be shown to have been taken direct from Herodian, on account of which Peter[21] entirely rejected the Dexippus intermediary theory a few years later. In the main, however, the general authenticity of the sources, whether Greek or Latin, was accepted up to the year 1889, though one or two discoveries had been made which weakened their hold and prepared the way for the general attack.

The first was made by Czwalina[22] of Bonn in 1870, who declared that the documents and letters in the Life of Avidius Cassius were spurious ; and in 1880 Klebs[23] destroyed the authenticity of those at the end of Diadumenianus' Life. Things were more or less quiet until the year 1889, when Dessau[24] opened his attack on the general authenticity

---

[17] Giambelli and Plew, *opp. citt.*

[18] *Op. cit.* p. 82.

[19] *Marius Maximus als direkt und indirekt Quelle der S.H.A.,* Strassburg, 1878

[20] Boehme, *Dexippi fragmenta,* 1882, pp. 10-11.

[21] *Die S.A.H.,* pp. 49, 102.

[22] *De epistularum auctorumque quae a S.H.A. proferuntur,* Bonn, 1870.

[23] " Die 'Vita' des Avidius Cassius," *Rhein. Mus.* vol. xliii., 1888.

of the Scriptores' work, asserting from the strongest internal evidence, such as their mention of persons and things—in lives dedicated to Con-stantine as Emperor—which did not happen till after his death, that the lives were the work of a forger in the later part of the fourth century; a man who had been stupid enough to give an appearance of antiquity to his work by the use of names and dedications borrowed from older sources, but not smart enough to avoid the inclusion of glaring anachronisms.

Mommsen[25] at once undertook to defend the authenticity of the collection, asking saliently why a forger of Theodosius' time should undertake to praise the extinct dynasty founded by Constantius. The very patchwork, he says, is enough to prove the collection no forgery. Again, the use of pre-Diocletian geographical names, such as those given to the legions, all date from a period prior to Diocletian. Mommsen then proceeds to his criticism, in the course of which he divides the lives into primary and secondary, which to his mind solved the problem, and on this basis he drew entirely different conclusions from the facts which Dessau had adduced as proofs of forgery. The progress of Mommsen's study forced him to admit what he had so entirely repudiated at first, that the lives do contain hints of a later period, all of which, he asserts, can be accounted for by the manner in which the collection took form. Mommsen's opinion, as finally stated, was that about a.d. 330 an editor collected the available material and then filled in the gaps with his own work. Again, at a later time a reviser retouched this whole collection and added the evidence of the latest period, which has caused all the trouble. By him also the work resembling Eutropius and Victor was inserted. It is not the clearest of statements, and had to be so modified, as it proceeded, that it certainly has not the weight attaching to it that others of Mommsen's works carry.

During the year 1890 two works appeared, the first by Seeck,[26] who attempted to assist Dessau, the other by Klebs,[27] who had accepted a modified Mommsen estimate of the authenticity of the Scriptores. Seeck began by pointing out that a work which was first heard of in the latter part of the fourth [28] century was not likely to arouse sufficient interest to induce any one to revise it during the earlier part of that century. He attacked the work attributed to Vopiscus, Pollio, and Spartianus in particular, pointing out, in the case of Vopiscus, that had he written under Constantine he would not have put him

---

[24] Dessau, " Über Zeit und Persönlichkeit der S.H.A.," *Hermes,* xxiv. 337-92, 1899.

[25] "Die S.H.A.," *Hermes,* xxv. 228-92.

[26] "Die Entstehungszeit der S.H.A." *Neue Jahrbuch Phil.,* vol. cxli.

[27] " Die Sammlung der S.H.A.," *Rhein. Mus.* vol. xlv.

[28] Seeck, *op. cit.*

second in the dedication,[29] or, if Pollio had written in the third century, when the title Mater Castrorum was commonly given to the Empresses, he would never have spoken of it as a speciality in Victoria's case.[30] If Spartian wrote under Diocletian, it is obvious that he must have had a prevision of that Emperor's sudden change of plan as to the succession. Klebs[31] in the same year further modified Mommsen's position, and explained the similarities to Victor and Eutropius as due to the use of the same sources by these authors and by the Scriptores, and rejected the idea of a revision by a late hand on the ground that no one would be so foolish as to imitate the style of the original writers for the sake of inserting nonsense; certainly not the most convincing of the arguments which might have been used by a man who presumably had at least heard the history of the Gospel additions. A later article (1892)[32] was more conclusive, as here he attempted to prove that no one forger could have adopted the variety of attitude towards both the Senate and Christianity which we find expressed in the various sections of the " lives," while the presence of geographical names and official titles, lost before the beginning of the fourth century, point to earlier authenticity, not later forgery.

Woelfflin[33] in 1891 supported Mommsen on textual grounds. He traces the differences of style to the fact that certain authors had used Suetonius, others Maximus, while others again had trusted to their own retentive memories, not altogether a safe historical criterion. He states that the traces of similarity running through the works are due certainly to a reviser, but that the reviser was Vopiscus,[34] which either puts Vopiscus at a much later date than had ever been done before, or resigns the idea of a late reviser in the Mommsen sense.

Dessau[35] in 1892 replied with a scathing attack on this same Vopiscus, from the point of view of his age and the impossibility of his having seen and heard all he claims to have done. Seeck[36] in 1894 published a second article supporting Dessau with six points culled from titles and names not known till after the reputed dates of the

---

[29] *Carinas,* xviii. 3.

[30] T. Pollio, *Trig. Tyr.* v. 3, etc.

[31] Klebs, " Die Sammlung der S.H.A.," *Rhein. Mus.,* vol. xlv., 1890.

[32] *Ibid.* vol. xlvii.

[33] "Die S.H.A.," *Sitzungsber. der philos.-philol. Klasse der Bayer. Akad.,* 1891.

[34] *Op. cit.* p. 479.

[35] " Über die S.H.A., " *Hermes,* vol. xxvii., 1802

[36] " Zur Echtheitsfrage der S.H.A.," *Rhein. Mus.* vol. 49.

Scriptores. He now considers that plurality of authors, or forgers, as the case may be, is certain, and that they wrote, or forged, as Diocletian and Constantine gave command, using for their work many sources, including the Imperial Chronicle. But it is an inconclusive article.

In 1899 an American, Dr. Drake[37] of Michigan, published some studies in detail on the life of Caracalla, which tended to establish the genuineness of certain portions which had been thought spurious. Heer[38] of Leipzig followed in 1901 with a critical survey of the life of Commodus, dividing it into two parts, the first chronological, the second biographical, and came to the conclusion that, though the chronological part was trustworthy, the biography was derived from very poor sources, and was only in part contemporaneous. Schulz[39] in 1903 applied the same methods to the lives from Com-modus to Caracalla, in 1904 to the life of Hadrian,[40] and in 1907 to the lives of the house of Antonine,[41] unfortunately leaving out Elagabalus.

Kornemann[42] in 1905 attempted to bring together the materials of the lives from Hadrian to Alexander Severus, much on the lines of Schulz's work. He points out that the characteristic note was to be found in the author's interest in the affairs of state, as opposed to those of war, and how Alexander Severus has been raised to his pinnacle of smug propriety on account of supposititious favours to the senatorial body, while extreme animus is betrayed towards the warlike Emperors or those who, like the paternal despots of the Antonine House, trusted in the army and only used the " slaves in togas" for ratifying any decree that they might think necessary, a mode of procedure in government to which that body had long been slavishly subservient. Kornemann goes on to suggest that this fondness for Alexander presupposes the writer's work having been published during that Caesar's reign, especially as no trace is found of his work later. Kornemann then invents a new name for our old friend Marius Maximus, and calls him, with some further show of scholarship, one Lollius Urbicus,[43] a theory which still only interests Kornemann. Heer[44] in 1901 had given him a certain support, however, in

[37] " Studies in S.H. A., " *Amer. Journ. Phil.* vol. xx., Baltimore, 1899.

[38] *Der historische Wert der* Vita Commodi.

[39] *Beiträge zur Kritik der Uberlieferung der Zeit von Commodus zu Caracalla,* 1903.

[40] *Leben des Kaisers Hadrian,* Leipzig.

[41] *Kaiserhaus der Antonin,* Leipzig.

[42] *Kaiser Hadrian und der letzte grosse Historiker von Rom,* 1905.

[43] Quoting Diadumenianus, ix. 2.

refus-ing to believe that any one could have credited Maximus with any part in the chronological side of the lives, and Schulz in his Life of Hadrian adopted the same view, assigning the references to Maximus to a later hand. It was Peter[45] who, in 1905, asked pertinently why Maximus should be ousted from the authorship of the chronological source in favour of an *unknown* contemporary, though he admitted, with some freedom, that many of the citations from Maximus stood in passages of questionable value, or seem to have been thrust into the text.

In 1899 Tropea[46] of Padua published a treatise on the general literature of the S.H.A., in which he shows that the aim of the collection was political, and in the interest of the reigning house ; in consequence of which he postulates that it is either falsified in fact, or wholly fabricated in the sense that Czwalina had already suggested. Tropea was followed by his pupil Pasciucco,[47] who examined the life of Elagabalus in detail in 1905. The result of this examination was to show that Lampridius had not only failed to examine his sources of information, but had exhibited a singular lack of order and

proportion in his imaginations. Pasciucco concluded with the illuminating remark that Lampridius' sources are either fabulous or of little value, and answer only to the political complexion which that writer had adopted.

In 1904 Lecrivain[48] published an admirable conservative presentation of the available material, which, with Schulz's work on the Imperial House of Antonine in 1907, leaves the textual criticism of the sources in a sufficiently nebulous condition to please the majority, at any rate for the time being.

In the light of the foregoing criticism and the almost universal conclusion, drawn by both parties, as to the obvious want of impartiality not only amongst the sources but also in the lives themselves, the scope of this work will limit itself to a psychological criticism of the life of Elagabalus, as contained in the Augustan Histories. These documents, as will be remembered from the foregoing summary, are a collection of heterogeneous and unenlightened com-positions, to which Lampridius, by no means the ablest contributor, has added the life of the Syrian boy-emperor Marcus Aurelius Antoninus. Lamp-ridius exhibits to a striking degree the want of method and order, the vain repetitions and frequent contradictions, the lack of historical insight and love of petty detail which characterise the whole collection. This he shows to such a degree

---

[44] *Op. cit.* pp. 145 ff.

[45] *Berlin, phil. Wochenschriften,* xxii. p. 489, xxv. p. 1471.

[46] *Studi sugli S.H.A.,* Messina, 1899

[47] *Elagabalo,* Feltre, 1905.

[48] *Etudes sur hist. Aug.,* 1904, Paris.

that it would be as obviously unfair to regard his biographical compilation on Elagabalus as historical fact, as the more than questionable " ten denzschriften," which were his sources of information; the perusal of which must have left the compiler with a distorted view of events, even had he started with a fair and unprejudiced mind. This certainly was not Lampridius' outlook, as is evinced by the obvious animus against his subject portrayed on every page both in his unsupported accusations and in his puerile fault-finding.

In all probability this series of lives was never intended to be more than a succession of scandal-loving biographies, designed to take the place of the improper little novels which used to be imported from Greece, but whose supply was falling short with the decadence of Greek literature.

In the result, the biographies of the Augustae Historiae Scriptores are for the most part an inartistic farrago of unordered trivialities, which modern criticism has shown to be late in date, and with little or no individual significance. Their whole value depends on their source, or sources, and these have been proved, at least biographically speaking, to have been only too often untrustworthy. The Life of Elagabalus, as caricatured by the particular Scriptor, or forger, is not even an attempt to portray historical events in either their chronological or natural order; it makes no mention of the origin of the Emperor, his claims to the throne, his fight with Macrinus, nor yet of the facts of his subsequent government. It is merely one vast stream of personal abuse and ordures, directed against the memory of the great exponent of that monotheism which was the chief danger to Constantine's theories in a similar direction ; while Lampridius' sources are vitiated by the fact that they are Imperial attempts to blacken the memory of a murdered Emperor, whose popularity with the masses made his murderer's position insecure on the throne of the world.

It may not be altogether fair to charge the young Alexander personally with the murder of Elagabalus, and even if one does, it is only right to remember that he claimed a certain justification for the deed.[49] Alexander affirmed that he had himself been in danger of death at his cousin's hand on more than one occasion. Undoubtedly, the true instigators of the murder were Mamaea, Alexander's mother, and Maesa, the common grandmother of the cousins. Both of these women saw power and authority passing from their hands, and could ill brook a second place in the direction of the government. By their machinations, bribery, and corruption, they had endeavoured already three times to suborn the Praetorian Guard. But the effort had failed. Sufficient men had always been wanting for the project, and only an unlucky chance threw the Emperor into the hands of those few on the day of his death. Alexander's complicity in this crime might have been overlooked, on account of his youth, had not his strenuous efforts to justify the deed called atten-tion to his attitude, not of regret, but of exultation in the

---

[49] *Vide* cap. vi. *Vita Alex. Sev.*

crime. This attitude is most clearly seen in the scandalous literary productions which alone disgrace the name of Elagabalus, all issued from the pens of Cassius Dio, Herodian, and Maximus, —or Lollius Urbicus,—all three servants and bedesmen of Alexander and his female relatives.

Surely if it had been possible to give proof of cruelty, tyranny, bloodthirstiness, deceit, or guile, the record of these deeds would have filled the pages of the paid traducers; but contemporaries, who loved Elagabalus too well for his generosity, charm, and beauty, would know better. The only course open to the writers, therefore, was to attack personal habits of which the outside world knew little and cared less, because they were habits that affected no one save the boy's familiars, who were perfectly free to depart if they objected to his manners or conversation.

As regards the later compilers of Imperial histories, mention must be made of Zosimus and Zonaras, the twelfth-century editors of Cassius Dio, who, however, add little to our knowledge. They are of a certain value because they omit many of the scandals before produced, while the same may be said for Aurelius Victor and the *Breviarium* of Eutropius.

The Church historians make little mention of the period ; they were undisturbed by persecutions, and had no emperor or praefect to abuse. They were, in fact, so busy inventing the difficulty of the diphthong and developing Pauline theories on the doctrine and position of Christ, that they had but little time for the real facts of life and progress around them. Origen is a slight exception, but then his pride had been Mattered by a summons to Court, where, Eusebius tells us, he discussed astronomical theology with the now visionary Julia Mamaea— who seems to have aped her aunt, Julia Pia, in these matters. Origen's pride was further nattered by the dignity of a Praetorian escort on the journey to Antioch—he does not mention the return voyage —which was certainly a most astonishing honour, for which one would like to have other than sacer-dotal confirmation.

Further literary authorities, such as Sextus Rufus, Orosius, John of Antioch, and Jordanis, though inferior in weight, have obviously got some of their information from sources other than those open to the Scriptores, and their statements may be accepted with reserve, unless they can be shown to be irrational and contrary to known facts.

When all is gathered in, the sum total of the recorded history, as Mr. Cotter Morison[50] says, is meagre to a degree. The investigation of the various isolated records in the light of what is known of the movements and tendencies of the age —combined with the psychology of the boy's char-acter—is and must be the key to much that at first sight seems contradictory and obscure in the scandals reported—none of which, as Niebuhr has said, are capable of historical treatment with anything like an assurance of accuracy. In this part of the biography Lampridius himself is of considerable use. In the

---

[50] *Life of Gibbon.*

course of his vituperation he is continually letting fall allusions and observations revealing a character, instincts, and religion which he is quite incapable of comprehending, and can only malign with a vitriolic vehemence worthy of a better cause. His very vehemence is fortunate, since it has left the way open for psychology and science to proclaim the abuse, what we now know it to be, both malicious and untruthful.

The evidences from the jurisprudence of the reign are certainly unsatisfactory. Later codifications have left us with but few dated laws of a reign that stands in the golden age of Roman juris-prudence. Ulpian, Papinian, and Paul were not men to allow a break in the order of legal succes-sion, and though Ulpian was presumably banished in connection with Alexander, it was not until within a few months of Elagabalus' death. Sufficient remains to show us that the Empire suffered no break in the perfect autonomy of jurisprudence, justice, and government, throughout a period which Forquet de Dorne[51] has dignified under the pseudonym of the reign of military anarchy.

Cohen and Eckhel are of great importance in fixing, as nearly as possible, the chronology of the period, by their records of the medals and coins of the reign. The same may be said of the inscriptions which have escaped the vandalism of the Emperor's enemies. Duruy, in his great history, is unwilling to give the medals much biographical weight, comparing them to the governmental journals of all times, which give only the account of events as seen through official spectacles, and on which as little reliance can be placed as on the published bulletins of victories : witness the Parthian medal of Macrinus, the record of a great victory for the Roman troops over Artabanus; the real fact being a colossal defeat followed by a peace, the latter purchased in a manner disgraceful to both the people and the arms of Rome.

Inscriptions are unfortunately few and far between, owing to the fury with which Alexander and his relatives pursued Elagabalus' memory. Undoubtedly it was no new thing to call upon the Senate to execrate the memory of a murdered rival. It was, in fact, one of that body's most important functions during the period under discussion. Rarely has the work been done so thoroughly and effectively, which says something for the zeal of Alexander and the money he spent in extirpating all reference to the memory of Elagabalus.

The works of Valsecchius[52] and Turre,[53] amongst seventeenth-century scholars, are illuminating on the subject of the length of Elagabalus' reign. Tristran's[54] attitude shows

---

[51] *Les Empereurs syriens*

[52] *De M.A.A.E. trib. pot.,* **Florence, 1711**

[53] **Bishop of Adria.**

[54] **Tristran Sieur de St-Amant,** *Commentaires historiques,* **Paris, 1635.**

the slavishness of tradition ; certain of Saumaise's[55] emendations show the same tendency despite his usual impartiality; in fact, all have accepted the tradition of wickedness without the least question as to its *fons et origo*. This work proposes to take the texts as they exist, and endeavour from their unwitting statements of the boy's psychology to convict them of untruth. From their unsupported charges of secret crimes, to show that real crimes were largely non-existent, and to throw the burden of all the ordures which have covered this Emperor's name on to the shoulders of his relations and murderers, to whom alone it was a vital object to destroy his fair renown before a world which loved him. That his world did love him, de-spite all, there are manifold traces. The prodigal Emperors always were adored; so were their suc-cessors, the wicked popes. Man was too near to nature to be aware of shame, and infantile enough to like to be surprised. That was Elagabalus' scheme ; he amused his people and surprised them at the same time.

The whole spirit of tolerance of the unusual makes it difficult for us to picture Rome. Modern ink has acquired Nero's blush ; yet, however sensitive a writer may be, once Roman history is before him although he may violate it, may even give it a child, he never can make it immaculate. He may skip, indeed; and it is because he has skipped so often that you may fancy Augustus was immaculate. The rain of fire which fell on the cities that mirrored their towers in the Bitter Sea might just as well have fallen on him, on Virgil, on Caligula, Nero, Otho, Vitellius, Titus, or Domitian [56] why, then, condemn Elagabalus alone unheard, save for the fact that his relations hated him, and as far as we can see, hated him without a cause, or perhaps because he was growing too strong, and his unfortunate disease gave them their opportunity to gain that power after which the women were striving like grim death ?

---

[55] C. Saumaise, *S.H.A.* vi., *Notae et emendationes*, **Paris, 1620.**

[56] *Vide* Suetonius, *Lives of the Emperors.*

CHAPTER II. THE FAMILY OF THE EMPEROR MARCUS AURELIUS ANTONINUS

Great houses, says a historian, win and lose undying fame in less than a century ; they shoot, bud, bloom, bear fruit; from obscurity they rise to dominate their age. indelibly to write their names in history, and after a hundred years give place to others, who in turn take the stage, while they descend into the crowd and live on insignificant, retired, unknown. This is true, in some periods, but not of the Imperial houses of Rome. Their flight across the stage was meteoric in its rapidity. A generation saw the rise and total extinction of many of those families who aspired to the Roman Purple, particularly the revived house of Antonine.

On the borders of the Orontes, in that part of Syria which is known as Phoenicia, lies a small, disagreeable, and melancholy-looking town, which to-day bears the name of Horns, or Hems. It is a construction of yellow and black stones mixed with mud and broken straw, and is the rendezvous of Curds. Bedouins, and Turkomans, a straggling village, where dirt, squalor, and misery proclaim the absence of trade, roads, or contact with an outside world. A short distance away are the ruins of an ancient castle, built by the Crusaders to dominate the route to Antioch. Here alone is there a trace of fruitfulness, a sort of oasis of green gardens, extending along the river-bank towards what was once the graceful and beautiful capital of the Elagabal monarchy, the famous city of Emesa—celebrated under the independent High-Priest Kings of the family of Sohemais for the splendour of its palaces and the magnificence of its temple, and because it was the headquarters of the worship of the God of Gods, Elah-Gebal, or Baal, which is the name more familiar to Christian ears. For us the chief interest in this wretched village lies in the fact that it is the home of that race of Syrian Emperors who ruled Rome during the period of her greatest renown and prosperity—a period when the splendour of the Purple reached its apogee. Rome had been watch-ing a crescendo that had mounted with the ages ; it culminated in the revived Antonine house; but the tension had been too great, something snapped, and there was nothing left. So it had been with Emesa ; her splendours endured sorrowfully until the twelfth century, and then were engulfed, as her house had long since been, in a great earthquake which devastated that part of Syria, along with lesser-known parts of the earth's surface.

Little is known of the early history of the hereditary High-Priest Kings of Emesa. Strabo tells us that, like the neighbouring sovereigns of Jerusalem, their origin was sacerdotal, to which functions they had attached the title and jurisdiction of secular rulers on the breaking-up of the Seleucid monarchy.

The most famous princes of the Emesan dynasty of High-Priest Kings were Samsigeramus and his son Iamblichus, the friend of Cicero. In the war between Octavius and Antony this prince found he had taken up arms on the wrong side, and was killed by Antony for fear of treachery. In the year 20 b.c. Augustus re-established the kingdom of Emesa in favour of the son of Iamblichus, which kingdom certainly continued until the time of Vespasian, according to Froelich, and probably until Antoninus Pius, during whose reign we have the first known Imperial coins of Emesa (Eckhel). The kingdom was small, and the wealth, except the revenue which came as religious offerings, insignificant— facts which undoubtedly decided the rulers of the time to yield gracefully before the advancing arms of the universal Emperor, who, in return, left the High-Priest Kings a certain amount of political as well as their inherent religious authority, much in the same way that he left the family of Herod their nominal monarchy, along with the support of a similar Babylonian religion. Certainly the fame of the temple at Emesa and the oracle of Belos at Apamea was widespread, and the hereditary High Priest in the year of grace 179 was an astute gentleman.

In that first year of the reign of the Emperor Commodus there was appointed to the command of the fourth Scythian legion then quartered in Syria, in all probability, as Peter thinks, at Emesa itself, an African, one Septimius Severus by name, a native of Leptis Magna in Tripoli, born in the year 146, and therefore about the age of thirty-three years.

Whether or not he was a widower at the time is uncertain. He had previously married a lady, by name Marcia, but as no children by her are known to have existed, it is probable that she was either dead or repudiated by that year, added to which his precocious inquiries as to the marriageable young women in the neighbourhood presuppose that the general was either free or at least travelling *en garçon*.

The High Priest of the period was—according to two references in the Epitome of Aurelius Victor —a certain Julius Bassianus, descended in hereditary line from the afore-mentioned Iamblichus. Certainly he was not a plebeian, as Dion says, somewhat sneeringly, when referring to his daughter's origin, unless, of course, Dion meant in point of comparison with the rank to which she eventually attained.

It was certainly a happy chance that Bassianus possessed not only a wise prophet, but also a super-stitious commander in the army of occupation, and was astute enough to work both for the miraculous profit of his house and lineage. Unfortunately he had no daughter old enough for an immediate marriage. She who is presumed the eldest, Domna by name, was at the time only nine years of age, having been born in the year 170, whilst her sister Maesa was presumably somewhat younger.

But to return to the Oracle. In the year of grace 179, when Septimus found himself in a peace-ful province, *en garçon* and very much admired, he took an interest in the marriageable daughters of important persons, like most young men of ambition in their more calculating moments, and—being a religious-minded man—he determined to consult the gods, especially the famous voice which spoke so near at hand. Here he learnt that to the elder daughter of Bassianus was reserved, according to her horoscope, the power of making the man whom she should wed a king. It was an ambitious height to which Septimius aspired, and an ambition which would have cost him his life had Commodus got bruit of the transaction. Never-theless, being a prudent man, and at the same time ambitious, he resolved to let no chance slip. He did what Bassianus expected—demanded the lady's hand and obtained the reversion thereof.

At what date the marriage took place is by no means certain; there are two references in Dion which are mutually exclusive. The first says that the Empress Faustine (who, by the way, the same Dion says, died in 175) herself prepared their marriage bed in the precincts of the temple, which sounds a highly unsatisfactory beginning to ordinary matrimony. But as he has just told us that the lady was of an age of five in the year above mentioned, it is highly improbable that her nuptial couch would be prepared by any one, or anywhere, for some time to come, especially as there is no indication that Septimius had heard of the lady before 179, when he consulted the Oracle.

Again, Dion assumes that Marcia did not die until Septimius was appointed Governor of Lyonese Gaul about the year 187, so that her husband could only have been playing with astrology, wise prophets, and other things against the time when the obex to solid matrimony should be removed. Possibly even Dion is referring—when he drags in the Empress Faustine—to Septimius' first marriage, or, as has been suggested, the whole thing was a dream of either Septimius or Dion, probably both, as both were much addicted to such proceedings. Considering the so-called scandal against the lady's character, her proclivities, and the knowledge that her eldest son Bassianus was born at Lyons on April 4, 188, it is most natural to conclude that the marriage took place sometime in the spring of the year 187, though the pledges may have been given when the child was nine years old or thereabouts, and the actual marriage deferred till Julia's seventeenth year, Septimius amusing himself in the interval, after the manner of soldiers. It must be admitted that, as the record of his scrapes is limited to two, he was more discreet than the majority of his profession.

His choice of a wife, if made on unusual grounds, was more than successful. Few Emperors have had more renowned ladies or more helpful spouses than Julia Domna Pia, the daughter of Bassianus, proved herself to Septimius. It was fortunate that she had more than a horoscope to assist her in her new position. Even the governorship of Lyonese Gaul was an important post, and there she had large scope for the use of her wit, learning, beauty, and wisdom, in addition to her Syrophoenician adaptability for amorous intrigues. By means of which combination the family became people of renown throughout the length and breadth of Pertinax's Empire, a circumstance which enabled them, on the murder of that Emperor, to assume the role of avengers, the deliverers of Rome, the saviours of the Empire, which had now three heads but no commander.

It was Julia, we are assured by Capitolinus, who decided her husband to assume the

Purple ; it was Julia who first amongst Empresses was Domna, or Mistress, Mater Castrorum, Mater Senatus, Mater Patriae, Mater Totius Populi Romani. Of course she had the sad notoriety of being mother to Caracalla, and late authors *(vide* Tertullian *ad Nationes)* have reproached her with many indiscretions—have even accused her of conspiring against her husband ; but Dion, who is by no means partial to her, mentions neither accusation, and the absurdity of the latter throws doubt, at least on the public knowledge of the former story. In any case her elevated mind, her four children, and her rank, even when combined with her sun-warmed nature, ought to have protected her from anything except occasional amusements, of which she might have preferred her husband ignorant. Julia's real fame rests on the basis of her character as a mathematician, an astrologer, and a wise counsellor. The fruit of her learning and philosophy has been handed down to all time by her friend and associate Philostratus in the dedication to her of his Life of Apollonius, the miracle-worker of Tyana, the Thaumaturge whose life and miracles are sup-posed to form so large a part of the traditional life of Jesus as it exists to-day.

In the palace Julia Domna had gathered round her a circle of learned men, where all subjects were discussed, and whence, in all probability, a contemporary derived his idea of the *Deipno sophistae.* It was a circle of rhetoricians, lawyers, astrologers, physicians, philosophers, and historians, which included men such as Cassius Dio, Ulpian, Papinian, Paul, Galen, and Philostratus—one and all names which speak volumes for the gravity of the lady and the perfection of her taste. If, therefore, any truth is to be attributed to the account of her frailties, the worst that can be imagined of the pious Julia is, that like the Virgin Queen of this country, she took her recreations in those ways which nature and temperament prompted, while the main business of her life was social, political, and philosophical. Many, like Bayle, have made merry over the carnal anecdotes, though surely for a true judgment of her character the preservation of a single conversation with Philostratus of Lemnos would be worth the record of a thousand dull intrigues—in surmise— for which familiarity has bred contempt.

Besides which, Severus lived in the bosom of his family, or rather of his wife's family, the Bassiani. With his two sons and two daughters there had come to Rome about the year a.d. 193 the family of his wife's sister Julia Maesa, a lady for whom fate had provided no Imperial horoscope, and who in consequence had no right to be anything like as ambitious as her sister the Empress. Maesa was, however, equally beautiful, equally clever, and equally determined to climb, if climbing were possible. To her mind Rome was the place where fortunes were to be made if you had an Imperial connection, so to Rome Maesa came. She had married, at an early age, the Proconsul Julius Avitus, by no means an undistinguished government servant. The fact that he held the governments of Asia, Mesopotamia, and Cyprus successively, and was Consul in the year 209, says something for the trust which was reposed in him. He seems to have been resident in Rome in his own mansion on the Aesquiline — according to Lanciani—

from the year 193, a fact which presupposes that he was already a man of wealth and position, who considered himself justified—on account of his relation to the Imperial home—in resigning the government of the provinces, though at no time was the proconsulship an unprofitable possession, even for the most upright. Herodian testifies most fully to the wealth of the family, lead-ing us to suppose that Maesa knew full well that " poverty is no recommendation anywhere," and had amassed money accordingly.

At the period now before us Maesa's political ability seems to have had little or no scope. It was gold she wanted at that time, and gold she was getting together against an emergency. This emergency fate provided under the Emperor Macrinus, and

she was thus enabled to use her stores of gold and statecraft with much profit both under Elagabalus and in the early years of Alexander's reign. She was then free, and showed herself in her true colours, a sort of Dowager-Empress after the Chinese pattern, greedy, with a terrible eagerness for power, authority, and a command such as Julia with more good sense had never thought of encompassing. It was a longing that she had to satisfy at the price of her treasure, her popularity—if ever she had any—even at the price of her own children's blood. Maesa's family consisted of two daughters, whose sons were both to become renowned Emperors, men whose names live by their very eccentricities, though their deeds are but far-off fables meet for the acrimonious discussions which make historians famous. Of the two daughters, Soaemias, or Symiamira, the elder, was less of the politician, had less of the calculating, self-possessed individuality which was so strong in both her mother and sister, who were both women with the true courtesan instinct, which could turn their very amours to substantial account. Soaemias was certainly no ruler. She was a living, passionate, human woman, full of the joy of life, generous both for good and evil, courageous too, according to Herodian. By common consent, she was voluptuous, devoted to those who loved her, willing to give her very life for that of her well-loved son. A woman who was bound to be popular with men, and hated by her sisters for all time, both on account of her qualities and her defects.   To such a nature the position Lampridius ascribes in the state would have been utterly impossible. Nor is this borne out anywhere by the existing inscriptions, which always make Soaemias take a place second to that of Maesa, except in the Senate on the Quirinal, which was her special concern.

Soaemias married some time before the year 204 Sextus Varius Marcellus. He was, according to Dion, a native of Apamea, and a man of some considerable prominence. As early as 196 we hear of him in the position of Procurator Aquarum, and his advancement, presumably helped by his connection with royalty, was very rapid. Through the usual grades of procuratorships he reached the rank of Praefect in early life, and thence the height of ambition, the Praetorian class of the Senatorial order. At the time of his death he was about to complete his term of office as Legatus Legionis III. Augustae, Praeses provinciae Numidiae, or may just have vacated that position ; at least such is the reading of the inscription according to Domaszewski, who puts his death sometime in the year a.d. 217. The young couple seem to have had an estate at Velletri, a city some twenty-five miles south of Rome ; as here Varius Marcellus' funeral inscription was found some short time back. Whether or not her husband's praefectorial duties left Soaemias much to herself can be judged by the statement, made by all authorities, that she spent the greater part of her time with her aunt at Court, which she could scarcely have done had her husband been at Velletri.   There is a question raised by Eckhel as to the number of her children; he cites from a Bilingue Marmor, which contains the inscription —"Julia Soaemias Bassiana cum *filis*" but as this is the only mention of any children, apart from Bassianus himself, the others have passed into obscure oblivion. Probably this mention is responsible for more than one of the many scandalous stories which centre round her name. She certainly had one son, Varius Avitus Bassianus (sometimes also called Lupus). Whether he was first, second, or last, we have no sort of information. Various writers give the boy different names in early life; few agree even as to the year of his birth. Dion says that he was born on October 1, 204. Herodian, for no discoverable reason, puts it as early as 201, while both Ammianus Marceliinus and Julianus imply that his birthplace was Emesa, which latter fact seems most improbable. Bassianus' very parentage is obscure, on account of the re-putation which his mother had acquired during her residence in Rome. Certainly her cousin Caracalla admired her, but he admired most women of the type, and if we can believe any of the scandals, Soaemias was in no way averse to passing her time in amorous converse with her very vigorous cousin, or indeed with any other strong and healthy soldiers who thronged the imperial ante-chambers. This state of affairs seems to have been one of which people in Rome were well aware, as was testified by the vestal whom Caracalla, having im-potently failed to violate, burned alive, protesting her innocence on the grounds that Soaemias had put it beyond the power of Caracalla to violate her when he tried.

In one way it was a misfortune for her son that no one could fix exactly—perhaps his mother least of all—the paternity of Bassianus, though, on the other hand, this very uncertainty had its peculiar uses at the psychological moment. Certainly the discovery that she had other children, whilst Bas-sianus alone comes to the front, lends countenance to the official story that her attachment to Caracalla was not unfruitful, while the name Bassianus, which her son bore, was the name by which Caracalla was always known until the time of his proclamation, and even afterwards. At any rate there is nothing unlikely in the imperial paternity which all authors mention, some as conjectural, some even assuming as a fact, with, however, very little chance of ascertain-ing the arcana of the circumstances. There is and can be, at any rate medically speaking, no truth in the abominable suggestion of Lampridius, that the boy was named Varius on account of the variety of gentlemen who contributed to his *mise en scene,* especially when Lampridius knew, if he knew any-thing at all, that the lady's husband was by name Varius. What, therefore, was more natural than that the lad should bear the family name along with the other belonging to his natural father the Emperor Bassianus ?

The reputed birthplace is certainly a mystery. Why Soaemias should have taken the long and tiring journey to Emesa, when she could have enjoyed herself so much better in Rome, has never been explained. Even though the birth were an accident which she wished to conceal from her husband, why go to Emesa, where she was best known out-side Rome, and where people could talk just as well as in the imperial city ? Her husband may have been absent on military or civil duty for too long a time to stop people talking about the interesting event (in some provinces the tenure of office was five years), which would suggest things best left undiscovered, but even then there were many such accidents happening in the best-regulated families. No one would be shocked, her family was in too good a position to allow any such expression of feeling; she was a married woman and could claim the protection of that state of life at Terracina, or Baiae, or any other seaside resort, until the time was safely over. There seems no suggestion possible that will accord with Julianus' implication. It may be true, though we can see no earthly reason for the journey, and, in the absence of corroboration, we may conclude that in all probability it is merely a loose way of saying that the family of a man belongs to a certain village or island, without necessarily implying that the person in question was himself born there. It may even be a backhanded way of disparaging the birth of him whose memory had to be slighted, by saying that he was a mere provincial nobody, whilst the birth of his murderer and successor is vaunted and raised to great splendour by circumstantial untruth, in order to prove him fully *capax imperii.*

The second daughter of Julia Maesa was Julia Mamaea. While still abroad with her family, she had married another Syrian, by name Gessianus Marcianus, a native of Area. Nothing is known of him except from Dion's statement that he had filled, more than once, the office of Imperial Procurator. By this marriage Mamaea incurred the *capitis diminutio* on account of the inferior rank of her husband, but by means of a privilegium from Severus and Caracalla she was allowed to retain her own Senatorial rank. Of this admirable woman none of the frailties so common amongst her family and rela-tions are reported. She lived and died a model of unswerving rectitude. This affectation she carried almost to the Jesuit extreme, when she made use of her reputation and wealth to obtain the murder of the nephew of whom she so highly disapproved and by whose murder she would benefit so materially. There is, of course, the story of one indiscretion with Caracalla, by means of which she consented to gain popularity for her son. She, as well as her sister, claimed the distinction of having been Caracalla's mistress, and Alexianus, as well as Bassianus, was claimed as the result of that cousin's too amorous embraces. The admission was doubtless due rather to a hypocritical affectation of wickedness, prompted by the political exigencies of the moment, than to the fact that her cold and stately beauty had unbent to tempt a too ardent cousin by the offer of those seductive attractions which he could get so easily elsewhere. Especially as the assumption of this role of temptress might

cause her in after-life all the reproaches of a misspent youth, with little to show for the sacrifice. Perhaps mention ought to be made of the opinion of Dexippus, that the boys Bassianus and Alexianus were cousins-german *paternal,* which, as we know from theologians, when they are fitting facts to theory, is the same thing as brothers by the same father. Certainly Mamaea's beauty is remarkable. As we see it in her bust at the Louvre, she is a younger edition of her aunt Julia, perhaps without the humanity and gentleness expressed in that lady's portrait, which is to be found in the Rotondo at the Vatican, but there is a real resemblance between the two. Both, though Syrian by race, are remarkably Western in type, whereas the features of Julia Soaemias—in the statue representing her as Venus Coelestis, also in the Vatican museum—are dis-tinctly of a more Oriental cast. Soaemias' form is most beautiful, though it must be confessed that her head and arms would have pleased Rubens' taste better than they do our present pre-Raphaelite ideas of attractiveness. Soaemias' history, however, leaves no doubt in our minds that all men considered her the more attractive at the time ; and certainly, if but a tittle of the stories concerning her be true, she must have been as fascinating as the goddess in whose form she has been portrayed.

We have now before us the main personages in the political revolution of the year a.d. 218, a revolution which displaced the Moor, the beloved of the Senate, and replaced the house of Severus, the beloved of the army, upon that peak whereon the young Emperors of old Rome balanced them-selves—a peak with a precipice on either side.

First, there is the *Empress Julia Domna Pia,* clever, witty, sagacious, and beautiful.

Then her sister, *Julia Maesa, Sanctissima,*—for so her religiosity is described—the widow of Julius Avitus, wealthy, hard, crafty, and domineering, but a woman with a policy and limitless determination, as her later history shows. Then her two daughters—

Julia Soaemias Bassiana, the wife of Varius Marcellus, beautiful, voluptuous, religious, neurotic, the mother of Elagabalus, a woman with few, if any, political aspirations, tendencies, or abilities.

Julia Mamaea, the upright (except when other things paid better), classic, cold, calculating, philosophic, mildly interested in Christianity, and devoted to the interests of her own family.

Finally, the two successive Emperors, their sons, *Varius Avitus Bassianus,* the impulsive, affectionate, headstrong child of about thirteen years, with all his mother's hereditary sexuality, neurotic religion, and love of life ; and *Alexianus,* a child of approximately nine, Mamaea's son, and bearing her reputation, of whom more at a later time.

Let us follow in outline the actions and movements of this family from the death of the Emperor Antoninus Caracalla to the inception of the movement which placed his, at least reputed, son in his place.

Without doubt the family had lived securely and delicately in Rome through the reigns of Septimius Severus and his son, growing in wisdom, stature, and prosperity, and, as far as we know, in favour with God and man, until the tragic events of the year 217 made it appear that the fortunes of the family had come to a sudden and decided collapse. The circumstances of the death of Caracalla were typical of that age of sovereignty. As a general rule the knife gave what a dish of mushrooms took away. Caracalla's government had been cruel and severe in the extreme, but he was adored by the army, with whom he lived and worked, not as Emperor, but as comrade. For them he could never do enough in the way of privileges, for them the treasury was depleted, and cities turned into cemeteries that they might have the booty. Fighting was as natural to him as to a tiger cat; and fighting he died. It was for the pursuit of a campaign against the Parthians that the Emperor and Court had moved to Antioch in Syria, where Julia, his mother, was acting as Secretary of State, while the Emperor was bounding like a panther upon the various cities of Mesopotamia. In the pursuit of her duties, it happened that there came into her hands certain letters warning her of a plot against her son's life.

With the army at that time was a praefect, Opilius Macrinus by name, a Moorish lawyer of low birth and pedantic habits. He had been procurator to Plautianus, the so-called traitor, whom both Julia and Caracalla had hated. Now Macrinus had been honoured by Severus after Plautianus' murder, and still stood high in the imperial favour—though he was treated by the Emperor, says Dion, as a sort of buffoon. Macrinus had dreamed that the purple should be his, and was supported in his wish by the African astrologer Serapion, who was obliging enough to prophesy the speedy demise of Aurelius Antonine in Macrinus' favour.

Julia immediately sent dispatches containing the account of what was going forward to her son, who, as usual, was absent from the city. When these arrived in the camp, Caracalla was just mounting his chariot, and gave orders that the mail should be taken first to Macrinus, who would sift its contents and only bring what was necessary to the Emperor. Thus did Macrinus learn that his treachery was discovered and a death-sentence for real or supposed treason imminent, which un-pleasant certainty he resolved to obviate without further delay. In a very few days he had discovered a discontented person willing to do his work, one Martialis, a centurion, whose brother, according to Herodian, had recently been executed for some military offence, or, in Dion's version, because he was angered at his own tardy promotion. These two discussed the matter and resolved on the extermination of their mutual grievance, Martialis to do the deed.

The opportunity came on the 8th April 217, when Caracalla was on a journey to visit the temple of the Moon at Charrae in Mesopotamia. By the way, he had occasion to dismount for purposes of natural relief, and withdrew somewhat from his staff, thus leaving himself unprotected. Martialis saw his opportunity.   On the pretext of having been called, he rushed up and stabbed the defenceless Emperor in the back, then made off, followed by the German officers, who immediately got wind of what had been done. He was the cat's paw, and suffered the penalty that Macrinus had foreseen would be his. Four days later, *and, faute de mieux,* the army offered the Empire to this same Macrinus, little wotting for the moment what his part had been in the tragedy they deplored, desiring only a leader against the approaching forces of King Artabanus. As usual, according to Herodian, the Senate breathed a sigh of relief when the Emperor died. In their effete condition they were only too anxious to change masters as often as possible. With a want of politi-cal sense and ability, which so well merited the treatment they received at the hands of their tyrants, that august body continually preferred—with an entire lack of statesmanship—the unknown to the known evils of their future.

At the time of Caracalla's death, Julia's chief grief was at the loss of her influence. During the last quarter of a century she had had the world at her feet, and not the world of sycophants by any means. Latterly she had enjoyed the supreme power, and must have had enormous patronage in her hands ; naturally her nominees would be men eager in her interest and support. Dion seems to say that her first idea was one of suicide, as a means of escaping her loss of prestige, but he shows us that her fears proved groundless, since the new Emperor left her in Antioch with the outward marks of her dignity unaltered.   It was certainly not a wise policy from Macrinus' point of view. Julia, knowing at least of his treachery, and ably assisted by her crafty sister, took advantage of the mismanagement of the Parthian campaign, and the insensate strictness with which this pedantic lawyer immediately attempted to reform the manners of his young soldiers, to suggest that she herself would make a better ruler than this pedagogue (at least, so one gathers from Dion, 78-23). It was a chimerical scheme at best, and as Julia knew her Rome so well, she must have realized that no woman could have a chance, as sole ruler, in such an environment. It is therefore more natural to suppose that if she attempted anything at all, it was to suggest some youth to the army in whose name she could exercise the power she loved; and who was more natural than the son of Soaemias and Caracalla? It is conjectural, of course, but the report of his paternity seems already to have been abroad, and will account for the extraordinary alacrity with which the troops re-ceived the lad a few months later. At any rate, something caused Macrinus to change his mind as to the advisability of allowing Julia and her rela-tions to remain longer in the Eastern capital. Thus he ordered them to return at once to Emesa, whence they were sprung. Julia was too proud to submit to the condition of subject under the adventurer whom her family had raised from nothing, or to become after so much grandeur an object of public pity. She resolved, therefore, to escape from her distress like a Stoic of ancient days. Moreover, she was suffering from a disease which is still considered incurable. Death was approaching her; she went out to meet it, and either allowed herself to die of starvation or pierced her cancer with a poisoned dagger. The report that Macrinus had ordered her suicide is quite incompatible with his other dealings towards the family of Bassianus.

Maesa, more prudent and more far-seeing, resolved to obey the order literally, and returned with her widowed daughters (Dion), their two sons, and all her vast treasure to her native city of Emesa, some 125 miles south of Antioch. Here, as we have already pointed out, the family was of immense importance, not only on account of their hereditary position, but by reason of their wealth and imperial connections. Macrinus' short tenure of office is one continual record of gross blunders, of which this is about the most futile, comparable only with a few similar acts perpetrated by our own Stuart dynasty and the last hereditary kings of France. Emesa was the one place in the Empire where Maesa had real power and authority. A whole city would back her pretensions and further her schemes with a devotion that Macrinus could only expect from the handful of Moors who formed his bodyguard.

CHAPTER III. THE USURPATION AND FALL OF MACRINUS, 217-218

Steps to Empire

As we have suggested, Maesa saw more possibilities in living than in assaying that better part which can never be taken from men, which circumstance shows that she at least was not tainted with the growing superstition that a mythical eternity is preferable to a certain present. She promptly obeyed the edict of banishment which Macrinus had published against the relations of the murdered Emperor, and, as we have said, took with her to her native city the whole of her wealth and belongings. It was some time during the winter of 217/18 that Macrinus ordered the family of Bassianus to leave Antioch, and it was this very departure that eventually cost him his throne and life. Certainly he must have known that plans for replacing the house of Antonine on the throne were rife. The final result shows months of work, effected only by hosts of agents. In fact, we may almost surmise that government servants all over the Empire had never acquiesced in the usurpation of Macrinus at all, and were merely biding their time. There was only one safe plan for Macrinus, if he wanted the loyalty of the civil and military parties in the state, namely, to extirpate the whole house of Antonine. Instead of taking this sensible and necessary measure, he merely banished the relations of Caracalla, whom the soldiers regarded as their natural allies, most especially the son and impersonator of that Emperor, the young Bassianus, now aged about fourteen years.

They had more than one grudge against Macrinus. First, they felt the utter disgrace of the Parthian campaign, and were disgusted at the lying medal to celebrate a victory which all the world knew to have been a colossal defeat. Next, they were righteously annoyed at the restrictions put on their usual liberty. Third, they were quite unnecessarily relegated, on half rations, to uncomfortable winter quarters, their pay reduced, and their privileges stopped.

It is easy to imagine the soldiers' disgust at finding themselves subjects to a mere legal pedant, in the place of their popular idol and born leader Caracalla, subjects of a man whose prime object seemed to be the infliction of harsh and unnecessary punishments in all matters concerning the ordinary enjoyments common to their state and life—a ruler whose first reforms were to make criminal offences those natural pleasures which were alone con-sidered to make the strenuous military life endurable. Tristran, quoting from Dion, recalls a law which ordained the burning alive of a soldier and his mistress (*junctis corporibus*); or, as an act of grace, their walling up together (in the same interesting condition), and their being left to die of hunger and suffocation. This feeling of rebellion was by no means lessened when men knew that the new Emperor was taking his ease at Antioch, the Queen of the East, and they compared this treatment with what they had received from their friend and comrade the late Emperor. Macrinus was full of regulations for others, but fully impressed with the legal maxim that the lawgiver is above the law. It is small wonder, all things con-sidered, if the prayers of that host were that the Gods would favour their suppliants both in their hatreds and in their lusts, prayers that were offered in such right Davidic fashion that Forquet de Dome thinks the attempts made even during this period against the Emperor's life would have been suc-cessful, if it had not been for the fidelity of his fellow Moors. Macrinus, like other amateur soldiers, did not recognise the power of the army in the government of a military empire. He seems to have thought that the best way to play up to his electors was to adopt a title of Severus and display it towards them in all its rigour. Not that Macrinus' incapacity as a statesman and military leader ceased here; he made a yet greater mistake in leaving' a large and discontented army in winter quarters in Syria, partly at Emesa itself. These legions were nominally for the protection of Phoenicia ; actually, they kept Maesa in touch with the outside world, and were under the direct influence of her active brain and limitless treasure, for to such Herodian gives us to understand that her spoils approximated. Little could the Moor have imagined what a volcano he was preparing for himself when he left together the discontented legionaries, the aunt of Caracalla, and the representative of the house and name of Severus: whose title to bastardy henceforward became of prime importance to the family and their fortunes.

Julia Maesa had not lived for twenty-five years at the Roman Court for nothing. She knew the men with whom she had to deal, she was accustomed to observe and meditate ; further, she had gold which openeth the heart of man, and an intelligence quite acute enough to know where it could best be spent in order to yield the largest return. Besides this, she had a grandson celebrated for his remarkable beauty, his vivid intelligence, and his admirable gaiety. For such a youth employment must be found immediately. Here at Emesa was the very thing ready to hand, the sacerdotal position which was the property of the family. Maesa knew that a high position in the Church is an acquisition which, even in this life, is of lucrative and social advantage to the holder. The High-Priesthood of one of the most important religions of Syria was Bassianus' possession for the mere trouble of undergoing the ordination rite, while with it there still went a certain amount of the former princely kudos of that house. No sooner had the family, with apparent grief and tribulation, covered the intervening miles, than Bassianus was endowed with the family offices, dignities, and emoluments, while his cousin Alexianus was most probably associated with him as a sort of priest or acolyte. A very fitting figure the boy made as High Priest of the Semitic Elagabal or Sun God, the God of Gods made without hands, supreme, fecund, potent, and glorious. Elagabal was wor-shipped under the symbol of a great black stone or meteorite, in the shape of a Phallus, which, having fallen from the heavens, represented a true portion of the Godhead, much after the style of those black stone images popularly venerated in Normandy and other parts of Europe to-day. The temple itself was of great renown; its celebrity was gained from the fact that it represented the greatest natural force of all time, and its magnifi-cence was in proportion to its renown. Gold, silver, and precious stones had poured into it, not only from the countryside and from Judea, but from kings, satraps, and vassals all over the Eastern provinces. Solomon's temple, though nominally the last word in barbaric ostentation, was easily surpassed in taste, richness, and splendour at Emesa. Herodian paints vividly the sensuous beauty of the worship, the vestments, the music, the dances, the sacrifices, and the mysteries, till one has only to substitute Jehovah for Baal, and one has a familiar scene; rather more splendid, rather more cosmopolitan than the Jerusalem mysteries, but equally designed to entrance the beholder and to mystify the devout. But whereas Baal drew all men within his warm, natural, fecund embrace, Jehovah was at best a local deity whom no one — save those urged on by tribal necessities—had ever thought it worthwhile to propitiate, let alone to serve, at least if we can form any idea of his importance from the Semitic literature and philosophy when compared with that of the Western Empire.

Into all this power and sensuous beauty Bassianus stepped proudly, as supreme lord, knowing how well it became his own splendid magnificence. He must have been warned that it was but a means to an end, that here he had no abiding city; but unfortunately he had a strong strain of mystical devotion in his blood, and immediately became an enthusiast for his deity. From the first moment that he appears upon the scene the boy is always the same, impulsive, enthusiastic, mystical, continually dominated by that effete neuroticism which still trades under the name of religion. Thus Bassianus gloried in the beauty, which to his mind expressed, however inadequately, the potency of his ineffable deity. Here was a God who was able to make men happy, and had taken him into a very specially protective embrace ; a God who was evidently supreme, only, and alone, the God of the Universe. Further, Bassianus gloried in his own beauty, the perfection with which he had learnt to dance that indolent measure to the kiss of flutes, robed in garments the like of which he had not imagined during his resi-dence in the city of the Caesars.

Now, it will be remembered that Caracalla's soldiers were wintering, half-fed, loveless, and discontented in that place, and, as is not uncommon with simple men of that profession, they were easily attracted by the mysterious and the unusual. Soon they heard of this wonderful boy, in whose face was the enigmatic beauty shared by Gods and women ; and further, it was rumoured that, unlike most religious functionaries, this priest was more ready to give than to receive. They came in scores to watch and worship, and found, when they came, that he possessed the charm of the dissolute and the way-ward, heightened by the divine. On his head was a diadem set with precious stones, whose iridescence sparkled like a luminous aureole about his brow. His frail tunic was of clinging purple silk diapered with gold, the sleeves were wide, after the Phoenician fashion, and fell to his feet, and he was shod with fine gilded leather reaching to his thighs. Many of those who gazed upon him must have seen and remarked his beauty in the great City of the Empire, whilst those who ascended to the temple and beheld its rites believed each day more strongly (assisted, of course, by

Maesa's well-spent incentive) that they beheld the child of destiny. Never had his beauty appealed as now; never had the soldiery felt the need of a deliverer as much as at present. Still the numbers — attracted by rumour — grew greater till the lad, feeling the return of Rome to himself, ceased to dance, and strolled amongst his beloved soldiers, surveying them with the bold feminine eyes they loved. Amongst the troops was a certain Eutychianus, called by Xiphilinus, Comazon, because he took part in mimes and farces. He was a soldier of some age and renown who had served in Thrace under the Emperor Commodus, and was a man of growing influence and ability. Publius Valerius Comazon Eutychianus was the full name of the man, who was highly honoured for his part in the subsequent proceedings. It is impossible to believe that this man was merely an actor, indeed it is most probable that the abridger of Dion has thought fit to introduce a bit of gratuitously impossible information when he remarks that Eutychianus was only a freed man of the Emperor and an actor. During the reign of Elagabalus he was once Consul and twice City Praefect, and was again appointed to this same office under the Emperor Alexander.

This man and the tutor Gannys seem to have been the means of forcing home on the neglected legionaries two most important items of information. Through them the soldiers were reminded that Bassianus was their murdered comrade's son and heir, issue of the Emperor and his equally popular cousin Soaemias—that fiery-eyed woman of superb bearing, before whom fire had been carried as before an Empress, and yet one whose favours had ever been for the strong, whose pre-dilections were for the military. Here they found her again, passionate as ever, banished on account of her relationship to their dead leader, and banished by the man they now knew to be his murderer. And further, they found her rich. Sedulously she caused the rumour of her generosity to circulate, until all men knew about the lumps of gold she was ready to give to anyone who would place her Antonine on the throne of his father. It may have been that more than one in that camp could have traced a resemblance to himself in the young priest's features, but none did, the lumps of gold had a language all their own, a persuasive power so potent that not only was Bassianus recognised with a frenzy of loyalty, but his less attractive cousin Alexianus was accepted as his half-brother, a youth whose imperial paternity was at least as possible as his own.

Now the question was, could anything be done to put these protestations of loyalty to some practical use ? Bassianus was certainly accepted by the legionaries early in the year 218 as the legitimate bastard and heir of Caracalla; the true Augustus, deprived of his throne and heritage by the hated Moor,—the man who had killed their idol, and was now oppressing them (which was perhaps more to the point) with the multitude of his civilian parsimonies.

Already Maesa's plans (or were they those of Julia Pia?) were taking shape in a manner almost too good to be true, when, to the help of the youth and his relatives, came the divine portents, which were the accustomed foreshadowings of important events. The great God veiled his face. Elagabal signified his displeasure at the rule of the murderer by an eclipse, and following on the eclipse came a comet, a daystar from on high (another frequently recurring sign of the rise of a redeemer and of the rejuvenation of the world). These signs and portents were doubtless adequately explained to the soldiers, and seem to have decided them to redeem their promises. Within four days, according to Wirth, it was decided that Bassianus should repair to the camp with his treasure, and be proclaimed Emperor by the whole army in that province. Of course, all this took time. Authorities differ, not only as to the method adopted, but also as to the month in which the proclamation took place. Dion states definitely that Bassianus was proclaimed Emperor at dawn on 16th May 218. Wirth, criticising Dion, decides that the proclamation took place almost immediately after the eclipse, which we know from Oppolzer took place on 12th April. He quotes Dion's own words that the proclamation took place *ὑπο τας ημέρας έκεινας* of the eclipse ; therefore 16th May is obviously a scribe's error for 16th April, as the phrase is quite incapable of bearing the meaning within thirty-four days. Further, Wirth goes on to explain that haste was an obvious necessity, as no troops would ever be left in winter quarters till the middle of May. The middle of April, in that province, was more than late enough to account for Dion's statement that the troops had been unduly delayed in winter quarters that year. Undoubtedly, Wirth's suggestion as to an earlier date of procla-mation than that stated in the present text of Dion is the most likely ; the difficulty lies in the fact that from 16th April to 8th June, the date of the battle, there is a period of seven weeks in which the active Maesa apparently did nothing; but more of this later. To continue with the story. When the preparations were ready, and the portents of the eclipse had decided the superstitious, Dion says that Bassianus, Maesa, and the family of the Bassiani, with wagons bearing their treasure, the ransom of the Empire, left the city, and took up their quarters within the camp on the night of 15th April (or 15th May) 218. Herodian says that only Bassianus and Eutychianus went, and by stealth, as Maesa was ignorant of the final plans, though both agree that at dawn on the next day the High Priest, Bassianus, was brought out, shown to the soldiers, habited in the clothes that Caracalla had worn, and then, Macrinus having been deposed, Bassianus was elected Emperor in his stead, under the title of Marcus Aurelius Antoninus, Antonini Filius, Severi Nepos, Augustus, Pius, Felix. Herodian adds that the camp was at once fortified, both to protect the young Emperor—who, like his putative father, preferred the camp to the palace— and also to withstand the punitive expedition which Macrinus was bound to send as soon as he heard of the revolt and mutiny. The news would take at least a couple of days to reach Antioch, if not consider-ably longer, considering that the soldiers had taken care to keep the proceedings within the camp. In due course Macrinus heard of their audacity. He was astonished and disgusted, and frankly said so. The account which he sent to the Senate was not pleasant reading for any of those it concerned ; but except by means of the pen, the nominally deposed Emperor did not think that much need be done. Still, that a mere boy, with a handful of women, should have seduced the defenders of a province was preposterous. Something must be done to show the soldiery that, though Caracalla might have stood such freedom of choice (which by the way he never did), he, Macrinus, was now master of the Empire, and incidentally their master as well. It was a veritable storm in a tea-cup, of course, but really upsetting to the man who thought that his troubles were now over, that rest remained for the elect of the Gods. The remarkable thing about Macrinus is, that he seems to have been absolutely in the dark as to the state of public opinion, and the extent of the plot for replacing the Antonine House on the throne. As we read the history of Bassianus' phenomenal rise to power, there is a ring of the English Restoration. It is impossible to account for his universal success except on the grounds that the government officials everywhere as well as the soldiers recognised in him a legitimate sovereign and an obvious ruler. From the moment at which he set up his standard there seems to have been no sort of adequate opposition either from the civil or military government of Macrinus; while, on the other hand, Bassianus obviously had a party organised in every city and province, which was sedulously kept informed of his progress from day to day. Not only a party, but the party, as there is no instance—except at Alexandria, where the Antonines were scarcely popular—of Bassianus' legates being received otherwise than with open arms. None of which facts argue well for the position of the Moor in the state. Macrinus was inclined to overestimate his popularity, and he certainly under-estimated the influence of youths and women. Perhaps he had no experience of female tactics, and the persistency with which they prosecute their own designs; he obviously thought a sententious letter to the Senate, full of smug platitudes, abuse of the army and the house of Antonine, was what that august assembly wanted. So far he had not missed his mark ; but when he went on to inform them that they would never have any desire to wish him any hurt, one of the Senators, Fulvius Diogenianus by name (who was obviously better informed than the majority as to the likelihood of their having to put up with Macrinus much longer), answered immediately and with surprising candour, " But that is what we are all longing for " ; whereupon the Senate sent word to the army that their general and Emperor was not to be trusted on several counts.

Macrinus, however, was not entirely idle; he had at least begun to think. True, he had, for himself, preferred the pen to the sword, and then found that the pen was a double-edged weapon like the sword, only rather more dangerous, because it constituted documentary evidence. Still, he would not let others err in the same way. He sent for his Praetorian Praefect, Ulpius Julianus, to attend at his silken couch and talk business. The result of this conference was that Macrinus resolved to strike fear, by proxy of course, into the hearts of that " child and idiot," his two women, and the legion who supported him ; and where, he argued, would the revolt be when their hopes, centred in a child, too young to know even the rudiments of politics, were suddenly blighted ? Of course, he would like news, and yes, he thought he had better say it, the boy's head in a charger —stone-dead hath no fellow. It would put the Emperor quite at his ease once again to know that his rival was dead. It was perhaps foolish to be concerned about so effete a crew, nothing could come of it all; but still he would feel relieved if Julian would go at once to Emesa.

We are not told how long Julian took in his preparations, or on the journey. From Macrinus' attitude of disregard, probably he was not specially pressed, though from his selection of troops Julian must have thought the rising more important than Macrinus had pretended in his letter to the Senate. Julian's chief anxiety was to secure loyalty to Macrinus amongst the men he took for the sup-pression of this revolt. Certain incautious specu-lations amongst the men led to the execution of several before the expedition started. From his position as Praetorian Praefect, Julian would take a fair contingent ; his dignity demanded it, and probably his knowledge of the state of politics would tell him that a strong movement was necessary at the outset. Apparently about three legions went in all. Julian added to his forces a large number of Moors, unless Herodian means that he took the Moorish cohorts of the Praetorian Guard as main body, and added other men to these; in any case, it seems obvious that, even if the government had not got wind of what was going forward, the army had, and in consequence the Moors, as Macrinus' own countrymen, were considered the most trustworthy soldiers for the work, besides which they were never over-particular in their methods. There is evidence that, no matter how much he might belittle the movement in public, Macrinus knew that the " Idiot " and his two women were likely to have a full dog's chance, and get a good run for their money.

The journey from Antioch to Emesa is, as we have said, a matter of 125 miles. The report of the meeting *inside the camp* had to reach Macrinus ; he had to get his mind attuned to the extraordinary circumstances; then appoint Julian, who had to make his inquisition and other preparations, and then get to Emesa. Conjecturally, he could not have arrived with an effective force much before the 28th of April, or settled down to attack the fortified camp outside the city till that day. On the first day, Dion tells us that Julian all but took the camp in a long day's fight; but it was heavy work, and, contrary to Macrinus' expectation, the arrival of Julian had not struck fear into the heart of the "effeminate and debauched Syrian lad," who was still with his soldiers, and showed no intention of giving way even when the sun began to decline in the west.

Unfortunately for Julian—and incidentally for his master also, as things turned out— the Praefect thought that " the night cometh in which no man can work," and gave his Moors leave to retire to their lines at sunset. With them went certain of the Emesan legionaries, displaying a hardihood truly heroic, unless they were fairly sure of their ground. All that night they worked, spreading their evangel, talking, persuading, and promising on behalf of Antonine and his gold ; talking until even the besieging Moors knew full well that those walls held not only the son of Caracalla, but the limitless wealth which he was ready to give to all those who would assist him in reaching the throne of his father and their hero. It was enough. When morning broke, the vision of his Augustitude was seen above the walls of the camp, dressed in garments which they could recognize from their colour and shape as having belonged to Caracalla, and surrounded by his money bags. There he stood, boldly and proudly, certainly in imminent danger of death from the besiegers, but without fear, while all around him rose a great shout, " Behold the image of your benefactor! can you fight against him and us, who stand by him for his father's sake ? " Now, the resemblance, as shown on the coins given by Cohen (vide com 8, p. 324, and coin i, p. 243, vol. iv.), is quite remarkable ; whether it was merely a family likeness or entirely paternal, it was quite good enough for men who at some little distance were already con-vinced, and entirely anxious to share in the largess that they had seen was already the prize of others.

There was no further fighting, for all Julian's orders. The soldiers threw down their arms and refused battle against the popular idol. True, there was still a question of heads, but the head of the " Idiot" was not thought about in the old connection ; it was too valuable where it was. It was the officers of Macrinus who suffered at the hands of those who were candidates for their offices, and to whom the position and property of the defunct had been promised by the new Emperor. The last to fall was Julian. That trusty favourite of the deposed Emperor had managed to escape when he saw the way that the tide was flowing, but for a general commanding-in-chief to escape is not easy, and there were doubtless many aspirants for his responsibility and position. Herodian tells a dismal tale of the Praefect found in hiding, where he was given a short shrift, because his head was wanted for a use other than that of commanding the Praetorian Guards. The ingeniousness of the conquerors had designed it as an evangel, or announcement of good tidings to Macrinus, impersonating the head he wanted, that of Bassianus the Impostor.

But to return to Macrinus. Julian departed on his mission, the Emperor seems to have got more and more worried; people must have told him things which he had never heard before, and he appears to have worked himself into a fever of excitement, a simple longing to do something, no matter what, to get on the move, to propitiate somebody, chiefly the soldiers whom he had neglected, and well, perhaps, just a bit persecuted. It had all been for their good, of course, but now he had to think of his own good; and so he set out towards Emesa. Not that he had any intention of endangering his precious person by going anywhere in that vicinity himself; but there was the second Parthian Legion, enrolled by Severus, and very loyal to the house of Antonine, which was wintering at Apamea, about half-way between Antioch and Emesa. Perhaps it would be as well to modify that precious title of his by gifts, largesses, and other privileges, especially in the case of this particular legion of Albano, as it was called, a legion which was so near the danger zone, and whose defection might simply mean flight for Macrinus. Gold had worked miracles at Emesa, but Macrinus was not so foolish as to expect miracles, he only wanted mercenary service; neither did he want any more talk of bribes, which everyone would accept very readily, and would as readily repudiate the responsibility thereby incurred. But surely what had paid at Emesa ought to pay at Apamea too. If a boy Emperor Bassianus was popular there, why not set up a child yet younger than the impostor; in fact, why not make his own son, Diadumenianus, Associate Emperor with him-self? The boy was quite ten years of age, and would make a fitting set-off to the "Idiot" of fourteen, whose youthful pretensions he had just derided so conclusively before the Senate. Besides which, it would be an additional security for his family if anything untoward should happen, and would furnish the occasion for a largess, which Macrinus was wanting. It would be an occasion at which no one could cavil, no one pretend to sneer.

Neither would it be a craven act, such as the late dealings with Parthia had been stigmatised. It was quite a budget that the ponderous lawyer had thought out in so short a space of time. Travelling, he knew not quite whither, had sharpened his wits wonderfully, and he did more than plan ; he executed his design without delay. The legions rejoiced once more in their demoralising privileges, and in more than they could have hoped for in the way of extra pay. Dion tells us that on the day when Macrinus declared his son Antonine and Augustus (with no senatorial patent, of course) he promised to each legionary 5000 drachmae, of which 1000 were to be paid down. Further, in the letter to the Senate which announced his son's elevation, he promised to each Roman citizen a congiary of 150 drachmae. Obviously Macrinus was changing his views ; in his last letter he had played up to the Senate and despised the army; he was now playing up to the army, and showing the Senate and sovereign people of Rome that he estimated their worth at just one thirty-third of the amount at which he valued a base soldier — a man who would continually suffer himself to be bribed, to the enormous hurt of the state, as he had so recently enforced upon the senatorial attention.

Macrinus was certainly not clever, his acrobatic feats were never graceful, never gained him much applause even from the gallery. The occasion of this congiary and donative was certainly a good bid for general popularity; rejoicings went on apace; the obedient Senate, having taken their bribe, poured contumely upon the house of Antonine with a hearty goodwill, and declared its members enemies to the state and commonwealth of Rome. But somehow no one was quite satisfied, certainly not Macrinus; the news he was expecting did not come; the head he wanted had not yet been sent.

There is a certain difficulty about the date of Diadumenianus elevation. Neither Dion nor Herodian state definitely when it was effected. Mommsen postulates that it must be late in May on account of the scarcity of evidence on the point. There are several known coins which call him Emperor, one struck at Antioch, another at Thyatira in 218; a third obviously earlier in the same year omits the title. Certainly the writer of Macrinus' letters to the Senate places it after the proclamation of Bassianus, and leads one to suppose that it took place as given above, at Apamea, and was the means adopted to conciliate the legionaries.

Meanwhile at Emesa busy brains had been busily at work. A gentle reminder of his perilous position was on the way to Macrinus. By way of showing him that Julian had forced a battle, and was sending the spoil to grace the festivities arranged for the Child Emperor's elevation, Eutychianus Comazon, the soldier whose per-suasive power and influence had been of such use to Maesa, bethought himself of a pleasant surprise. He took the Praefect's head and wrapped it in linen cloths, tied it with many and elaborate cords, then, taking Julian's own signet, he sealed the bundle carefully and sent it by the hands of a trusty and cunning soldier. " From the victorious Praefect Julian to his august Emperor, with greeting. The head and source of our offence, according to the commandment." Judge of the fright and disgust which arose in the breast of that Moor on discovering, when the bundle was opened, not the features of his despised enemy, but the death-mask of his trusty and well-beloved lieutenant, the man who had saved him from Caracalla's vengeance at the outset of his own plot. Merely that, and no further news to hand, because the bearer of the tidings had departed without waiting for a reward. Bit by bit the news trickled through: at least four legions had deserted, and, greatest blow of all, the very Moors in whom he had trusted. The hated Antonine was triumphant and in the ascendant. It was enough to wake even the comatose parody of the great Marcus Aurelius. After waiting to recover his senses, he took to his heels and ran— discretion being the better part of valour—not, however, as Herodian suggests, with characteristic untruth, towards Emesa, but back to Antioch, as Dion discreetly remarks, with Bassianus and his paltry, though rapidly augmenting, forces soon to follow. The boy and idiot was ready to fight the Praetorian Guards, ready even to face the brunt of opposition from the conciliated legion at Apamea if necessary.

Bassianus' army must have been enthusiastically loyal and keen. It was a motley crew of men, with new officers and a disorganised commissariat ; certainly it had no adequate head. Indeed, had Macrinus taken the bull by the horns at once, he was bound to have cut up Antonine's forces and silenced the revolt; but he escaped, hoping to fight another day, and Bassianus instead came to Apamea. Here Severus' legion of Albano was in no mood to offer opposition to the heir of Severus, and promptly took the suggested oaths, which added yet more strength to the rush that was about to be made on Antioch, where Macrinus was sheltering himself and shivering with appre-hension, having left the field clear to his adversary, and given him just what he wanted, time for acces-sion of strength.

To return for a moment to the length of time during which this campaign lasted. If we accept Dion's date of 16th May for the proclamation, there will only be three weeks left before the battle, in which time much has to happen. First, The news has to be brought to Macrinus 125 miles away. Second, Macrinus has to appoint Julian, who has carefully to choose his men, to reach Emesa, and lose his head in the effort to take Antonine. In the meantime Macrinus has written to the Senate to announce the revolt, and get that body's con-demnation of the Antonine house. He has then gone to Apamea with the court and baggage, declared his son Emperor, and, as he thought, pacified the legion and organised festivities, during which festivities he receives ocular demonstration of the failure of Julian's attempt.   He then writes to the Senate a hurried letter announcing his son's accession, and receives an answer to his first letter condemning the house of Antonine. He then retires to Antioch, and here there seems to be a lull, during which time the patrolling parties, for whom Macrinus has sent, come in to Bassianus' standard, not Macrinus'. Herodian says that this happened in driblets, but that these amounted to such a number before the 1st of June, that Antonine's generals advised him to tempt a battle. All this, especially the wait for gradual accessions of strength, would have been impossible to fit into less than a fortnight.

But there is further evidence. According to Henzen, the Collegio Fratrum Arvalium were concerned on 30th May with the " precatio co-optionis Antonini," to be admitted a member of the College. If the proclamation had only taken place on 16th May, the Brothers could not have known about it and arranged a meeting by 30th May, especially when we consider that (according to Dion) Macrinus' letters to the Senate had caused that august body to declare war on the family of Antonine after that time. Had Bassianus been proclaimed on 16th April and the Brothers heard of his phenomenal success, they would naturally hasten to be on the safe side by 30th May. Within a month from that date they would have heard of the defeat of Macrinus, so that in all prob-ability the meeting which admitted Bassianus and sent Primus Cornelianus to announce his admission was held about 28th June. On 14th July there is the record of a third meeting, which merely takes further vows for Antonine's safety, as the Emperor, who has been already admitted a member. Dion's date is, therefore, simply impossible. Neither Macrinus nor Antonine could have accomplished what they did in a fortnight, even three weeks. Rome could not possibly have heard and answered under five weeks, even by express post. Bassianus could not possibly have got together forces enough to assure success under that period. We must therefore conclude that Dion's date, 16th May, is a mere slip for 16th April, as Wirth has postulated.

This is very forcibly brought home to us when we realise (as Herodian tells us) that when Bas-sianus did move on Antioch, it was with forces scarcely inferior in number to those with Macrinus, and by so doing he managed to frighten the Moor out of his lair, because there was a fear that Antioch might fall and he would be caught like a rat in a trap. Thus was Macrinus forced out to meet the child. Again the ancient Procurator-Fiscal made an error of judgment by taking command himself. He would have done better to stay in the city and give the command to a trained general; but not a bit of it, he was too anxious, too worried to trust anyone. When he heard that Antonine was nearing Immae or Emma, not twenty miles from Antioch, he went out suddenly, resolved to trust to his Moors and Praetorians for the result.

In this battle the valour of both armies seems to have been indifferent. Herodian tells us that the soldiers of Antonine fought like lions, fearing the results of doing anything else; preferring to die like men than to be hanged like dogs; a report of valour which was probably picked up from that army itself. But the stars in their courses seem to have fought against Sisera in the person of Macrinus, while Deborah and her leman Barak, otherwise Maesa and her similarly related Gannys (neither of whom had ever seen red blood before save in the circus) managed so to shut up the forces of Macrinus in the narrowness of the village, that their numbers and superior agility, divested as they were of their cuirasses and bucklers for that end, were of small effect. Nevertheless, the issue of the battle would have been not a little doubtful if Macrinus had not given it away by his cowardice. The guards made so vigorous a stand, that Anto-nine's army turned to fly. It was then that Maesa and Soaemias showed their bravery, according to both Dion and Herodian, for, having leapt from their chariots, they rushed into the midst of the failing troops, and with tears and entreaties urged them to return. The palm of victory seems, how-ever, to lie with the boy Emperor. Both Dion and Herodian tell us of his bravery and the mighty fury which (like a divine inspiration) breathed from him, when, sword in hand, he galloped through the failing ranks and cut down all those who showed an inclination to turn from the fight. It was a good beginning, and shows that the boy was not entirely what his biographers have painted him—the craven, miserable, religious sensualist known to common report.   He showed in this battle that he could glory in his manhood, could forget that salvation was by faith and prayer alone ; could forget that only the Gods can settle the great issues. It was thus that Antonine carried his successful arms right into the opposing camp, hoping to find the Moor ; but to the disgust of all that host, the Emperor had vanished ; being tired, he had gone home. His Praetorians had sought for some time for the ensigns that announced the presence of the Em-peror, but they had sought in vain, and deserters had told Antonine the story.

Antonine now made a proposition to the op-posing host, namely, that they should turn and become his guards, should retain the privileges granted by Caracalla, and above all, should fight no more for the craven. Nothing loath, they did as they were bidden, and by nightfall on 8th June 218 the proclaimed Emperor Marcus Aurelius Antoninus was the acknowledged head of the greater part of the army, and ruler of the Roman world which acknow-ledged Antioch as its capital. Maesa's bold attempt had succeeded beyond all her hopes. The one source of trouble was that Macrinus was still at large.

The Antonine policy had never been that of Macrinus. They had always eradicated the source of their offence as far as they were able, and to that end Marcus Aurelius sent messengers to take the ex-Emperor's person. From the battle-field that caitiff had gone, first to Antioch, sending heralds on ahead to announce their master's victory and the destruction of the Antonine host, lest the populace should seize the city for Antonine and kill him, or, as Xiphilinus puts it, in order to induce them to receive him into their city at all. Had there been time, we might have had another medal, in correspondence with the Parthian fraud, announcing the victory of Macrinus at Immae; but stragglers began to come in, and with them the news that Antonine would arrive shortly at the head of the whole army, an announcement which caused bloodshed and strife in the city, and decided Macrinus to reconstruct his plans. He would not stay, he decided, where he was not wanted; he would make his way to Rome, in the hope that his kindness to the Senate would at least secure them as a bodyguard—though what use some 600 portly and middle-aged gentlemen were going to be to him against the legions of a military empire was a question that had not yet occurred to his distracted mind ; but at any rate Antioch was no place for him or his son. The latter he entrusted to Epagathos, one of the few men on whom he could rely, with orders to take him to the King of Parthia for safe keeping; whilst he himself, having cut off his hair and beard, and laid aside the purple and imperial ornaments for his successor's use, set out for the capital city by the route used for the ordinary post. It is a most significant fact that this man, the acknowledged Emperor, should on the very day of the battle itself have distrusted all his own lieutenants, governors, and civil officials to such an extent that he felt the only safe mode of progress was, disguised as a countryman, to travel by the public carriage. It presupposes that by this time all men were merely waiting for his fall, which was anticipated everywhere as a foregone conclusion, the inevitable result of a weak usurper's unsuccessful attempt.

It is incredible that all the government servants and other accredited agents of Macrinus would have dared to give credit immediately to the ambassadors of an unknown pretender, and only in Alexandria (where the name of Antonine had acquired an unenviable notoriety and there was a personal friend of Macrinus as governor) were Antonine's ambassadors put to death as upstart traitors. True, there have been fugitive kings before and since, but never after one battle and to make way for an utterly unknown child, who by some miracle has got the whole functionaries of imperial government, both civil and military, into his own hands in less than a couple of hours, without even the use of the field telegraph.

From Antioch, Macrinus went on horseback to Aegae in Cilicia, and thence by the public post through Cappadocia, Galatia, and Bithynia, with great expedition, giving out that he was a mes-senger from the Emperor Macrinus. He intended to cross into Europe by way of Eribolus, and thus to avoid Nicomedia, where the Governor Caecilius Aristo was seeking his life to take it from him, in favour of the new Emperor. The distance that Macrinus travelled was, so we learn from the *Itinera Hierosolymitana*, 750 Roman miles, covering in his haste, so Friedlander thinks, about 130 Roman miles per diem, which would bring him to Eribolus (barring accidents, of course) about 15th June. Thence, we are told, he took shipping and attempted to reach Byzantium ; but the battle was not to the strong; the attempt was rendered abortive by the avenging deity in the shape of a great north-west wind, which threw him back upon the coast near Chalcedon. There the well-informed agents of the Emperor Antoninus came up with him, and dis-covered his whereabouts by means of Macrinus' imperial procurator, to whom, being short of funds, the Moor had foolishly sent in his extremity.

The discovery was tragic ; the lord of the world, the man whose sceptre threatened the Gods and commanded the sun, was discovered by his pursuers hidden in a small house on the outskirts of Chal-cedon, trembling with a fever and fright, brought on by the fatigues and emotions of his hurried journey. He was promptly put into a chariot and taken back towards Antioch by his captor Aurelius Celsus. By the time the party reached Cappadocia news was brought that Epagathos had failed in his mission, and that Diadumenianus was killed, which so utterly upset the poor gentleman that he deliber-ately threw himself from his chariot, in the hope of ending his disappointed existence and escaping a worse fate. In so doing he broke his collar-bone instead of his neck. There was certainly no luck for Macrinus till he reached Archelais, about 75 miles from the frontier of Cappadocia, when, pre-sumably acting under fresh orders, the Centurion ordered him to be put to death, a merciful release from the sufferings which his stupidity and incapacity had brought upon him. The date is not known, though it was in all probability some time before the end of the month of June. Dion allots fourteen months less three days to his tenure of power, counting to the day of the battle.

As far as we know, he left neither friends, enemies, monuments (except the arch at Tana in Algeria, erected by his compatriots), children, nor evils to live after him. Certainly he meant well, and acted in a manner more futile and less imperial than any of his predecessors. There was no attempt of any sort made to revive his memory; no resuscitation of any party in favour of his rule ; no enthusiasm or even loyalty betrayed towards him from the moment that Antonine claimed the throne. Antonine's campaign, on the contrary, was one triumphal procession, feebly resisted by a countermarch on the part of the reigning Emperor; after which time, and without even waiting to hear of their Emperor's death or abdication, the whole governmental world settles down without the least suspicion of disloyalty under the headship of Antonine. Nothing is dis-organised. In less than half a day everything is absolutely at his disposal throughout the empire, and no further question is asked as to where the late Emperor may be. Travel quickly as he will, Macrinus was not able to take from men's minds what must have been a foregone conclusion, namely, that he was doomed, and another was reigning in his stead. It was an obvious case of a usurper about whom no one cares sufficiently to make further inquiries.

The Roman world had wearied of Macrinus and his pretensions, just as it had wearied of Claudius; both were fantastic, vacillating, abstracted, and cowardly tyrants, declaring themselves to be of the opinion of those who were right, and announcing that they would give judgment in favour of those whose reasons appeared the best. Slipshod and tattered they both went through life; Emperors whom no one obeyed and at whom every one jeered ; men who, when they heard that conspirators were abroad, were not indignant, but merely frightened. Perhaps it was the purple which had driven so many

Emperors mad, that made Macrinus an idiot; certainly he acted like one, and made way for yet another Phaeton for the universe: a prince for whose sovereignty the world was too small, as Tiberius had remarked of his nephew Caius, nick-named Caligula, the man without whom neither Nero, Domitian, Commodus, Caracalla, or Elaga-balus could have existed. The lives of all are horrible, yet analyse the horrible and you find the sublime. The valleys have their imbeciles, from the mountains poets and madmen come. Elagabalus was both, sceptred at that, and with a sceptre that could lash the earth, threaten the sky, beckon planets, and ravish the divinity of the divine.

CHAPTER IV.THE WINTER AT NICOMEDIA

Saluted by the whole army on the evening of 8th June 218, the young Emperor, Marcus Aurelius Antoninus, set out to cover the 20 odd miles which separated Immae from Antioch, the Eastern capital. Next morning, we are told by Dion, he entered the city amidst the customary rejoicings. It had been a principle with the late Caracalla to give conquered cities over to the rapacity of the soldiers, and here the conquering host imagined, nay, strongly urged, that this laudable custom should be revived, but the present Antonine saw no reason for any such pro-ceeding. With a singular lack of subservience, which is, we are told, the first mark of a born sove-reign, he informed them that a regular toll would be taken from the citizens instead, and each man paid a sum of 500 drachmae from the imperial exchequer ; he thus satisfied their natural expecta-tion of reward, and promised the population that no pillage would take place ; that, on the other hand, the ordinary contributions to the exchequer (the marks of settled government in times of peace) were sufficient, while pillage would suggest the wars and disturbances which were now over.

It was certainly a bold act, this crossing the will of the soldiers at the very outset, too bold for either a woman or a boy of fourteen to have devised ; but Antonine intended to make that city his tempor-ary capital, and had in consequence more than soldiers to conciliate.

As to the question of principal adviser and chief minister, we have a most difficult matter to face from the outset. Lampridius asserts that Soaemias was in the position of absolute director of the Emperor and his government, an assertion utterly ludicrous to anyone who understands that lady's character, as Lampridius himself has expounded it. Soaemias would have been, psychologically speaking, quite incapable of directing any operations other than those of the nuptial couch ; though she may have thought out some of the details of costume, etiquette, and precedence which later fell to her share as president of the Senate on the Quirinal; besides which, her name always follows that of Maesa on inscriptions and records where the two names appear together. Herodian, on the other hand, states that Maesa was the ruling spirit, which is much more likely. Maesa's character is very different, if less attractive; crafty, cunning, able, and persistent, she had not schemed, fought, and expended her treasure except for her own ultimate good, and to her the ultimate good was the possession of power and - authority. Besides which, she was fully *au fait* with all governmental procedure in Rome, and was, in consequence, the fit and proper person to direct the immediate policy.

But there was much to temper her power. There was an element which even she, far-sighted as she was, had forgotten, and left out of count, namely, the Emperor himself.

From the moment of his elevation he showed that he had a mind and will of his own; probably he had possessed them all along, but his grandmother had never thought that they would get in *her* way till she was brought face to face with them.

By nature Bassianus was gentle and affectionate, with no other passions than an innocent fanaticism for the cult of the only God, and a hereditary temperament, which we know to-day is less of a vice than a perversion ; a temperament which Suetonius assures us he shared with the majority of his pre-decessors, and Dion says was common amongst the Syrian clergy. Caracalla had, innate in his being, jealousy, hatred, and revenge. Bassianus hated no one; he was, in fact, only too prone to love his fellows, but, like Caracalla, he had a strong and imperious will. He had no sooner grasped the limitless possibilities of the imperial position than vertigo seems to have overtaken him. But fancy the position! On a peak piercing the heavens, shadowing the earth, a precipice on either side, the young Emperors of Old Rome stood. Did they look below, they could scarce see the world. From above, delirium came ; while the horizon, though it hemmed the limits of their vision, could not mark the frontiers of their dream. In addition, there was the exaltation that altitudes produce.

The Emperor was alone; henceforward his will was unopposed. His grandmother tried to make herself felt; on each occasion she had to give way, to retire beaten, till one can well imagine that lady's despair at the unforeseen development,—almost anticipate the final resolve of that crafty old sinner, to rid herself of the grandson whom she had set up, fondly imagining him her mere puppet. Still, advisers were necessary. From what we can see of the available men (and a man would certainly be Antonine's choice) there is but one for whom con-sistently through his life the Emperor had respect, namely, Eutychianus. He had, so Dion states, con-ceived the plot of the proclamation, and carried it out by himself, while the women were still unconscious of what was going forward. He was immediately made Praetorian Praefect, later he was Consul, and twice City Praefect, which frequent recurrence of office, being unusual in one person, is put down by Dion as a gross breach of the constitution—where no constitution existed except the imperial will. The sneer of Xiphilinus at his buffooneries is obviously an untruth, considering the fact that we know of him as a soldier as far back as Commodus' reign. If he had been a mere nonentity or a worthless person, it is incredible that, in the proscriptions and murders that followed that of Antonine, Eutychianus should have been reappointed to the office of Praefect of Rome for at least the ensuing year. Taking all the evidence into consideration, it is probable that from the outset the soldier Eutychianus was chief minister and director of the government, and as such supported Antonine against his grandmother. To him therefore, as well as to Maesa, may be attributed much of the sane common-sense work that was done; work which, especially in the dealings with the soldiers, shows a man's hand, a soldier's touch, indeed that of a soldier who knows, by reason of his position, just how far he can go.

The first recorded act of the new government was to announce to the Roman Fathers the restoration of the house of Antonine. Now the Senate of the Roman people was in no very pleasant position, considering the possibilities and the knowledge that the imperial house had not a few grudges to settle with their august assembly. Rome, as we know from the record of the Arval Brothers' meeting held on 30th May, was expecting some announcement almost daily, either of the accession or extirpation of the late imperial con-nection. The last communication from the East had been signed by Macrinus. It was a distracted and illiterate epistle announcing the elevation of his small son to the empire, and the speedy fall of the pseudo-Antonine. In all probability the news which had reached the Arval Brothers was common property, and the Senate was not so sure of the result of the revolt as Macrinus would have liked them to be. The main cause for anxiety was their answer, which was probably still on its way to Macrinus: a dutiful response to his demand—made about 20th April— that the Antonine family should be proscribed and declared enemies to the state. With their usual subservience, the Conscript Fathers had decreed as desired, had even gone out of their way to level invectives and ordures against the memory of the house of Severus, and this with a hearty good-will that showed their genuineness.

Now, if these tactless epistles, as the Fathers feared, had reached Antioch either just before or just after the new monarch's arrival, they were likely to cause an infinity of trouble, especially if they fell into the wrong hands, which, as luck would have it, they promptly did. This circumstance quite decided Elagabalus on the amount of respect which it was necessary to pay to the " Slaves in Togas" either in his own or in any other state. Judge of their apprehensions when an answer to their obedient proscriptions was brought into the Senate House, within the first fortnight of July, if not earlier, by a herald declaring his mission from the august Emperor, Marcus Aurelius Antoninus, Antoninus' son, Severus' grandson, Pius and Happy, Tribune and Proconsul, without so much as by your leave or with your leave from the assembled Fathers. (Dion omits the title of Consul, despite the fact that there are inscriptions which call Antonine Consul at that date.) Think how willingly now the Fathers would have given their right hands to repair the egregious mistake they had just made. They had been too precipitate, too hurried altogether, and they knew from past experience that the house of Antonine did not visit such mistakes in a chastened spirit.

At last the imperial message was laid before the house.   It was as though the Gods had been for once propitious to human stupidity. The letter contained gracious words, "dropping as the gentle dew from heaven." Was it a mere ruse, such as former Antonines had played, or was it in reality the herald of a new world to come ? Surely yes, for it promised amnesty, on the word of the Emperor, to the Senate and people of Rome, for all words, acts, and pro-scriptions formerly promulgated against the divine Caesar, by command of the usurping murderer Macrinus; to whom the same Senate and people were commanded to give neither help nor assist-ance, but rather to condemn and execrate, in the precise terms they had so recently applied to the divine

Emperor now happily reigning. For was he not an enemy to the state who had not only murdered his master, whom he had been appointed to guard, but also in that he, who was neither Senator nor otherwise worthy, had pretended to Empire, being a mere slave and gladiator, whom Caracalla had raised to the rank of Praetorian Praefect ?

There was some more biting sarcasm on the ease with which that august body had accepted the pretensions of the ex-slave without question, and had been persuaded to confirm him in the position of his murdered master. For himself, Antonine makes the mere announcement of his succession, much as Macrinus had done on the occasion of his son's elevation, with the obvious implication that the Fathers will confirm the accomplished facts with as little delay as is compatible with the usual decencies. He tells them that to err is human, but Antonine, *mirabile dictu,* will forgive, on the conditions mentioned, of course ; which conditions taken as fulfilled, the Emperor continues with an explana-tion of the happy auguries for the commencement of his reign. He was come, he said, a second Augustus; like Augustus he was eighteen years of age (an obvious lie, and they knew it, but an Emperor of fourteen did not sound well); like Augustus his reign started with a victory which revenged the murder of his father, and the success, with which both he and Augustus had met, was a good omen for the people, who might expect great things from a prince who proposed to unite the wisdom of Augustus with that of the philosopher Marcus Aurelius, and to rule after these truly admirable examples. Another letter to the soldiers was delivered at the same time, which contained extracts from Macrinus' correspondence with Marius Max-imus, Praefect of the City. In this the vacillating duplicity of the late Macrinus and his opinion of the army generally was made the most of, his innate civilian distrust of the military held up to ridicule and scorn.

To crown these admirable productions of literary persuasiveness was a promise to the soldiers of their immediate return to the privileges and conditions existent under Caracalla in the case of each and several of the Emperor's beloved comrades. They were certainly admirable letters, designed to rejoice the hearts of both guards and people, and to leave the Senate in pleasurable anticipation of favours to come, if they took immediate advantage of the opportunity now given them to change their minds,— otherwise—well, the more stringent methods of Augustus might have to be employed, and orders were sent to Pollio, Consul Suffectus, to this effect. Undoubtedly the Fathers made up their minds with admirable promptitude—they do not seem to have made a single inquiry as to the fate of the Moor who was nominally reigning Emperor. Never was their voice more willingly given; public thanksgivings were decreed for the restoration of the house of Antonine, and the acts of an Emperor who had treated them as so much garden refuse were lauded most fulsomely. Proscription was the lot of the "Tyrant and Murderer," who had usurped the imperial styles, titles, and addresses ; in fact anything that lay in their power to oblige with they were most happy to offer; more than he had ever thought of asking the Fathers hastened to lay at the feet of the child whose origin, whose sentiments, whose feminine beauty, whose very female relatives breathed divinity from every pore.

There is no better example of the vast comprehensiveness of mind possessed by bodies of men fulfilling the functions which Aristotle calls the " collective wisdom of the many," than this instance of the wonderful facility with which they are able to see all points of view in succession, especially the more advantageous. Only a few short weeks back the infallible wisdom had decreed that the new deities were enemies to the state. Now they knew that the existence of these very enemies was only another way of stating the life and being of the state itself. Their one regret was that they had not known it sooner ; as it was, they were forced to admit that, if the well-bred can con-tradict other people, the wise must contradict themselves.

Of course the young Emperor was pleased with the transports of loyalty with which Rome greeted his accession; Maesa and Soaemias at the joint title of Augusta which the Emperor and Senate conferred upon them; but for precaution's sake, Pollio might as well keep the soldiers on the *qui vive,* as a sort of reminder to the Conscript Fathers that it would be as well to take no more comprehensive views of the circumstances just at present, especially as the Emperor had no intention of proceeding to Rome just yet. But it was not wise to talk, and the Fathers knew it; they were content, for the present, to praise the Gods for their safety, and to register any decrees which august personages might see fit to send for their confirmation, otherwise they decided to keep their mouths tightly closed as to the inner thoughts of the heart.

The announcement of his succession having been posted to Rome, and agents dispatched to secure the person of the ex-Emperor, Antonine seems to have turned his attention to rewards and the management of the army. As was quite natural, the first offices were bestowed on Eutychianus, the man whom we have just mentioned. In all prob-ability it was to him that the success at Immae was actually due; he was the soldier, the trained leader, while Gannys, the boy's tutor, to whom Xiphilinus ascribes the victory, was admittedly an effete and uxorious leman of both Soaemias and Maesa, who could never have been a real leader of men, even though he were personally popular with the troops, as the Valesian Fragment states. It is obvious that the work and abilities of the two men (Eutychianus and Gannys) have got muddled. Xiphilinus(78.31.1) ascribes the plot to Eutychianus ; later (79.6), still presumably quoting Dion, he states that Gannys was solely responsible for the whole plot. Dion (Frag. Vales.) states that Eutychianus had contrived the whole revolution. Clearly some scribe has erred in the insertion of names, or Xiphilinus is not a trustworthy abbreviator. If we can judge by results, we see that Eutychianus was immediately appointed Praefect of the Prae-torian Guard in the room of Ulpius Julianus, deceased, while Gannys, the personal favourite of the Emperor and his women, got no sort of dis-tinction. Eutychianus' elevation was not altogether popular. Xiphilinus considered that he had no right to the post (though he had just remarked that he alone set the

Emperor on the throne), and that the frequency with which he was reappointed was actually a constitutional scandal; but he certainly did good and useful work throughout his tenure of office.

The first move was to rectify the error of Macrinus in keeping troops out in the field un-necessarily. The new government sent back to their quarters all the soldiers gathered for the Parthian war by Caracalla, and that with expedition. There are various inscriptions at Lambesa, in Pannonia, and other places which testify to this, while at Moguntiacum in Upper Germany there is a record of the arrival of a legion as early as 23rd July 218, and which, by the way, gives the Emperor the title of Consul, as well as the other imperial addresses which Dion has mentioned that he assumed as of right.

This dismissal of the soldiers was a prudent measure. It not only pleased them, and gave them something to do besides stirring up strife, but also made it possible to preserve discipline without resorting to the enormous gifts which had im-poverished the government heretofore. This may certainly be traced to Eutychianus' influence rather than to that of Maesa, who would probably have preferred to keep the soldiers a little longer, in order to see how things settled down; whereas the troops must have been sent back to their quarters the very week of the battle, and before Macrinus' death, in order to have arrived in Upper Germany by 23rd July. This action, to whomsoever attributable, shows the perfect confidence of the new government in its own stability from the very outset. It was also a bold measure, and a measure which could only have been taken by a general who knew his troops, who to keep and with whom to dispense, because trouble was sure to arise through ambition and similar causes.

Dion tells us of at least two notables who thought themselves *capax imperii,* because they imagined that the state was disturbed, the occasion propitious. One was Verus, or Severus, tribune of the third Gallic, another Gellius Maximus, tribune of the fourth Scythian Legion ; both were Senators who aspired to empire and found futurity. The same historian mentions three others, insignificant persons; one the son of a centurion in the third Gallic Legion (which legion, by the way, on account of these two bids for notoriety, was practically disbanded, the men being transferred to the third Augustan Legion). Another was a clothier; the third a mere private person, whose temerity led him to an attempt, the object of which was to subvert the fleet stationed at Cyzicus during the winter of 218-219, presumably for the protection of the Emperor when he arrived at Nicomedia. The attempts of these persons met with the reward due to folly, and did but strengthen the position of the Emperor by giving him an excuse to put to death others, whose complicity or sympathy pointed them out as perilous to the state. They were all friends of Macrinus, says Wotton, who were making difficulties for the new government. All authorities state very clearly that there was no man who suffered for any assist-ance given to Macrinus; neither was there any inquisition made after enemies or neutrals. The heads of the opposition party were merely put to death when they refused to acknowledge the *fait accompli* when they did so they were confirmed in their offices as a matter of course. The number put to death, besides the five aspirants to the imperial position, is placed by Dion at eight—no enormous holocaust, when one thinks of the legions of imperial servants confirmed in their offices. The names include Julianus Nestor, Captain of the Guards to the late Emperor; Fabius Agrippinus, Governor of Syria; Pica Caerianus, Governor of Arabia; Aelius Decius Triccianus, a man of mean origin, whose death the 2nd Parthian Legion demanded on account of his cruelty towards them ; Castinus, a friend and officer of Macrinus; Claudius Attalus, Lieutenant-Governor of Cyprus, a man who had been expelled from the Senate by Severus and stupidly readmitted by Caracalla. It was not clear on what count this man actually suffered, and in consequence the story of an enmity between him and Eutychianus, during the campaign in Thrace—when he is said to have cashiered the new Praefect of the Praetorian Guards—is regarded as sufficient reason for saying that Eutychianus demanded his death.

During this same winter there was another pre-tender to kingship, helped by another governor friend of Macrinus, a certain Senator Valerianus Paetus. This man's crime lay in the fact that, after the imperial custom, he had coined gold pieces bearing his own image and superscription, and distributed these amongst the people of Cappadocia and Galatia, which was considered tantamount to a declaration of imperial proclamation. His defence, when appre-hended, was that the medals were actually intended for the adornment of his mistresses. The court found, however, that no sane man could reasonably possess this luxury in sufficient numbers to justify the coining of the amount of medals discovered ; besides which, his accomplice Sylla, Governor of Cappadocia, who had just before been tampering with the loyalty of the Gallic Legions, on their way through Bithynia, was mixed up in the plot quite inextricably. So the judgment given was, "guilty of usurping imperial functions, and aspiring to empire " ; rather a larger count, all considered, than the kindred count of " coining," which merited death in this enlightened and humane country up to the year of grace 1832. Throughout the trials we are given to infer that the usual course of judicial procedure was adhered to; the condemnation was after trial and just cause found ; while those who know anything of Roman legal procedure are aware that every chance was given to the accused, and that the burden of proof lay on the accuser.

But to return to the chronological arrangement of the events during this sojourn in the East. As we have said, on 9th June 218 Antonine entered Antioch amidst the applause of the world. As far as we can judge from Herodian's statement, he must have stayed there for some months. The pressure of immediate government business would be enor-mous, the various legates had to be sent forth, the submission of governors received, and the army question settled, along with other outstanding difficulties, and in consequence the season was far advanced, says Herodian, when the imperial family reached Nicomedia, too late for them to attempt the cross-ing into Europe. Besides the business delays, much time must have been wasted by the Emperor's determination to take the image of the Great God with him, and wherever he should reign, there to set up the temple of that supreme ineffable Deity.

Duruy states that during his residence at Antioch, or on the journey across Asia Minor, the Emperor reconsecrated to Elagabal the temple of Faustina which Marcus Aurelius had erected on Mount Taurus. If this be so, it could only have been as a temporary resting-place. The Deity, we are assured, had no settled home after leaving Emesa until the great temple or Eliogabalium was erected on the Palatine. There was one person to whom these delays appeared as highly unnecessary, namely, the Dowager Empress Julia Maesa.

In the full flush of her newly acquired position, she had every intention of wintering in the capital. It was much more to her liking than the provincial life to which the late Emperor had relegated her. In consequence of this intention, we are led to infer that the lady gave orders. Here the Emperor showed his paternity. Maesa may not have fully credited her own assertion before, henceforward she was called upon to believe it whether she would or no. Her grandson, perhaps merely self-willed, perhaps wishing to settle business, certainly intending to stay in the voluptuous East, told the lady to be quiet, and revoked the orders. She tried reasoning, but was told that it wearied his youthful augustitude. She persisted further, and then thought that she had triumphed, because the Emperor, with true Antonine guile, packed up and commanded the Court to set out for Rome. Not that he had the slightest intention of facing the Tramontana, possibly even snow, but it looked gracious, and many things might be done *en route*. For many reasons the journey was slow and difficult; the dignity of the God had to be considered ; the procession across Asia would take some weeks. We have no idea as to the route taken, though Roerth has informed us of an inscription from Prusias, where, he says, the Emperor stayed ; if so, it was probably his last halting-place before Nicomedia, where he had decided to winter instead of trusting himself on the billows of a wintry sea. It was here that Antonine's imperial life actually began; here, under the eastern sky and surrounded by the pomp and colour of the Orient, that the Emperor shaped his reign, and developed the two main features of his life—his religion and his psychology.

Before discussing either of these, however, it will be well to sum up what we know of the work done during this winter spent in Asia Minor. According to Hydatius' statement, drawn from the *Consularia Constantinopolitana,* Antonine ordered the records of indebtedness to the fiscus to be burnt, which burning took thirty days. If the story be true, it was either a foolish waste of indebtedness to the government, or an acknowledgment of the hopelessness of collecting the debts, though how the new government could have grasped this fact so quickly is not recorded ; in any case, it was a real bid for popularity.

Much time would also be spent in the legal proceedings which settled the fate of the various pretenders, malcontents, and traitors. Again, the consideration of grants to legions, fitting rewards for assistance given in time of need, in fact the thousand and one things which occupy the official mind in the ordinary course of events, let alone on the restoration of a house banished and proscribed by imperial predecessors, had all to be discussed and would certainly take time. Cohen tell us of one of these measures, of which we know nothing save from the coins of 218, some of which bear the legend " Annona Augusti," which he says is a reference to some measure relative to the grain supply, instituted for the benefit of the people.

There was certainly enough to occupy every one's attention, but it does not quite account for the whole Court staying at Nicomedia until May 219. Cohen has, however, discovered a fact that no historians mention, namely that during this period the Emperor was unwell, as some of the coins of 219 bear the legend " Salus Augusti," " Salus Antonini Augusti," which are supposed to announce his recovery. If this illness had happened after he arrived in Rome, we should probably have heard about it, besides which it might have been a bar to his matrimony; if in Nicomedia, as Cohen thinks, it accounts for the length of the stay.

Business apart, of which they say little or nothing (facts have to be culled from coins, inscriptions, reports, etc., not from the pages of paid traducers), the historians now begin their tirades against the Emperor's conduct and religion. The obvious inference is that the self-willed boy was already beginning to get on somebody's nerves ; on whose more likely than on Maesa's and his sensitive aunt Julia Mamaea, who so ardently desired her own son to occupy his room. Maesa must have learned by now, from her own sense of the fitting and the insistent representations of Mamaea, that she would have been much better advised, even from her own point of view, if she had set up her younger grandson instead of this headstrong youth who was flouting her at every turn. Of course, it was a question whether Alexianus' elevation would even have been possible, while an elder and a more charming son of Caracalla was known to the soldiers, nevertheless Maesa ruminated and left records which her scribes have copied.

" One of the blackest of his crimes," to quote Xiphilinus, the monk of Trebizond, the abbreviator of Dion Cassius, " was the worship of his God, which he introduced into Rome (though it was a foreign God), whom he revered more religiously than any other, so far as to set him above Jupiter, and to get himself declared his priest by decree of the Senate. He was so extravagant as to be circumcised and abstained from hogs' flesh. He appeared often in public in the habit resembling that of the priests of Syria, which caused him to be named the Assyrian. Is it necessary to mention those whom he put to death without reason ? since he did not spare his best friends, whose wise and wholesome remonstrances he could not bear." These are the sum total of the great crimes which during this period Xiphilinus brings against the Emperor, to which Herodian adds the accusation of a disordered life. Let us examine the statements in order.

" The blackest of his crimes was the worship of his God and the introduction of a foreign God into Rome." To Xiphilinus the ecclesiastic, in all probability the worship of any God except his own was a foul and insolent crime, best dealt with by the holy office of the Inquisition, or whatever took the place of that most useful body (for general purposes of extermination) at the period. But at the moment the knowledge and worship of Xiphilinus' God was, for all practical purposes, confined in Rome to washerwomen or to people of their mental calibre. Xiphilinus' idea that Rome had no foreign Gods is equally ecclesiastical, since only the wilfully blind did not know that Rome was comprehensively, sceptically polytheist, and that she admitted and was deeply attached to many similarly monotheistic Eastern cults, notably those of Mithra and Isis. Why then decry the worship of Elagabal alone ? One can see no reason except the exclusiveness of that worship, the vast monotheistic ideal to which the Emperor had attached himself, and which he was minded to spread throughout the length and breadth of the empire, by every fair means in his power. It was this idea, later centred in Mithraism, which was the most deter-mined opponent of the similarly monotheistic ideal of Xiphilinus, and, as its strongest opponent, called forth the monk's hatred. Rome, however, had a different reason for disliking Elagabal. It was because he, like Jehovah, dethroned all other deities. Rome would willingly have accepted the Syrian Deity amongst the lupanar of divinities whose residence was the Pantheon and whose rites were obscene; but such was not Antonine's scheme, even *primus inter pares* was impossible. Elagabal was over all supreme; even Jupiter Capitolinus, Jehovah, and Vesta must serve the one God. But Rome, whose atriums dripped not blood but metaphysics, knew too well the futility of all Gods to wish for any exclusive cult ; such must fall to the washerwomen, because they were unwanted, unlearned, barbaric, and out of date. But the Emperor persisted, which annoyed his grandmother and other people hugely (she seems to have been generally annoyed, however, so this may be taken as said on other occasions). She had told the boy at Emesa that religion was only a means to the end, and he, with his usual contrariness, had flouted her opinion, backed up by his mother, and persisted in making it the main end of his life. In so doing he went clean contrary to the *Zeitgeist,* and eventually suffered for his folly in not hanging up the fishing-net when once the fish was landed. Xiphilinus makes another egregious mistake in declaring that Antonine caused the Senate to declare him priest of Elagabal, since it was the possession of that hereditary rank or office which had paved the way to empire at all. Again, we are asked to believe that to this period belong his circumcision and resolve to abstain from hogs' flesh, whereas Cheyne considers that these two religious peculiar-ities were common to all Syrian religious, as well as to the Egyptian and Semitic peoples, and dated with him in all probability from the usual age at which circumcision was performed, the age of puberty, which corresponded with his assumption of the priesthood in 217 or early 218. Lampridius, on the other hand, dates the commencement of these observances as part of the fanaticism of the later period in Rome ; when the Emperor formulated his scheme for one universal church, which was to include the distinctive rites of all religions, an inference which is not by any means necessary. Antonine's religion was undoubtedly exclusive and fanatical, though even here it was not peculiar, as the Christian history gives us far more pitiable records of these vices. Antonine's religion was never cruel, it never persecuted, whereas from the moment that Christianity attained the ascendancy she has considered persecution her especial role. There may be joy in heaven over the sinner that repents; in Christendom the joy is at his downfall. We can fancy the difference with which the monk would have treated this Emperor's memory had he been successful, had he even had the foresight to affiliate his church with the kindred worship of Jerusalem, to call his Deity Jehovah in the later adaptation of the term, and had then died as other martyrs had done, a victim to the conviction that in him resided the fulness of the godhead bodily, and further, in the prosecution of a scheme for monotheistic worship, such as no Emperor had ever yet formulated. It is a thousand pities for his reputation that he did not see ahead. In that case, though he would not have formed a fourth part of the ineffable Trinity, his life would at least have become blameless, not only by the baptism of blood, but also in the pages of ecclesiastical historians. We might then have seen St. Antoninus " Athleta Christi," a holy martyr worshipped throughout the length and breadth' of Christendom, as the upholder of monotheism against the forces of his polytheistic surroundings.

In connection with this question, one act of pride is recorded of the sojourn of Nicomedia, an act which well shows the temper of the boy, namely, his assumption of the latinized name of his God, Elagabalus (though, apparently, this was not done for official purposes, as it never occurs on the coins or inscriptions of his reign). Earlier Emperors had been deified at their death ; latterly it had been customary to accord divine honours during the lifetime of the monarch. Elagabalus did not believe that, a senatorial patent aiding, he could become a new God. He did believe, unfortunately, like so many prophets and other religious maniacs, that he could associate himself with his God as his earthly emanation or expression; and henceforward, says Lampridius, none might address him officially except on the knee. It was a weird fancy, but no uncommon delusion, and the world has connived at his conceit by giving him that title when all others are for-gotten save amongst numismatists. That Antonine intended others to regard him in this light, and was thus a constant menace to Christ, is certain from the fact (recorded by Herodian) that he sent to the imperial city during this winter his portrait, painted in the full splendour of his Aaronic vestments, with the command that it should be placed in the Senate House, immediately above the statue of Victory, and that each Senator on entering should offer incense and an oblation to Deus Solus in the image of his High Priest on earth. Herodian records another effort, made during this winter, to introduce the worship of Deus Solus into the minds of men. This was an order sent to magistrates officiating at the public sacrifices that this name should take the first and most important place ; an order which, we are told, even Montanist Christians were able to obey, especially as there were no penalties attaching to the refusal.

It had obviously been a gross error of judgment on Maesa's part to introduce a boy of such a tem-perament to a religion of any sort, much more so to have made him the directing force thereof; but it was done, and with it went the clothes she now hated so cordially. At Emesa, Antonine had accustomed himself to the clinging softness of the silken raiment worn by that priesthood ; now he declined to lay it aside. He hated wool and refused to wear it, neither did linen take his fancy. Silk and cloth of gold encrusted with jewels was his ostentatious conceit, and he was going to wear what his soul delighted in, now that he was free to indulge his proclivities, but what had been entirely proper and fitting at Emesa would not do for the War Lord of the Roman Empire. One knows that circumstances alter cases, and can fancy the state of Maesa's mind when she contemplated the wide-eyed astonishment which would greet the painted priest as he made his entry into Rome the conservative. The Emperor thought he knew better than his elders ; he had found the secret of popularity with the army, and thought that similar attractions would bring the city captive to his feet. Money, beauty, and voluptuousness, says Capitolinus, had brought him to the throne of the world, and he had artistic taste enough to realise that his beauty, height, and grace were enhanced when he was robed in the silken garments of his choice. He did not realise that the clothes were too rich for a soldier ; that bracelets, necklaces, and tiaras were the means by which priests rule women, not soldiers the hearts of men ; that now he must put away childish things, since he had begun to be a man, the leader of armies. Again Maesa was right, but she was overruled, and made more entries against the day when the sum of this grandson's iniquities against her should be so complete that she might put another in his room. It is only fair to state, however, that Dion totally disagrees with this other "eye-witness" when he remarks, that Antonine always wore the Toga Praetexta at the games and shows, thus restricting the use of the Syrian clothes to religious and family appearances.

But, to proceed to Xiphilinus' third charge, that of putting men, even his best friends, to death without reason. This almost certainly refers to the death of Gannys, his mother's and grand-mother's obliging servant, and the Emperor's tutor, to whom, Herodian tells us, he was much attached. Forquet de Dome says that this man considered himself authorised to remonstrate continually with the Emperor on his conduct, just as though his relations' grumblings did not weary him sufficiently. Further, Wotton tells us that a marriage had been arranged between him and one of the imperial ladies, and that there was an idea of declaring him Caesar. Probably these two circumstances led to the tragedy or accident which resulted in Gannys' death, and which, we are told, Antonine always bitterly regretted.

The tutor was nagging and pedagogic. Further, a plot was unmasked. Gannys did not realise that the Antonine temper, when developed, was not a thing to play with. The Emperor forgot himself, and in a fit of mad anger rushed at his tormentor with his sword or knife drawn, struck, and even wounded him. As was only natural, Gannys drew to defend himself, and the guards, fearing for Antonine's life, interposed, and the unfortunate man was no more. Gannys' fault lay in neglecting the boy's training for amorous converse with his female relations; putting off his duty of moulding the plastic character until all was set, hard as bronze, in a misshapen and distorted mould. He had put everything off till a time when reformation was impossible, and the reckoning must be paid by the defaulter. There is no other murder or act of cruelty, either recorded or hinted at .by any one of the men who were paid to ruin his reputation. The worst that they can say is, that his character was debased, and small wonder.

As we read this Emperor's life, we are bound to admit that his nature was debased; but we are struck, not so much by this fact, as by the necessary conclusion that he could never have had the opportunity of being anything else. His faults are admittedly the faults of children, magnified by the fact that he was a child suddenly placed in the unfortunate position where all restraint from outside was impossible, and where his wayward petulancy forbade any to tempt the trial. To him the posses-sion of supreme power meant the holding of limitless privileges, with practically no training for the responsibilities involved. The whole position calls for our pity rather than our censure, if we realise that his only training was neurotic or religious, and phallic at that. All things considered, it is a marvel that no deeds of murder, rapine, envy, hatred, or malice have been laid to his charge, even by his enemies ; such as have been laid to the charge not only of his predecessors, but even at the door of those whom the world honours as the righteous, the salt of the earth. No history is immaculate. If it were, it would relate to a better world ; unable to be immaculate, history is usually stupid, more usually false. Concerning Elagabalus, it has contrived to be absurd, by means of the impossibility of the statements for which it attempts to offer neither proof nor likelihood.

It is during this period at Nicomedia, we are told by the historians of the reign, that his popularity disappears—a statement which, on the evidence of the medals and inscriptions, as well as from what we know of his extraordinary generosity, is and must be utterly false.   A further statement that the soldiers already regretted their action in deposing Macrinus is equally absurd, as they had no sort of reason to do this, and, being largely returned to their quarters, would know little or nothing of any scandals of which they had fully approved a few months previously. The impression left by the adjectives used on inscriptions, medals and coins is, that the Emperor was wildly popular, not only with the military, but also with the civil population. The titles are fulsome, the use of superlatives unparalleled. The frequent use of the adjective *indulgentissimus* tells its own story, explains what Rome thought of his character. There is not the smallest doubt that his generous prodigalities endeared him to the whole population as few, if any, of the Emperors were ever endeared, and the adjectives are indicative of the popular sentiment. Another reason for the popularity of the Emperor was the Pax Romana which he brought to the whole world. That such was popular and advantageous is abundantly testified by the inscriptions and many coins still known to us.

The fatal influences of peace were as yet un-recognized, and a happy scepticism tranquillised the mind, gave free play to the senses. Life was nonchalant, though the world still had its one great passion—Rome, its greatness and renown. The wheels of empire were well oiled ; they now ran with wonderful smoothness, even in provinces which the rigidity of the Republic had alienated. It was a time when, even in far-distant Dacia, the lover quoted Horace to his maid under the light of the moon, a time when the toga protected the world. Life was sweet, because of the abundance of its pleasant things. The treasure of the world was such as has never been realised since, the resources of wealth wonderful. During three hundred years, from Augustus to Diocletian, no new tax was created, and at the beginning of the third century the contributions of the citizens, fixed two centuries earlier, had become so nominal, with the growing power of money, that their weight was almost infinitesimal. The Roman world owed all to its Imperium ; small wonder that its people adored the youth who personified its all with such grace and liberality.

CHAPTER V.EARLY GOVERNMENT IN ROME

The Government in Rome to the Year 221 a.d.

To write the history of the years from 219 to 221 (as we have it in the Scriptores) is a task which can only be undertaken adequately in a language not understanded of the people. Not that these years differed materially from those which had gone before, or those that followed. " Every altar in Old Rome had its Clodius "—so Juvenal has told us—"and even in Clodius' absence there were always those breaths of sapphic song that blew through Mitylene. Rome was certainly old, but Rome was not good—not, at least, in the sense in which we use the word to-day. Of this no one who has even sauntered through the catacombs of the classics preserves so much as a lingering doubt. This is because the Roman world was beautiful, ornate, unutilitarian ; a world into which trams, advertisements, and telegraph poles had not yet come; a world that still had illusions, myths, and mysteries, one in which religion and poetry went hand in hand, a world without newspapers, hypocrisy, and cant," a world into which this boy Emperor, his mind attuned to the whole surroundings, entered proudly during either June or July in the year of grace 219.

The date of the imperial family's departure from Nicomedia is uncertain, on the information at present available; and we can only approximate to the date of their arrival in the city by means of a comparison between the statement of Eutropius that he reigned two years and eight months there, and the statement of Dion that he reigned in all three years nine months and four days, neither of which is definitely certain, as they do not agree with other authorities. If the date, if even the month, of Antonine's death were capable of definite interpretation, the date of his arrival would be clear. As it is, most authorities have placed his entry into the city within the first fortnight of July; Wirth suggests, on the foregoing data, nth July, to be precise. There are, however, various circumstances which incline us to an earlier period, most probably during the month of June.

It seems incredible that, unless the illness already alluded to was of a most serious nature, the Emperor, with Macrinus' failure before his eyes, should have stayed away from Rome for more than a year. It will be remembered that the Emperor Caracalla had been absent for some years before his death, warring against the Parthians ; that Macrinus had spent the whole of his fourteen months' precarious tenure of the imperial power in or about Antioch the voluptuous; and that the restored house of Antonine had ruled with undisputed sway from 8th June 218.

Rome had, therefore, been for about five years without her Court and her God, the personification of her greatness. All that time Rome had clamoured and grown weary, waiting for her essential life to vivify her magnificence. That Antonine was wanted and wildly popular there can be no doubt, both from the statements of Lampridius and those of Eutropius, which record the spontaneity with which both Senate and people condemned the usurping house, and rejoiced at the restoration, as also from the record of the warmth with which Antonine was welcomed on his arrival. In fact, all men seem to have been pleased; the army with their Antonine ; the Senate with their Aurelius ; the people with their Augustus, or their Nero, as the case might be. Save for her strength, Rome had nothing of her own. Her religion, literature, art, philosophy, luxury, and corruption were all from abroad. Greece gave her artists; in Africa, Gaul, and Spain were her agriculturists; in Asia her artisans. Rome consumed, she did not produce; except for herself and her greatness, she was sterile. She was bound to desire the fount of her greatness, the embodiment of her power in her midst.

This is, of course, supposition of a merely circumstantial kind, but there is more than supposition that the family arrived earlier than July. There is the record of the Emperor's first marriage, which must have taken place early in that month. This is commemorated by Alexandrian coins dated LB, *i.e.* prior to 28th August 219. The marriage took place in Rome, and the news of its accomplishment would take at least three or four weeks to reach Egypt, after which new coin dies would have to be cut, and the money, ordinary debased coins in common usage, issued. The latest possible date, therefore, at which the marriage could have taken place, to find coins in circulation recording the event, before 28th August, was the second week in July. This leaves neither time to the Emperor for the choice of his consort after his arrival—which would, after all, have been only a natural wish on his part — nor, which is more important, time to make the necessary preparations for what Herodian tells us were the most stupendous celebrations that Rome the magnificent had yet witnessed. Wirth's date is just possible, especially if Maesa had chosen the wife and had made the preparations beforehand ; otherwise, knowing Maesa's propensity for manage-ment, we must suppose an earlier date of arrival, especially as no two of the biographers agree as to the length of the reign, which is variously stated as having lasted from six years (Herodian) to thirty months (Victor).

Unfortunately, the one known inscription is mutilated. It is set up to the Sun in honour of the return of somebody and Totius Domus Divinae. It was found in 18S5 under the Via Tasso on a pedestal, and bears only the date of its erection, 29th September 219, not the date of the return of the house. It seems therefore safest, in order to allow time before 21st July for the marriage and festivities, to conjecture a start made either late in April or early in May, which, after a journey of 1600 miles, would bring the family to Rome sometime in the early part of June. It is, of course, conjectural, but allows time for the known events.

Once in Rome, we hear little good of the Emperor's life, conduct, administration, or abilities. Unfortunately, we have to deal in the main with Constantine's friend, Aelius Lampridius, a man whose biography is a cheap glorification of Alexander, combined with ignorant and perpetual abuse of Antonine's religion and psychology. All his statements in the way of fact could be compressed into half a page of any ordinary book of reference, and even these he manages to arrange so badly, or to draw from such conflicting sources, that they comprise simply a mass of futile contradictions.

The entry into the city is the record of a scandal which only Herodian perpetuates. This writer, as we have remarked, is nowhere famed for his accuracy; he tells us that the cortege was a rabble of women, eunuchs, and priests of the Sun who surrounded the Emperor. The boy was dressed in the silken robes worn by the priests of Syria. On his head was a jewelled tiara of Persian design, whilst his body was laden with rings, neck-laces of pearls, bracelets, and other signs of vulgar ostentation ; his cheeks were painted, his eyebrows darkened ; in fact he was the very picture of an Egyptian or Assyrian courtesan. To finish with, we have a bit of morality, which tells us how he not only spoilt his real beauty by such extravagances, but made himself ridiculous in the eyes of gods and men by these borrowed plumes.

This is all very circumstantial, obviously the work of an eye-witness, but it is not supported by the evidence of any coin struck to commemorate the event. The *Adventus Augusti* shows the Emperor riding into the city laurelled and habited in military accoutrements. Nor is the scandal mentioned by either Lampridius or Dion, which means that, at least as far as Lampridius goes, his source, Marius Maximus, the then City Praefect, who would certainly be an eye-witness, had not noticed anything unusual. This, one imagines, he would have been only too anxious to do, since he appears to have vacated this office immediately afterwards in favour of the Emperor's friend Eutychianus, which circumstance was not likely to be specially pleasing to Marius, and ought to have encouraged him to keep his eyes open for indecencies. Dion, too, as we have said, is silent, and he has lost no other chance of recording Antonine's frailties. Surely, then, it is at least allowable to relegate this record of inexcusable folly to the limbo of other picturesque lies, and proceed to sift the similar accumulation which Lampridius has collected for our amusement.

Undoubtedly, the first act was to make an alliance with the daughter of the well-known jurist, Julius Paulus, and to celebrate the event with a colossal magnificence. All the authors, with the exception of Lampridius, who ignores the marriage entirely, furnish picturesque details. They describe the games, in which only one elephant and, to balance him, fifty-one tigers were killed (the numbers are peculiar, but incapable of verification); the general distribution of wheat, the unusual magnificence of the whole scene, and the congiary in which even the wives of Senators took part. The sums of money given are most noticeable ; everyone in Rome received 150 drachmae per head, except the soldiers, who only got 100, or very slightly more—a diminution of the promised privi-leges formerly granted by Caracalla, which could scarcely have been pleasing to the Lords of Rome, especially if, as Lampridius says, the Emperor had already begun to lose his popularity with the army. It almost presupposes a change of idea in the body politic, and argues that the new government was bent on the same reforms which had ruined Macrinus, a circumstance which would not turn out advantageously for all concerned. Certainly it was neither wise nor conducive to peace thus to reduce the donative on such an occasion ; but of this more must be said later.

Directly after the festivities in honour of the arrival, and, as has been suggested, of the marriage as well, because we can only trace one congiary and one set of rejoicings during this year—which circumstance rather leads one to suppose that the extraordinary generosity cited did duty for the two occasions—the Emperor set to work to pro-vide a shelter for his God. In point of fact, he provided two. The first and most magnificent, was on the Palatine ; the other, almost as vast and beautiful, was a sort of summer resting-place in the suburbs. Wissowa considers that this second was in the eastern part of the city, near the site of Sta. Croce, near also to the Porta Praenestina, and that it was built on a tract of land known as " Ad Spem Veterem " ; in other words, in the garden belonging to Varius Marcellus, the Empress Soaemias' late husband, and, therefore, imperial property.

Concerning the position of the first temple, we have more certain evidence. Baumeister has identified certain ruins on the Palatine as the Eliogabalium, and though his conclusions are not generally accepted, all the Greek authors agree as to the Palatine being the centre of the cult. Victor tells us that the God was established in " Palatii penetralibus," and Sextus Rufus corroborates Lampridius' statement that it was on the site of a temple of Orcus (Pluto) on the Circus Maximus side of the Palatine Hill.

Some idea of its general magnificence may be gathered from a coin struck in the year 222, which is described by Studniczka. " The temple," he says, " rises to a great height in a glorious symmetry of columns, and is partly covered by the figure of the Emperor and his attendant. Below the group appears the entrance to the temple courtyard, which is crowned with statues." On either side of the entrance are wing-halls, singularly reminiscent of the Bramante porticoes at St. Peter's, eagles taking the place of statues as acroteria.

We must not suppose, despite Xiphilinus' statement, that the cult of this Sun God was first heard of in Rome at this period. All the imperial money coined at Emesa had borne his temple, stone, and eagle on the obverse for many years past, besides which the worship of Mithra, the Persian Sun God, is considered by Cumont to have been the most popular religion in Rome at this time. Septimius Severus had built a temple on the Palatine in his honour, doubtless with the help and counsel of the family of Elagabal worshippers, and there seem to have been many others in the city; a fact which would tend to pave the way for Antonine's scheme. This however could not develop itself until the temple was completed, which from the evidence that can be gathered from coins and inscriptions does not seem to have been an accomplished fact until the late autumn of the next year, 220.

No sooner was the temple finished than the scheme for the unifying of churches, which the Emperor had himself conceived, and intended to promote with the full strength of imperial command, was put into operation. As we have said, Antonine had no more idea of making Elagabal a mere rival to the Roman Deities than Constantine had of putting Christ into that unenviable position. He intended that the Lord should swallow up all other Deities, should make captive all the gods of old Rome. To do this it was necessary, first, to impress the world with the splendour, the beauty, the power, and the magnificence of that being who had so miraculously delivered the family of Bas-sianus from Phoenician obscurity, and brought them into the fierce light of the Roman noonday; secondly, he had to make some alliance with the head and centre of the old Roman worship of Vesta, the one religion which symbolised Rome, its perpetuity, and its undying fame; thirdly, he had to acquire all the objects of sacred devotion, and transfer them to Elagabal's temple, as well to attract worshippers as to stimulate devotion.

For the accomplishment of the first of these objects he ordained the most magnificent worship that had as yet been devised. He, as High Priest, used to descend daily from the palace in order to sacrifice vast quantities of oxen and sheep upon innumerable altars laden with spices and odours. The libations were more ample and more costly than any that had yet been heard of. Herodian further tells us how the rare and costly wines min-gling with the blood of the victims made great streams in every direction ; but even this waste was insufficient: with Davidic persistency the Emperor danced, encircling the altars, followed by the Syrians, men and women, who formed his court, while the display and waste of energy was accompanied by the clashing of cymbals and other instru-ments of music which had been brought from the God's home in the East. At these orgies the Senate sat in a great semicircle, and were, fortun-ately, mere spectators of the show. It was the generals of armies, the governors of provinces, and court officials of all sorts who were less fortunate. These worthies Antonine habited in a replica of his own trailing garments, and ordered to perform menial offices about the altars of God, a proceeding which caused them to gnash with their teeth and run about the city declaring very plainly (to one another, of course) that they infinitely preferred the tents of ungodliness to all and sundry offices of divine religion, especially in its Semitic forms. From the very outset Elagabal was unpopular with the upper classes. They had cause to dislike this insensate show. With the populace it was probably different, at least for a time. One can imagine their joy at beholding, tier upon tier, the Conscript Fathers assembled each morning as most unwilling spectators of a show which they abominated.

As we have already pointed out, other Eastern cults were making considerable headway in Rome amongst all classes, and had attracted not a few of that august body. We have mentioned the worship of the Sun God Mithra, which, with other similar religions, had constantly increased in importance since the year "204 b.c., the date of its introduction into the city.

Now the Eastern cults were popular because they supplied a felt want, namely, a personal spiritual religion, whereas the religion of Rome, though fine, virile and strong, was purely political. The God of Rome was Rome, and concerned itself solely with patriotism. With the individual, with his happiness or aspirations, it concerned itself not at all. It was the prosperity of the Empire, its peace and immortality, for which sacrifices were made and libations offered. The antique virtues, courage in war, moderation in peace, and honour at all times, were civic, not personal. It was the state that had a soul, not the individual. Man was ephemeral, it was the nation that endured.[57] Naturally, this was unsatisfying to the uneducated; their Rome was the abridgment of every superstition, their Pantheon an abattoir of the Gods who presided over death and whose worship was gore.

Added to this had come the worship of Isis, the secrets of Mithra, of which the chief note was one of mysticism. There was something terrifying and yet alluring about the abluent functions, the initia-tions, the secrets that it was death to divulge. Now, the rites that Antonine introduced were entirely blatant, Semitic, Syrian. They con-tained, as far as we can judge, nothing specially mysterious, either in the way of initiation or progression, little which could even attract the curiosity of the devout. All that Elagabal could appeal to was the public curiosity ; his worship was, in fact, designed to appeal to such and nothing more, *at the outset;* even with such an end in view it might have become popular had it not been that Antonine made this all-embracing deity too easy of access, in consequence of which he became too cheap. The Emperor seems to have recognised this early, and to have evolved a scheme for uniting the already popular mysteries of all other Gods with his own ; to which resolve we may attribute the stories of his initiation into the priesthood of Cybele and the rest; he thought that it would enhance his God's attractiveness and assure his popularity in the eyes of the mob.

As far as we can judge from the evidence of coins and medals, there was little or no parade of Antonine's religious ideals or his comprehensive cult until the later part of the year 220, until, in fact, the temple was ready and the necessary adjuncts to hand. With its opening came the transference thither of the most venerable objects of Roman superstition: all the sacred stones, even the Palladium from the temple of Minerva, the sacred fire which was the symbol of Rome's existence, even the shields which had fallen from heaven, and to which the oracles had attached the very destinies of the city itself. But of this more in its proper place.

Certainly, for all his attempts, Elagabal did not become a popular divinity. Men began to fear his propensity for swallowing other cults. His rapacity in absorbing the deities of centuries made the superstitious uneasy for the continued existence of Gods whom, they believed vaguely, they might someday need, and who would then have lost their power and authority. But there was yet another reason for Elagabal's unpopularity, namely, the Emperor's attempt to unite the Hebraic and Christian mysteries with those

---

[57] As Tiberius, " **Principes mortales, rem publicam aeternam esse** " *(Ann.* **iii. 6).**

of his own God.

Neither Christian nor Hebrew was ever popular in old Rome. Their characters, their rites, and their machinations were sincerely disapproved of both by the rulers and the governed ; they were generally known as robbers, thieves, liars, law-breakers, cannibals even, men who were lacking in very virtue that Rome held dear; men who set up their own specimen of a creed to the exclusion of all others, the which was, generally speaking, subver-sive of government, law and order. They were men entirely displeasing to the high Gods, and therefore to be spared only when the master of Rome refused consent to kill.

Now, Antonine clearly protected these atheistic vagabonds, citizens of no state, troublers of every nation ; nay more, he attempted to tolerate their blasphemies by uniting them with his own religion. As we have said, Rome was probably familiar with Elagabal through the Syrian house and Emesan coins, but with the other Judean religion they had not a few disagreements, and had certainly no wish to amalgamate it with the venerated cults of the city, as Antonine seemed bent on doing. It was certainly a bad day for the house of Severus when the Emperor decided to mix himself up with the hated Judaism.

We must here leave for a moment the history of Antonine's religious changes and aspirations to recount the secular work accomplished between the summer of the year 219 and the autumn or winter of the year 220, it may be even up to the early weeks of the year 221, when the Emperor made that vital mistake in policy which threw him into the hands of his family, to his undoing.

Amongst the " facts" recorded by Lampridius concerning this period, we have two mutually exclusive statements concerning the admission of the Emperor's mother and grandmother to the Senate, and their governmental position in the State. The first (in Sec. 4) states that at the very first meeting of that august assembly Antonine sent for his mother; that on her arrival he called her to take a place alongside the Consuls; and that with them she signed decrees, Senatus Consulta, and other documents, an enormity which no other woman had ever perpetrated, and which was certainly never heard of again. He finishes with the remark that she obtained the title of Clarissima, the only woman who has ever had this honour conferred upon her— altogether a most circumstantial account.

A few sections farther on (Sec. 12) he recounts how Antonine always took his grandmother Varia with him whenever he went to the camp or to the Senate, in order to give him the authority and dignity which he lacked, adding, that before her no woman had been admitted into the Senate either to give her opinion or append her signature. It is significant, by the way, that Varia never was and never could have been Maesa's name—so much for Lampridius' ignorance of the family history.

Now, either Antonine took one, both, or neither ; Lampridius says both—each to the exclusion of the other, as each was first, each the only woman, but Soaemias was alone

Clarissima. Cannot one see the jealous wrath of the grandmother, the real poli-tician, at the promotion of her absolutely incap-able daughter over her head by means of that coveted title (a title, by the way, which would have bored Soaemias' temperament inexpressibly), while she was relegated to an inferior position ?

The only conclusion to be drawn is that which is recorded by *all* the inscriptions, namely, that Maesa was the predominant factor, since her name always occurs first where she and Soaemias are mentioned together. Maesa, in all probability, did slip into the Senate ; she would have appreciated the dignity of the position enormously, and the fact would give a basis to some story or other that had got about. Antonine would certainly have had no objection ; the Senate was no longer the government properly so called ; Maesa could do no harm there, and it would be a sop to her for the small power she was exercising in the actual development of events.

Soaemias, we can quite believe, was president of the assembly on the Quirinal which Lampridius sneers at as a foundation of Antonine's, and yet tells us had existed before his time. It was called the Senaculum or Conventus Matronarum. Fried-lander says that it was an ancient and honourable assembly as early as the year 394 b.c., when its members voted their jewels to help raise the tithe in connection with the spoils of Veii. Seneca refers to it in his treatise *De matrimoniis* as a regular assembly. Again, in the year 209 b.c., the matrons met, in consequence of omens, to decide on expiation ; even in imperial times Suetonius says that the Assembly met to reprove Agrippina for her vagaries ; and Hieronymus counts amongst the dis-tractions of Roman life the daily attendance at the Matronarum Senatus. What, therefore, this petulant and carping critic can find to grumble about in this permanent assembly meeting to carry out the provisions of the Lex Appia, one simply cannot imagine, unless it be that, having been prejudiced in early youth, he declined to listen to any arguments for the furthering of either women's rights or duties in the State. At any rate, it is scarcely fair to stigmatise as an immoral and reprehensible act, the Emperor's grant to this Senate of women of the power to make necessary edicts on points which are now very ably supervised by the Lord Chamberlain's department. The points discussed were those relating to the length of a train or the Court uniform of a guardsman ; the precedence due to rank ; who must wait for another's salutation ; to whom a carriage; to whom a saddle-horse; to whom a public conveyance; to whom a mere donkey-cart was a fitting means of progression ; who might use mules ; or for whom oxen were considered sufficiently rapid; for whom the saddle might be inlaid with ivory; for whom with bone ; for whom with silver; or even when pointing out what persons might fittingly wear gold and jewelled buckles on their shoes without the imputation of plutocratic ostentation.

To-day, despite the fact that we have progressed by eighteen centuries, it is generally believed in governmental circles that such matters are possibly best settled by women, and such useful, not to say necessary functions concerning the polite amenities of civilised existence would be most readily conceded by authority to their sex, if only such would content and assuage that feline animosity which has of late disturbed social gatherings, even the intercourse between authorities in the state and ladies seeking a useful outlet for their superfluous energies. Alas; the world is grown older, and the female mind now knows itself capable of regulating both the social and political worlds, and has no intention of satisfying its aspirations, like Soaemias, with the social side of life, as long as mere man opposes her entrance into the political sphere.

Surely, everything considered, this cavilling at what was an ancient, and still would be a useful, body, is only another proof of the spirit in which the biographers have poured abuse on a boy who was so obviously striving to satisfy his relatives by giving them an outlet for their energies, while keeping the essential powers of government in his own hands. Of course he failed, mainly because his grandmother was not satisfied with her function in the state, she wanted to filch from Antonine what was *his* right, and what she wanted she determined to get at all costs. Whether she really aspired to the Senate and got there is another question. It is distinctly stated that under Alex-ander Severus no woman ever sat in that assembly ; further, that decrees were passed forbidding their presence there forever. Now, Maesa was almost sole ruler during the early years of that reign, and one can never believe that she deprived herself of one jot or tittle of a power which she had once acquired. There is one occasion, and one occasion only, on which we may well imagine, as the writers state, that the women were all present, officially, in the Senate, namely, at the meeting when Alexander was adopted. At other times, we can believe that they were there, just as the queen consort is present in the House of Peers, but without any real political significance.

To this period Lampridius assigns the winter spent at Nicomedia, which is a very fair example of this biographer's egregious carelessness and stupidity. Considering that both Dion and Herodian are perfectly explicit as to the actual date, it is monstrous that he should have put this period just a year later than it actually occurred, nor, as we have said, is it in this matter alone that he leads us to mistrust his accuracy, where either fact or fiction are at stake.

Lampridius, with a great show of moralising, and having already stated that the Emperor had lost his popularity shortly after Macrinus' death, re-ascribes its loss to this current year, namely, from the summer of 219 to the autumn of 220, and this without showing cause, reason, or mismanagement which would justify the statement, if we except the vague statement that he neglected public business for religion, though, as far as we can see, the Emperor did not begin to neglect the State for the Church until his temple was opened. After that time we can well believe that all his energies were centred on his cult, an error which, like that made by certain Stuart sovereigns of this enlight-ened country, equally lost, the one his head, and the other his crown. No act of cruelty is cited, no accusation of glaring or vital mistakes made, until the very end of the year 220.

Arrived at that period, there is much to be said —the mismanagement of affairs grows apace. First, there is his religion, which he makes a definite eyesore; second, he is accused of selling honours, dignities, and power, both with his own hands and by those of his favourites ; third, he appoints Senators without any reference to either their age, good sense, or nobility; fourth, he sells the offices of praefect, tribune, ambassador, and general, even those about the palace itself.

Now, all this may be perfectly true. Antonine must have wanted money, but, as we have remarked before, he had a passion for giving, not for receiving. The most likely supposition is therefore, that he gave offices indiscriminately to those who pleased him, and that his favourites, often debased and un-worthy people, sold what they could get hold of to the highest bidder. The accusation is vitiated by the fact that no names are mentioned, no instances given, except those of the two chariot drivers, Protogenes and Gordius, intimates of the Emperor and supervisors of his sports. It is quite possible that he admired and liked these men for their proficiency in sport, and that unwholesome minds saw more in the friendship than was warranted. Of Protogenes we hear no more. Cordus or Gordius—probably the same person as the above —was made Praefect of the Watch during the next year; perhaps he was useful, perhaps he was not; any way he was dismissed in the autumn of 221.

Amongst the last events of this 220th year of our salvation, or early in the year 221, occurred the divorce of the august Julia Cornelia Paula, Empress. We know that it was late in the year, as there are coins in existence struck at Alexandria after 29th August which bear her name, and others struck at Tripolis in Phoenicia after October 220 (Eckhel). In all probability this lady was in no way averse to retiring into opulent privacy, a woman with both a past and a future.

Certainly her husband had neglected her scandalously if even a tithe of Lampridius' stories of his infidelities are true, and, from what we can learn of his psychological state, a certain number are obviously so. Modern investigation of such psychopathic conditions inclines us to admit that the boy was a sort of nymphomaniac, if not entirely homosexual, at least heterosexual, with a strong homosexual instinct, and it would be unnatural for any woman to appreciate this temperament in a husband, especially when she knew, as she must have known, since he was perfectly frank about it, that he was already allied, by a species of matri-mony, with the chariot driver Hierocles—calling himself wife and Empress—and that he was not attached to this man alone but to many others, for whom inquisition had been made throughout the Empire, on account of their looks and ability to satiate his mania more satisfactorily. . This is, of course, Lampridius' version of the Emperor's character, and the same sources have been used by both Dion and Herodian with similar though varying degrees of grossness in expression. Undoubtedly the boy was by nature abnormal, as were almost all the Emperors of Old Rome. Antonine had his moments when he imitated a virgin at bay, others when he was a wife, still others when he expected to be a mother, others when he carded wool, others when he played the pandore (an instrument of music with three strings invented by the Assyrians, according to Pollux, or, as Isidore remarks, attributed to the God Pan himself). Again, he would play the hydraulic organ of the period, and loved to dress himself in the clothes of women, even in the customary undress uniform of the courtesan, adopting the positions, voice, and manner of the most expert.

Undoubtedly these pastimes were most repre-hensible and unpleasant, to be condemned one and all; though somehow to-day we are not altogether inclined to regard proficiency in music amongst men as quite so censurable and disgusting an art as the other foibles—to give them no worse a name —which Lampridius so justly censures. Unfor-tunately, many of these seem to have come quite naturally to the Emperor on account of his untrained and unrestrained nature, though Forquet de Dome thinks that it was not so much evil propensities as his innate desire to please, combined with his genuine efforts to spend all his energies for other people, which have been misinterpreted by the evil-minded, especially as this was not the only side to the boy's character, as the biographers would have us believe. And this because we are told, amongst the list of his enormities, that he loved driving chariots both in the palace and in the circus, habited in a green tunic, and that he was most dextrous in the sport.

To-day, racing is considered as the sport of kings; certainly it is not the obvious outcome of an effeminate or degraded mind; rather the reverse: it is a virile occupation, calling forth nerve, pluck, courage, and other manly qualities. In third-century Rome it was much the same, but for purposes of disgusting posterity Lampridius affected not to think so. He pointed out that it was a calling proper only to coachmen and lackeys, though he must have known, if he had thought about it at all, that his readers would listen with their tongues in their cheeks when he tried to maintain that the courage, nerve, and pluck which the boy showed in this sport were evidences of the same degeneracy which he was decrying when he recounted the carding of wool and the other feminine occupations. Hosts of men, kings, and emperors of all ages have indulged in the intoxication of horse-racing. The mere fact of Lampridius putting this story, with its palpably stupid and far-fetched moral, alongside the really serious scandals would be enough to make critics distrust, not only his information, but even his ability to understand and use such when he had got it.

To sum up, therefore, our investigations of the months between June 219 and November 220, we must admit that no gross act of folly had as, yet been committed. The Emperor had spent his time in building his temples, and in restoring the Flavian amphitheatre—which had been burnt down on 23rd August 217,—in finishing the baths of Caracalla, and in erecting his own splendid bathing establishments in the palace and on the Aventine. He had refounded the Senaculum, and built a hall for its use; he was attending to business, helped by his fellow-consul, Eutychianus, and was giving righteous judgment, as all biographers admit, when he attended the courts or the Senate. He was, moreover, most popular, liberal, and generous, though devoted to the pleasures of the table, and unfortunately hermaphroditic in tendency, which hereditary taint was certainly mitigated by the fact that he was devoted to outdoor exercises, especially those that demanded courage, nerve, and strength of will. Underneath all this there is a predominating religious feeling, and the simply monotheistic obsession which drove him to his doom.

The year 221 is the time of Antonine's utter failure. As far as we can judge from numismatic evidence, one of his first acts was to divorce, as we have said, the Empress Julia Paula, probably in pursuance of his scheme for religious unity. He had conceived a notion of rendering his God absolutely supreme by means of an alliance with the worship of Vesta. Now this Goddess and her Sacred Stone or Phallus, called the Palladium, her shields or bucklers, had been sent to Troy direct from heaven. Aeneas had brought them to Latium, and they were the head and centre of Roman greatness. Pallas, or Vesta, was too powerful to be absorbed in the ordinary way. Antonine therefore considered that his God, being unmarried, might well acquire possession of Vesta by a matrimonial alliance. As Pontifex Maximus, he was head of the Vesta worship, and had a perfect right to enter her shrine when and how he pleased, a circumstance which Lampridius entirely ignored when he said that the Emperor forced his way into the temple illegally. Antonine certainly did go to her shrine at this time, and took the sacred fire, carrying it to the Eliogabalium. Lampridius asserts that the high priestess, being jealous of the loss of her charge, tried to palm off a false vessel upon him, but that the Emperor saw the deceit and broke the jar in contempt for the foolish fraud. He also transferred the sacred stone at the same time, and in pursuance of his plan, celebrated the nuptials on which he had set his heart. This was bad enough for Roman susceptibilities, but he went one worse. Being himself free, he decided to marry one of the Sacred Vestals from the shrine of his God's new wife. He certainly seems to have been vitally attracted by the charms of Aquilia Severa, a woman no longer in the first flush of youth, to judge by her effigy, but one whom his religious as well as his personal predilections pointed out as a fitting consort. Pallas and Elagabal were united in a heavenly union like so many others amongst Syrian and Egyptian deities; why, then, should not Antonine, the chief priest of the Sun, and Aquilia, an important priestess of Minerva, unite in a fruitful union which would produce a demigod meet for the Empire ?

The theory had its points. Unfortunately, Rome did not see them. She stood obviously aghast, thoroughly disliking the notion. Then, as now, Rome disliked the public repudiation of vows ; it was an unforgivable scandal. As Clement VII. remarked some years later to Henry Tudor, with an equally genuine fervour, " Pray, please yourself by all means, but don't let me know." That was and always will be the true Roman attitude. Concubinage amongst these ladies was perfectly natural, in fact fairly usual, if we can believe Suetonius, but matrimony never; it offended the susceptibilities, and hence the subsequent trouble. Antonine does not seem to have grasped this fact, and, if any one told him, he was too much enamoured of his scheme to resign it without an effort. But even the Senate seems to have protested, and a plot, in which Pomponius Bassus and Silius Messala were implicated (probably inspired by that upright lady Julia Mamaea), was set on foot. It was an attempt to substitute some other personage for the youth who knew so little of Roman feeling as to commit this act of sacrilege. These two men were well-known busybodies, who had already dethroned one Emperor, and were obviously anxious for further employment in the same direction. Unfortunately for them, the plan was discovered, and their secret court, held to consider the Emperor's actions, raided. They were immediately arraigned before the Senate, and condemned for the crime of *lèse-majesté*, or treason, probably both, thus meeting the fate they had so richly deserved; but of these two men we shall have occasion to speak later on.

There is still another thing to notice in connection with this dual marriage (that of the two Gods and of the High Priest and the Vestal), namely, the erection of a shrine in the Forum to celebrate the event, the which was probably built, according to Commendatore Boni, somewhere in the summer of the year 221. Certain pieces of a capital discovered near that place between the years 1870-1872, display the God Elagabal between Minerva and Urania, his second wife, which leads one to the conclusion that the union with Vesta, though no longer of earthly, was at least considered as one of spiritual duration.

But to proceed. By the spring of 221 Antonine must have discovered for himself, even if his friends had not told him, that his religious ideals were far from popular. The very fact of the plot was enough to show him how public opinion was trending, added to which general pressure seems to have been put upon the Emperor to rectify the two glaring mistakes which he had just made, through his perverse religiosity. We know from both Dion and Herodian that neither marriage lasted any length of time. Numismatic evidence of his third wedding is dated prior to 28th August 221, which presupposes that Aquilia Severa had returned to her nunnery, while the celebration of the nuptials between the Sun and Moon implies, what we know to be a fact, that Minerva had returned to the seclusion from which she ought never to have been taken. It must have been a great blow to the boy, thus to relinquish his hold on one of the chief parts of his scheme, but he had seen that it would do Elagabal no good to slight the religion with which the destinies of Rome were inextricably mixed up, and that he had merely thrown open the way to his grandmother's machinations. Again, as Borghesi has pointed out, probably Eutychianus was back at his side as City Praefect, in which position that officer would be better able to judge of the feeling which Antonine's action had created, than as Consul. The result was that the Emperor published a statement, by no means conciliatory in character, which announced, that his God liked not so martial a wife, in consequence of which he had decided to return her to her own shrine, and send for Astarte from Carthage instead. Tanit of the Carthaginians, Juno Coelestis or Magna Mater as she was called in Italy, where she had grown in importance from the third century b.c., when she was first introduced, was probably a Phoenician Goddess with a cosmopolitan tendency. Cumont tells us that this maiden divinity was identified with Diana, Cybele, and sometimes with Venus. Gener-ally she was called a moon goddess, certainly she possessed a twofold nature — as queen of the heavens she directed the moon and stars, and sent down life-giving rains on the earth, and as the per-sonification of the productive force of nature, she was the patroness of fertility. Latterly in Rome she had been identified with the cult of Mithra, which had taken such a hold on the popular mind and was now at the summit of its power. Undoubtedly the introduction of this Goddess into their midst, especially since it could hurt no local superstition, would be a popular move, and Elagabal would gain the reflected glory; at least amongst the ignorant and religious-minded to whom such arrant nonsense would be sure to appeal. From the Emperor's own point of view the marriage was fitting, since the queen of the heavens was, not only second in authority to the Sun, but was also rich, and with her came the whole of her treasure, according to Herodian. This statement, however, Dion denies flatly, asserting that the Emperor refused to take anything from her temple except two golden lions, presumably as a sort of protection for the journey, while he himself provided her dowry by a general im-post on the whole Empire; so much for rival eye-witnesses.

About this same time, certainly (as we have said) before 28th August, Antonine married again, pre-sumably at the instigation of his grandmother, and to gain the allegiance of the patrician classes. The bride was widow of that busybody Pomponius Bassus, lately deceased. The alliance, like that of the God, was sure to be popular with all classes, and the lady, though by no means in her first youth (from the portraits on her medals she leaves one with the impression of being about forty-five years of age) was of Imperial Antonine lineage. Undoubtedly the Emperor soon tired of her charms, which were scarcely likely to please a boy of eighteen, and in consequence we are told he did not keep her long. She was a friend of his grand-mother, a well-known and ambitious woman, who was quite pleased to dry her eyes at once and fall in with Maesa's plan of appointing a sort of nuptial guardian for the boy, which would naturally be a great asset in the struggle that his grandmother and aunt had fully decided upon, from the moment when he made his mistake in underestimating the popular antipathy towards his unfortunate religious scheme.

Both Maesa and Mamaea were now working together, for both were determined to consolidate in their hands the power that was Antonine's by right. From this moment there is one continuous policy of corruption, vilification, and grab, while the women, their greedy claws ever stretching out, filch from the boy his popularity, his friends, and his reputation. Herodian tells us of the money spent to corrupt the guards. Every word of the biographies tells the same story. Even when they had encompassed his death and put another in his room they could not leave his memory in peace. The trump card in this game was played by Maesa's diplomacy; she knew that the only way to win the boy was to attach herself to his religious ideals, and she therefore seems to have fallen in with his scheme for the union of Elagabal and Urania. She sympathised with his endeavour to make his God popular; indeed, was not Elagabal her God also, hers by right of her position as the eldest of his hereditary house of priests ? Very insidiously she wormed her way into his boyish confidence, lulled his mind to rest, and then suggested her great plan, the appointment of Alexianus to help him in the government, to assist in the secular affairs which so sadly-hampered the Emperor's spiritual and sacerdotal functions.

CHAPTER VI.ANTONINE'S DEALINGS WITH ALEXANDER

Lampridius has given us, in his life of Alexander Severus, a mass of undigested information concern-ing the character and daily life of Mamaea's son. The narrative is as much concerned to prove the virtues of Alexander as it is to represent the degradation of his predecessor. Somehow the panegyric misses fire; Lampridius has produced a spasmodic and unenlightened discourse on trivialities, together with a haphazard essay on his hero's moral qualities. He assures us that Alexander had a regal presence, great flashing eyes, a penetrat-ing gaze, a manly appearance, and the stature and health of a soldier. Now, the practice of idealising the appearance of royalty is not unknown, even in these days. Unfortunately, this description is in no way borne out by the portraits still extant. Alex-ander, in the Vatican bust, has certainly the appearance of strength, but it is such as is possessed by a lusty coal-heaver, with a bull neck and a thick skull; the undecided features of the face, the weak mouth and chin, the low forehead, half hidden by the hair, all betoken mild-mannered vacuity rather than manliness, while the eyes, so far from flashing, seem, in the phrase of Duruy, to " stare without seeing." It is the figure neither of a Roman nor of a ruler of men, but just that possessed by the family to which he belonged, though cast in an effete and much-used mould ; it is the face of a half-caste Phoenician, such as he chanced to be. Alexander was an absolutely perfect tool for the purposes of his grandmother's scheme, and, in consequence, Lampridius records the series of omens portending his royal nativity. The entire menagerie of Egypt seemed to proclaim him king. Surely, argued Maesa, such evidences of suitability would convince the truly religious Antonine; and so, primed with her proofs, the lady repaired to carry out her scheme. But, as we have said, the Emperor was used to her wiles; she had tried cajoling him before and had failed; this time it was on the score of religion, on the necessity that he should devote his full energies to the furthering of his great and all-embracing scheme, that she attacked him. It is a pitiful sight for us, who know the results, to watch the guile of the serpent prostituting innocence for its own gain. Maesa must at this time have been close on fifty years of age, and we are assured on all hands that she was in close alliance with her daughter Mamaea, who had long since conceived a holy horror, not only of the sins of her nephew, but also for the person of the sinner. So strongly was she convinced of her righteousness, that she had already thought it her bounden duty, as well as her special privilege, to attempt the corruption of the guards, and to support the plots, all and sundry, which disaffected functionaries might attempt against the person of the Emperor.

Now, venality is a vice not confined to the modern world ; then, as now, it was possible to find men who considered that their usefulness was underestimated, and that their posi-tion inadequately represented their merits. The record of at least three such personages and their attempts has come down to us : the first was that instituted by Pomponius Bassus and his colleague Silius Messala, who had adopted Mamaea's line of argument as to the inadvisability of allowing Antonine's mistaken religious policy to continue ; the second, that of Seius Carus, who in 221 attempted the corruption of the Alban Legion in either his own or Alexianus' interest—and in both of these plots we are led to infer that Julia Mamaea had a considerable finger.

The question of Seius Carus is one of consider-able interest from this point of view. The gentle-man was wealthy and of the patrician order, which facts did not prevent him, according to Dion, from spending his money freely amongst the soldiery, obviously with an ulterior motive. Unfortunately for .him, he hit upon the wrong legion, the body which was now quartered near Rome and had joined Antonine so readily at Apamea in 21S. In the year 220 this legion had set up an inscription to Antonine's Victoria Aeterna, which monu-ment had expressed the greatest possible devotion to the reigning Emperor, and gave the lie direct to those stones of Dion and Lampridius, which assert that, as early as the winter of 218, the soldiers cordially hated Antonine, and placed all their hopes on Alexianus. Lampridius gives a very poor reason for this—because, forsooth, they could not stand the thought that he was as ready as they themselves were to receive pleasure through all the cavities of his body. Dion relates Seius' trial, but ignoring the fact of the plot, which he had just mentioned, he informs us that the gentleman suffered for a crime which was absolutely unknown to the imperial, as indeed to any other legal system, unless it be the ecclesiastical—"on account of his worth and abilities." Unfortunately, Dion does not point out why the millions of other men in the Empire, equally worthy and equally able, were allowed a greater longevity, though it is certainly a point which might be considered with some show of interest. But to return to the imperial ladies. As we have said, they were spending much time searching out disaffected subjects, and repeating stories not conducive either to peace or tranquillity; further, they were making use of Antonine's most foolish resolve to cut down military expenditure at the price of a possible unpopularity, by giving a decided preference to the civil element in the population, a proceeding which, as we have remarked on more than one occasion, was not only foolish but under the circumstances criminally wrong. Despite the manifold and splendid qualities which soldiers possessed, it must be confessed that they were as eager for gain as the average Hebrew grocer, and

almost as ready to accept coins from no matter what tainted source they might come. " Money," as Vespasian had said, " has no smell," a sentiment with which most men were in entire agreement.

This is a very fair view of the state of politics about the month of June, in the year of our Lord 221, at which time the Dowager Empress propounded her scheme; an attempt, she said, to transfer the odium of Antonine's neglect in secular matters to other shoulders, and so to set the boy free to carry out his great policy for the advancement of religious unity throughout the world. Maesa certainly agreed with her grandson's point of view, or said she did, which came to the same thing. The work which he had proposed was great and important, and it had been neglected for the good of the state. Now, to neglect the great God angered him to whom the family owed their position. To neglect the affairs of state angered the people, and gave rise to disturbances ; of this Antonine had had recent examples. Surely it would be advisable to appoint a coadjutor in the affairs of state, and, for obvious reasons, one of his own family, someone who would naturally have no other desire than to serve Antonine; there was a relative ready and willing. Why did he not adopt Alexianus ? Perhaps the boy was insignificant! Well, so much the better; but at any rate he might be used to advantage. All this was most plausible, and may have blinded the Emperor for the moment, but we can easily understand, from what we know of Antonine's nature, that even if he saw through the very specious pleas here put forward, he would quite enjoy meeting his grandmother on her own ground. He had done it before, and had played the game successfully.

But the suggestion seems to have really appealed to his sense of the fitting ; he *was* hard pressed ; he was more anxious for the fate of his God than for the fate of the Empire (a crime for which other sovereigns have suffered similar fates at the hands of infuriated populaces), besides which, Dion tells us that Antonine loved his cousin, stupid and namby-pamby as he undoubtedly was.

And there was yet another side to the suggestion which commended itself to the Emperor's favourable consideration. In his present position Alexianus was a distinct menace to the government. Since Antonine's mistake about Vesta and Severa, his cousin had been used as a lever wherewith to raise popular indignation. There had been two plots, as we have pointed out, to dethrone Antonine ; and, presumably, as Julia Mamaea was behind both, to replace him by Alexianus. Why not take the boy into his own keeping, adopt him as Maesa suggested, and, by taking their tool from their hands in response to their own appeal, neutralise the influence of both aunt and grandmother at one swoop ? He could then train him in his own way. Alexianus was young—Herodian says about twelve years old—and ought, if he were a natural child, to be easily won by kindness, friendship, and joy. This information of Herodian's as to age is, for a wonder, corroborated by several reliable sources ; not that Herodian knew he was right even in this case, because he puts the adoption in the year 220 instead of 221, which would have made Alexianus about eleven instead of over twelve years old, as he states.

This is the only rational view to take of the Emperor's apparent gullibility, as Antonine was far too quick-witted not to have scented trouble in any scheme, however specious, to which his aunt was party. He had already heard of her dealings with the soldiers, and of the money that she was spending with a purpose: obviously he saw in the adoption a loophole for his own escape, and at the same time for her undoing. His friends may have warned him to look out for rocks ahead. They knew that the boy was dealing with two able and crafty women made desperate by their continual disappointments; if so, he must have refused to listen to them, for some time early in July Antonine took his cousin Alexianus to the Senate, and there, in the presence of the women, this boy of sixteen summers went through the ceremony of adopting the child of twelve. He then solemnly declared his intention of training his son himself, fitting him for the business of Empire early, in order that he might be free from solicitudes about a successor. Now, this was by no means Mamaea's plan, and caused endless friction in the working.

Antonine obviously thought that some explanation of his decision was needed, and had the audacity to tell the assembled fathers that he was acting on the commands of the great God, who had designated Alexianus as the successor to the name and Empire of Severus,—this on the basis of a bastardy almost as probable as his own.

The name Alexander, which was then imposed upon Alexianus, is accounted for both by Lampridius and Dion by two equally untrue and mutually contradictory stories. Lampridius says that the boy was born in the temple of Alexander at Area, on the birthday of Alexander of Macedon, 18th June 208 ; as a matter of fact he was not born until the 1st October of that year, and it was highly improbable that a woman in the social position of Mamaea would allow an accident of the kind to happen in so public and unprepared a position. Dion accounts for the new name by relating the miraculous return from the dead of the Macedonian king, and his spectral journey through Thrace, where he buried a wooden horse which has not since been found,—neither has the consonance of the story been established, for that matter. The real reason for the change of name was perfectly simple ; it was in memory of the devotion which Caracalla, his putative father, had always testified towards King Alexander of Macedon.

The ages of the two principal figures in this ceremony form the peg on which Lampridius hangs not a few jeers. Perhaps it was absurd, but far more unnatural things had been extolled : witness Septimius' adoption of the defunct Marcus Aurelius as his father, which was certainly an even less possible performance in the natural order of generation. If Lampridius jeered later, no one did so at the time ; in fact, we are led to infer that all men were pleased. The soldiers, because Mamaea had made it worth their while to adopt that attitude; the Senate, because they expected consideration from a little milksop brought up entirely at his mother's apron - strings ; the people, because it was the occasion for Antonine's fourth congiary. Singularly enough, there is again no mention made of a donative, or distribution of money to the soldiers, which seems unfortunate.

It is difficult to ascertain the exact date of the adoption. Herodian's statement of the year 220 is easily refuted, both by epigraphic and numismatic evidence. These give, as near as possible, 10th July in the year 221, by means of the following deductions:— (1st) The fasti of a priestly college, probably the Sodales Antoniniani, dated either 2nd or 10th July in that year, describe Alexianus as "Marcus Aurelius Alexander

Nobilissimus Caesar," and either Imperii *consors* or *heres,* on which discrepancy of words hangs a future tale ; (2nd) the earliest Alexandrian coins which call Alexianus Caesar are dated or subsequent to 29th August 221; (3rd) there is an inscription found amongst those of the 7th Cohort of the Vigiles, which was set up on 1st June of that year, and commemorates the Imperatores Antoninus et Alexander. The earliest date is therefore 1st June, the latest the end of July or beginning of August. The probabilities lie between the two, as the early police inscription has been accounted for on the grounds that, along with her money, Mamaea had   circulated a report of the adoption before it took place. The numismatic evidence points to a middle date, because, as far as we can judge, the Alex-andrian mint was most expedite in issuing its coins, and here, if the adoption took place early in June, they would seem to have allowed a month or so to elapse between the time they got the news and the first issue of the coins. Other mints also issued their first coins, calling Alexander Caesar, towards the end of 221.

The one official decree is that of the Sodales. It is defective in its designation, and has caused much disagreement both as to Alexander's position once he was adopted, as well as about the date of the ceremony itself. At any rate, until more definite information comes to hand, we are forced to be content with the generally received date, somewhere about 10th July. The next question is as to the position of Alexander after that date, in the year 221. Certainly Maesa and Mamaea intended to have him "Imperii consors." As far as we can judge, both from the statement in the Senate and from his subsequent proceedings in the state, Antonine's intention was to adopt an " Imperii heres " ; now, this was a very different matter, and entirely nullified the major part of the plan of the schemers. Antonine certainly did defeat their plot in part by refusing to give Alexander any governmental powers. This is certain from the fact that on no coin does Alexander appear with the imperial insignia (the laurel wreath) before the month of March 222, though the titles which he received at his adoption—Augustus, Imperator, and Caesar—are frequently used before that date, because Antonine never had the least objection to other people using titles, so long as he kept the power. Maesa and Mamaea must have been wild with rage at having gained so little ; they had shaken hands repeatedly, and congratulated themselves so often because Samson had at last delivered himself bound into their hands and henceforth they were in permanent possession of the administration, that it must have been a very disagreeable awakening when they found that their plan had not succeeded.

If we can believe anything that Lampridius says, we would judge that Maesa was now genuinely frightened. She thought that Antonine's religious mistake had created a real wave of bad feeling in the city, and that, if anything should happen to the reigning Emperor, her position would be gone for good and all. Now, the last thing that she had a mind to do was to return to provincial obscurity. With a patience and determination worthy of a better cause, she set to work to gain for herself, and incidentally for Alexander also, what had not accrued when the adoption took place. As far as we can judge from the coins, Maesa had only managed at that time to obtain his association with Antonine as Pontifex Maximus, thereby lessening the Emperor's authority over the Roman cults, for which he had shown so little respect. One thing was, however, satisfactory: Alexander was " out"; people knew about him in Rome ; he was the heir designate, and, as such, a most useful lever in the hands of the unscrupulous.

It was certainly not long before Antonine found that his success had not been as unqualified as he had imagined. Alexander was Caesar by decree of the Senate; Severus by some utterly unconstitutional decree of the army; Antonini filius and Severi Nepos; but here it began and ended. The boy was utterly unresponsive to the affection that Antonine was anxious to lavish upon him ; utterly incapable, so the Emperor said, of any sort of train-ing for the position he was destined to occupy. Undoubtedly a great mistake had been made, the boy was a born prig, and the Emperor had given his case away by adopting him at all, by putting him into a position in which his popularity was bound to increase amongst those who did not know him personally. In fact, Antonine arrived at the conclusion before the wine harvest that he had played his aunt's game and not his own, and in consequence he became moody and uncomfortable.

Lampridius' contrast of the two characters is, as we have said, a caricature drawn for the laudation of the younger, the reprobation of the elder. If only a part is true, it must have been very annoy-ing for the Emperor of seventeen to be saddled, through his own stupidity, with a nincompoop of twelve, a boy who quoted proverbs to a purpose, and the maxims of a detestable crowd of female relatives at every turn. Of course, Lampridius' likeness of his little hero is stocked with ful-some adulation. One would think, on reading it, that there was at least one person in the world who did not deceive himself when he said that he was without sin, and therefore ready to cast the first stone. The account of his first meeting with the Senate is simply ludicrous ; no child, however disgusting, could have displayed the unction and greasiness which is recorded as having slipped off his tongue. Were he one-half as nasty as Lampridius asserts, we can well imagine that the whole devil in Antonine was striving to get hold of his cousin's prejudices, trying to persuade him to run, dance, play, to wake him up from the self-satisfac-tion which so ill became his years. All of this, we are told, Antonine did, under the generic terms of corrupting his morals, which is after all the sum total of Antonine's enormities.

But here Mamaea stepped in. She had spoilt her son's youth, as many another parent has done both before and since, and was not going to stand by and see her work dissipated, blown to the winds. Not that she need have feared. The Bassiani developed young ; Alexander's character was moulded, and he had no desire to change, to live his life as a man, instead of as a vegetable, or enjoy the gifts which the gods had given to men. Antonine had thought that something might be done for the cousin he pitied, by turning him loose; he found it was no good, and soon lost patience. He then realised the trend of affairs ; he saw the growing influence of the women, the stupidity of the boy, and chafed more each day under both. The nonconformist conscience, which was Alexander's chief attraction, and is still his only title to fame, annoyed the Emperor continually. Friction arose at every turn. It was Antonine striving to minimise the influence of the women, and the women striving to destroy the influence of Antonine, together with his crew of wretched favour-ites. Neither did the elderly Annia Faustina tend to mend matters. She as well as Alexander had been a mistake, and so the Emperor resolved to get rid of both his troubles at one swoop. To do this, however, he had to quarrel openly with his relatives, and by a *coup d'état* regain paramount authority in the state. The question was, would he be strong enough? Would a boy of seventeen, surrounded by friends who, however agreeable as sportsmen, however able in the histrionic art were anything but trained politicians, have much chance of regaining what statecraft, diplomacy, and guile had filched from him at a moment when he was com-paratively helpless ?

His first act was to follow the same tactics that he had adopted on 10th July. He sent to the Senate ordering the fathers to withdraw the title of Caesar which he had conferred on Alexander and which they had confirmed. That august assembly, we are told, preserved a discreet silence, not quite knowing whom to please, or which way the strongest cat was going to jump. Here, after all that the author has said about Alexander's popularity and the general hatred testified towards Antonine, occurs a strange statement. Lampridius, says they were silent because, "according to certain per-sons, Alexander was popular with the army." This, as we see, is a much-qualified expression of opinion when compared with those in the foregoing sections, and put in conjunction with the Senate's reluctance to commit itself one way or another, it is cer-tainly significant, and points to the fact that the real hatred towards the Emperor had yet to be worked up, like the similar hatred towards the aristocracy in this country. Another significant fact concerning the Emperor's honest and straightforward intentions towards his cousin is, that right up to the last he seems to have had command of the boy's person, and never took any decisive measure, either openly or secretly—in the usual Antonine fashion — for removing him to another sphere of usefulness in realms celestial, despite the plots formed against his own life, of which, before now, he had had ample proof.

It is probable that about this time Antonine made several official appointments which were considered thoroughly bad by the older politicians. Names are not mentioned, but we can well believe that the Emperor had grown suspicious of his old advisers ever since he had seen them paying court to the young Caesar and his mother. We are told that he put men into offices, especially those about the palace, who, from a personal and too intimate relation, he felt he could rely on. As ever, such appointments are a gross mistake. As mere friends such men would have tended to his undoing ; as officials they tended to revolution.

Following up his command to the Senate, Anto-nine sent messengers to the army.

These demanded that the soldiery should relieve Alexander of the title of Severus, or Caesar, or whatever designation they had taken upon themselves to confer on the boy, while the same messengers were ordered to deface the statues and inscriptions in the camp, as the custom was to treat those of dethroned tyrants. Now, this was unwise, without so much as by your leave, or with your leave, because the property belonged to the regiments, and not to the Emperor.

Next in order comes the record of an attempt made by Antonine to assassinate his cousin. It is a story which requires careful examination, because Herodian never mentions it at all, and Dion only refers to it casually in the following words: " Much as Sardanapalus loved his cousin, when he began to suspect everybody and learnt that the general feeling was veering towards Alexander, he dared to change his resolution, and did all in his power to get rid of him. He tried one day to have him assassinated, and not only did not succeed, but nearly lost his own life in the attempt." Lampridius is, of course, much more explicit. This we might expect, because he lived so much later and had a century of vilification to work upon as well as Dion's official story. From him we learn that Antonine sent men to assassinate Alexander, and also sent letters to the boy's governors (all of whom, be it remembered, were of Mamaea's appointment and consequently were working for her, not for Antonine) with promises of wealth and honours if they would only kill their charge in any way they thought best, either in the bath, by poison, or the sword.

This policy of bovine artfulness accomplished, Antonine went to his gardens in the suburbs *(ad span vetereni)* for an afternoon's exercise in chariot - driving, certainly without any sufficient guard. At this juncture Lampridius stops his fantastic story of the most futile attempt at assassination ever recorded, in order to utter a few sententious platitudes, which, however, cut both ways. He remarks with a verisimilitude of sincerity, that " the wicked can do nothing against the innocent." Now this is a maxim which is not always regarded as a truism, even on the Stock Exchange, but it was a convenient way of accounting for the incomprehensible ending to this absurd allegation.

Lampridius then continues that the promulgation of these orders, as carried to the soldiers, did not increase the popularity of the Emperor, at any rate amongst that party who were in Mamaea's pay; besides which, fratricide was by no means a popular, even when it was a fashionable crime. The result of these two supposed epistles when communicated to the soldiers (by whom or why is unfortunately not mentioned) was to rouse them to the highest pitch of anger. Quite spontaneously they ran, some to the palace, where Alexander was living with his mother, and some to the gardens, where, also by some unexplained power of divination, they knew they would find Antonine; their intention being to carry out Mamaea's wishes on the person of the Emperor without further delay. Soaemias, we are told, followed them on foot with the design of warning her son concerning the danger that threatened him. Antonine was preparing for a chariot race when he heard the noise approach-ing, and being frightened, says Lampridius, he hid in the doorway of his bedroom, behind the curtain ; surely not a very safe place to hide when thoroughly frightened by an angry mob, and quite unlike his usual procedure in times of danger. Next he sent his praefect Antiochianus to find out the reason of the tumult. This man easily managed to dissuade the soldiers from their murder-ous designs, and recalled them to their oaths, because, as Lampridius naively remarks, they were too few in number; the greater part having refused to leave their standard, which Aristomachus had kept out of the treasonable attempt.

At last Antonine's eyes were fully opened to his danger. He now knew how far Mamaea's money and persuasions had gone, and whither the influence of Maesa was tending. There had been a military rising; not strong enough to effect its purpose, it is true, but still able to cause confusion, strife, and divided allegiance in the city, and set people's tongues wagging.

The Emperor seems to have made up his mind at once as to his line of conduct. With a courage almost unprecedented in a boy of his age, he went -straight to the camp, resolved to show himself in their midst and settle this matter, once and for all, with the Praetorians. It was undoubtedly one of the finest acts of courage in his life, this going alone and unprotected into the midst of a camp which was supposed to be in mutiny ; a camp where he had just learnt that at least a section of the men were in his aunt's pay, and to which, if Lampridius' statement is correct, his aunt, cousin, and grand-mother had just retired for safety. Surely to go there utterly unprotected was simply courting the assassination he had so narrowly avoided, was making death absolutely certain, unless he knew that the number of the disaffected was very small, and that Lampridius' statement about the imperial family and their journey thither was pure fiction. There is not much doubt, however, despite the biographer, that they were still in the palace, and would rather have died than go to the camp, lest the Emperor should learn of their part in the conspiracy.

There is yet another discrepancy between the account of Dion and that of Lampridius ; the latter says that Alexander was in the camp for safety, the former is equally sure that Antonine took him with him when he went to find out the reason of the disturbance. Be this as it may, Dion states that the arrival of the Emperor put a stop to the trouble, and that there was a conference, at which Alexander's name was never mentioned. The subject of complaint and mutiny was, that certain freedmen had been appointed to offices for which, in all probability, there had been candidates better qualified than the Emperor's friends. With a con-siderable amount of good sense, Antonine acceded to the soldiers' demands; he dismissed four out of the five persons mentioned, amongst whom were

Gordius, from the praefecture of the night watch, Murissimus, from an unknown office, and two other friends, "who, mad as he was, made him madder." Hierocles' name was also mentioned, but the Emperor refused to listen to it; "he would die," he said, " rather than give up Hierocles, whatever they might think of his usefulness," and this was all. Antonine had recognised a grievance and remedied it; after which, in all probability, the affair was dealt with by the regimental court-martial as usual.

A comparison between Dion's account of this "terrible uproar" and Lampridius' account of the futility of the whole proceeding leaves one with the impression that once again Mamaea had failed in a dastardly attempt on Antonine's life. It is unthink-able that any assassin, however stupid, would have warned the friends of his enemy concerning his proposed attempt, as both Herodian and Lampridius testify that Antonine did. Herodian, speaking generally of Antonine's plots against Alexander, says that "the Emperor was of so shallow and wicked a character that he announced openly and without precaution what was in his mind, and did the same without any concealment." Lampridius says that he had the foolishness to write to the boy's guardians and tell them to do the deed.

As to the whole arrangement being a plot of Mamaea's, there is much more to be said. It would certainly not be to her advantage if Alexander's adoption was annulled: that project must be stopped at all costs; why, therefore, should she not circulate the report that Antonine was plotting a definite act against his cousin on a certain day ? She chose a day when, as she knew, the Emperor would be in a quiet spot and defenceless. She could pay for a military rising, which, being quite a usual occurrence, would account for everything, and then her troubles would be over, her position secure for her lifetime. Unfortunately for her, Soaemias heard of the plan and went to warn her son. When she got to the gardens, she found that Mamaea's money had not bought sufficient people, and that the attempt was frustrated. If there had been any real attempt made by an unpopular Emperor against a popular associate, some definite arrange-ment would have been come to as regards the protection of the person threatened, but, as far as we can see, things went on just as usual. The Emperor still had command of the boy's person, after as before the rising, and the family still lived on in the palace, trying to brazen out their treachery, facts which give the lie to Lampridius' remark that special regulations were made to keep the boys apart, as well as for Alexander's safety.

There is a phrase in Dion which is fairly conclusive as to the attitude which his family were adopting towards Antonine at this period. It reads: " this time" (in the camp conference, where it will be remembered that the soldiers never mentioned putting their Emperor to death at all) "he obtained mercy, though with difficulty, because his grandmother hated him on account of his conduct, and because, not being even the son of Antonine (Caracalla), her inclination was veering towards Alexander, as if he had been in reality the issue of that prince." This is a very fair indication of the stories by means of which these women were trying to ruin the boy ; stories inspired by hatred. It seems that they were perfectly willing to do anything, to say anything, to contradict anything, they had formerly said, to spend anything, if only they could collect a faction strong enough to support their schemes of replacing Antonine by Alexander. Here is a good attempt to crush his popularity by denying what they had formerly stated so enthusiastically— the bastardy of Varius—and affirming instead that of Alexianus as being the only genuine example ; in fact, they were limiting the performances of Caracalla to the unattractive sister, and denying Soaemias' position.   If they could do that, they were more than capable of working up fury by reports of a definite attempt on the only genuine bastard's life, and thus justify their attempt in the Gardens of Hope. The net result of this plot, by whomsoever instituted, was the retirement of Alex-ander from public notice.   Herodian states that he was deprived of his honours.   This, however, cannot mean what the mendacious author seems to imply ; namely, that Antonine took from him his titles of Caesar and Imperator, as both these occur on the Monza military diploma issued on 7th January 222, and on the majority of the coins issued up to the death of Antonine in the spring of that year. Mere empty titles were, however, of little or no use to the imperial ladies.

Defeated as they had been in one scheme, their ingenuity turned to yet another means of destroying the Emperor's authority. The attempt above mentioned cannot be dated precisely, but we may infer from Lampridius' arrangement of his matter, that it was between the wine harvest and the 1st of January, on which date Mamaea made her last and successful attempt to get her son into a definite political position. During the interval, both Dion and Lampridius assure us, with tears in their eyes, that the Emperor made daily attempts on the life of his cousin : a life so useful, so necessary to the state.

To circumvent these Mamaea refused to allow Alexander to eat anything from the imperial kitchens and set up a kitchen and establishment of her own in the palace, an arrangement which would scarcely have been sanctioned by Antonine if he had had any definite murderous object in view, because it would have interfered too materially with such plans. But there was obviously some gross negligence afoot. Any resolute ruler, given a couple of days (even without Locusta's famous stew of poison and mushrooms, which Nero, in allusion to Claudius' apotheosis, called the food of the Gods), would have given the lie to that pious generalisation of Lampridius about the impotence of the wicked, and done it in much the same manner that Nero, Domitian, Commodus, and Caracalla had done; not to mention others whose names it would be invidious to bring forward, but who still firmly believe that the wicked, when suitably backed, have a certain power in this world of woe, the wicked naturally being those whom we personally dislike. Antonine seems to have been quite indifferent as to what was going on; he knew that his position was precarious ; Syrian divines had told him that his doom was near; in consequence of which he prepared several devices for a unique and splendid suicide; and lived his life, a life in which the spintries — a form of amusement with which Tiberius had refreshed an equally worried frame— figured largely, along with other equally reprehensible enjoyments.

Of the actual politics we know little or nothing from the time of this so-called revolution, until by some means or other, unknown to the Emperor, Maesa got Alexander designated Consul for the year of grace 222. Here Antonine struck. He re-fused point blank to go to the Senate to be invested with the dignity unless someone else were designated instead of his cousin. He saw the game as clearly as you and I can see it, and resolved to create a deadlock in the constitution. There should be an Emperor, but no Consuls, unless, of course, the women and Senate were prepared to give way. He was *not* going to give official position and authority to enemies whose object he knew only too well. Up to this juncture he had succeeded in nullifying their machinations ; did they think he was going to give away his whole position now ? Not he, and so on, and so on. Here was a real difficulty—Rome without Consuls was unthinkable. Antonine without supremacy was almost as impossible a suggestion; still the women resolved to hold on, and try whether patience and diplomacy would not appeal to his sentimental nature, and thus overcome the last bit of opposition. After all, he was young, and affection with children is so much more powerful than reason.

This time Maesa herself does not seem to have tried to influence the boy. If we can believe Lampridius' statements, that crafty old sinner had already managed to worm herself back into the friendship of the boy and his mother, by putting the odium of recent troubles entirely on to the shoulders of her daughter Mamaea. In consequence, it was with a bold carriage that she appeared in public with the Emperor, and in private used her influence with Julia Soaemias, begging her to make it clear to the dear boy that his refusal to take the consulship would be his own undoing. Rome would never endure such a breach of the usual order. The obvious thing would have been for Antonine to go away, but he seems to have thought, right up to midday on 1st January, that the Senate and his relations would give way first. Then, suddenly yielding to his mother's entreaties, he consented to the plan, and, going to the Senate, he associated Alexander with himself in the consular dignity, thereby signing his own death warrant.

January 1, 222, was the beginning of the end. It is very pitiful to see the multitudinous wiles by means of which, all through his reign, craft circumvented what the Emperor obviously knew was his correct and proper course. Sometimes, as we see, it was his zeal for religion to which they appealed, sometimes his love for his mother. In each case the result was the same, the Emperor did what his political instinct told him was unwise, in response to what he considered a higher motive. The adoption had not carried with it the authority which the women desired; the office of Consul was, therefore, vitally necessary for Alexander's promo-tion. Antonine was bound to refuse his consent to the plan; he was permanent Consul if he liked, and would associate no one with himself of whom he disapproved. What did it matter to him if people talked of the discord ; had they not done so ever since Maesa and Mamaea started out on their elec-tioneering campaign ? The truth would certainly be better for him than his relations' lies; for himself, he was not afraid of danger, though Soaemias, the well-meaning and artless, was, and for her sake Antonine gave himself up, an unwilling victim, into the hands of his enemies. It was shortly after midday when he went to the Curia accompanied by the self-satisfied little enormity, and there, in the presence of his grandmother, he consented to give the women all that official power and authority which they had hitherto struggled vainly to obtain.

Henceforward, both Dion and Lampridius tell us that the Emperor sought his cousin's life to take it from him. Not that the continual reiteration of the accusation, when contrasted with the utter futility of Antonine's masterful inaction, is in any way convincing; this we have already pointed out, and can add nothing to the discussion here.

Lampridius recounts one quite amusing action, which, if it were true, would give a certain prob-ability to his stories. Antonine, having resolved to kill Alexander, because the tension of this continual running fight had become too great for his nerves, determined to dissolve the Senate first; fearing that, should they be sitting when Alexander died, they might elect someone else instead of the murderer. The chief reason for doubting this story is that no Antonine had ever yet had the smallest occasion to fear anything untoward from the action of that august assembly, and it is most improbable that this Antonine was going to begin now. Emperors had always taken the Senate's concurrence in their actions for granted, and had invariably met with entire subservience.

But to proceed with the beautifully circumstantial details, which, as usual, Lampridius makes as glaringly mendacious as they are circumstantial. The Senators, he says, were told to leave the city at once; those who had neither carriages nor servants were told to run ; some hired porters; others were lucky and got carriages. One only, a Consular, by name Sabinus, the personage to whom Ulpian had dedicated his works, and who, being Severa's father, one would have thought might reasonably have remained, did not go sufficiently rapidly for the Emperor's liking ; in fact, he stayed in the city in defiance of the order, and must have walked abroad very openly, for the Emperor saw him, and whispered to a centurion, " Kill that man ! " Now, the centurion was deaf, and thought the order was " Chase that man," which order he promptly executed. Thus the infirmity of a " mere common centurion " saved Sabinus' life, and gave the world the works of Ulpian with the dedication above mentioned. Now, if, as seems the case, Ulpian's dedication of his works to this Consular is dependent on Sabinus being the man saved from Antonine's rapacity and cruelty, the whole story is a lie, along with the palpable untruth about the dedication. Ulpian never mentioned this gentleman, either by name, implication, or in any other fashion, which is just a bit awkward for Aelius Lampridius, who might at least have taken the trouble to consult the title-page of Ulpian's works or have asked somebody else to do the job for him, if he was too tired with his former efforts at inventing fiction. The name is certainly mentioned in the commentaries which Ulpian wrote on the famous jurist of Tiberius' period, but that is naturally another story altogether.

There is yet another effort made to drag Ulpian into this same chapter, namely, when Lampridius says that part of Antonine's scheme for the murder of Alexander was to deprive him of his tutors, one of whom he banished (Ulpian), while Silvinus, the distinguished orator, whom the Emperor himself had recommended, was put to death. Both of these men suffered because they were great and good men. Now, Ulpian we know, Julius Paulus we know also (though quite why he was left by Alexander's side when good men were banished we are not told; unless it be that, for the moment, he was hiding his light under a bushel); but who on earth was Silvinus? His name is not given amongst that exhaustive list of nonentities marshalled out by Lampridius *(Alex. Sev. vita,* xxxii.) as the men who had failed to teach Alexander Latin, after an effort which lasted from his earliest babyhood up to the time of his death ; neither is he mentioned in any other place, either by this author or in any other record of Antonine's cruelties; on which account we feel inclined to relegate him, with other doubtful blessings, to the special limbo reserved for all similarly inspired terminological inexactitudes, and proceed to recount the rapidity with which Mamaea found means to make up for lost time in acquiring her authority.

Needless to say, even here Lampridius' fabrications are as difficult to reconcile with Dion and Herodian's stories as those two authors are impossible to square with one another. Of course the two last were both eye-witnesses of the scenes they recount, and tell us so, with some pride, a circumstance which in no way hinders them from seeing things double, and calling them different aspects of the same truth, after the manner of theologians when they are in a conciliatory frame of mind.

For the murder of Antonine Lampridius assigns no adequate reason, giving instead two suppositions of his own—first, that the Praetorians feared Anto-nine's vengeance on account of the attack which they had made on him some months previously, and for which he had then and there forgiven them ; but, says Lampridius, despite this forgiveness, the soldiers killed him in cold blood. Second, that on account of the hatred he had testified towards them (presumably in not seeing to their donatives), they resolved to rid the Republic of this pest, and began by putting to death, first, the friends of the Emperor by various foul and indecent means, and then, having got these out of the way, they openly attacked Antonine in the latrinae, and killed him.

Dion's account is more circumstantial, and brings Alexander and Mamaea into the horrid scene. His story is that the two Consuls, during a meeting of the Praetorians, summoned on account of one of the multitudinous plots against Alexander, went into the camp, that their two mothers followed, fighting one another more openly than usual, each imploring the soldiers to kill her sister's son. We are then told that Antonine, quite contrary to his custom, got frightened, rushed from the scene and disap-peared into a chest. This was apparently a foolish and obvious hiding-place, whence he was soon dragged in order to have his head cut off, while his mother held him in her arms. Naturally, as the operation of killing one without the other in such a position was difficult, Soaemias perished along with her son.

Herodian, always the most circumstantial and picturesque liar, substitutes for the story of the sudden dissolution of the Senate, a report which he says Antonine caused to be circulated. It was to the effect that Alexander was ill, so ill that he was likely to die at any moment. By this means Antonine hoped to keep the boy shut up in the palace until the soldiers and citizens had forgotten him, when he would be able to put him out of the way quietly. Of course this would have been an admirable plan if the boy had had no fond mother or grandmother to look after his interests, but was rather futile when one considers that these ladies, after striving to rule for four years, had at last got the power into their own hands by appointing Alexander Consul. It was extremely improbable, therefore, that both Maesa and Mamaea were going to keep their mouths closed and say nothing when, in the full flush of their triumph, they saw their puppet, and with him their own power, being put *hors de combat* in a slow and lingering manner. As usual, Herodian never thought of these things, and ascribed the whole action to the Praetorians. These turbulent guardsmen, when they began to miss the young Consul, decided to mutiny again, the present form being a refusal to turn out the palace guard until Alexander should reappear in the temples.

On the face of things, this was a most irrational proceeding. If the Praetorians wanted to save Alexander and suspected that foul play was about to be perpetrated in the palace, surely they would have gone to their posts as usual, and then used their official position to rescue the boy, instead of shutting themselves up in their camp, and leaving him to his fate quite unprotected. This apparently did not occur, either to the soldiers or Herodian, who announces that when the guards refused to come to the palace, Antonine (instead of finishing the work and showing the dead body in the temples) was simply penetrated with the usual fear—always imputed and never lived up to, unfortunately for Herodian. In order to demonstrate to the soldiers just how frightened he was, the Emperor did the one thing that no terrified person could possibly have done, he set out in a litter for the camp—utterly un-protected, of course, because he had no guards. The litter is fully described, namely, the state litter, sparkling with gold and precious stones. With Antonine went Alexander, presumably, as the story develops, in order to foster the hatred which the soldiers felt towards the Emperor, and raise to a frenzy the love they bore Alexander. It was as usual a journey in which the Emperor courted death; in fact, the number of times that Antonine imperilled his precious life is simply astounding to anyone who studies these delightful romances. But to proceed. When the litter arrived, the gates of the camp were opened, and the Consuls were conducted to the chapel, which occupied a central position in the enclosure. This leads one to suppose, considering also the magnificence of the carriage, that the visit was one of an official nature, in which the two Consuls were bound to go together. The chapel also was an ominous place, as it was here that Caracalla had played the farce of regretting his part in, if not of exculpating himself from, the murder of his brother . Geta. Of course, things happened just as was expected; the visit did foster loyalty to Alexander, who was received as a deliverer with acclamation, and raised to fever pitch all the evil passions against Antonine, who was received with perfect coldness. Despite this inauspicious reception, the Emperor elected to stay the night in the camp chapel, the better to meditate on his wrongs, which was obviously an unlikely proceeding on the part of the young Sybarite.

Next morning he held a court-martial to try the soldiers who had made themselves conspicuous by the warmth of their reception of Alexander. Herodian and the Emperor seem to have quite forgotten that the guards were mutinying, as we hear no more of that story, though obviously they ought to have been tried for that offence first. At any rate, Antonine, still penetrated with terror, condemned these men to death as seditious persons. The soldiers, transported with rage at his treatment of their companions, and filled with hatred of the Emperor, conceived the notion of succouring their imprisoned brethren by upsetting the dishonoured Emperor. Time and pretext were admirable; they killed Antonine and with him Soaemias, who was present, both as his mother and as Empress; they then included in the massacre all those of the cortege who were in the camp, and known to be Antonine's ministers or accomplices in his crimes. They then gave the bodies to the mob, to be dragged about the streets of Rome, finally throwing that of the Emperor into the Tiber from the Aemilian Bridge. All this was presumably done under the eyes of, and with the consent of Eutychianus, the Emperor's friend and chief minister, who was, it will be remembered, in command of the Praetorians at the time.

A careful comparison of these three stories reveals the fact that none of the eye-witnesses saw the same things, and none ascribe the deed to the same motive. All agree, however, in shifting the responsibility from the shoulders of the former conspirators on to those of the Praetorians. No one except Dion Cassius mentions either Maesa or Mamaea, and he merely says that Mamaea and Soaemias both urged murder each of her sister's son. No mention is made of Antonine's supposed plot against his cousin ; in fact, all reference to plots against Alexander, Maesa, and Mamaea is here carefully eliminated, surely with an object; since it has been the great reason given heretofore for the Emperor's unpopularity, and precarious position. But let us attempt to recon-struct the events of this memorable day. From Herodian we learn that the state litter was used ; that in it travelled the two Consuls, accompanied by at least the Empress mother; Fulvius Diogenianus, the Praefect of Rome ; Aurelius Eubulus, who, as chancellor of the exchequer, had made himself extremely unpopular by robbing hen - roosts (Dion), and was in consequence torn to pieces by the mob; Hierocles, the Emperor's friend and husband (who had recently been designated Caesar, presumably as a sort of set-off to Alexander), and two out of the three Praetorian praefects.

Dion and Lampridius both suggest that the Emperor tried to escape. Herodian, with the fullest account, makes no mention of this fact ; neither Lampridius nor Dion agree, however, as to the mode of Antonine's proposed escape.

The incident of the latrinae, mentioned by Lampridius, suggests a murder similar in circumstance to that of Caracalla. What would have been easier than for one of Mamaea's party to seize the boy, alone and unprotected in the latrinae ? The Emperor once gone, the obvious thing would be for the conspirators to remove as quickly as possible all those persons who might make things difficult for his successor. Of these, Soaemias would certainly be the most troublesome. Hot and passionate, devoted to her son and to his memory, if she had lived, Rome would have resounded with the noise of the crime. It was obviously neces-sary to close her mouth with expedition. Why Eutychianus did not suffer the same fate is quite incomprehensible. The only theory that has been suggested is that neither Maesa nor Mamaea felt themselves capable of undertaking the whole admin-istration alone ; they felt that they must have at least one man who knew the ropes at their back.

To account for the treatment of Antonine's body at the hands of the mob is certainly difficult. We know that he had done nothing which could have rendered him obnoxious to the populace. To ascribe it to intolerance of his psychopathic condition shows, not only ignorance of Roman susceptibilities, but also a foolish antedating of popular prejudice. We certainly have no record of this Emperor's sepulchre ; and to dismiss as mere fable the one point on which the authors all agree is equally impossible. The probable solution lies in the fact that Mamaea's money, which had caused the murder, invented this scheme for disgracing her nephew's memory, and thus averted trouble from herself. It would raise a popular tumult, or at any rate a disgust for the idol of the masses, if they could have Antonine's body dragged through the city publicly, as the perpetrator of unmentionable crimes, concerning which the populace knew nothing. Suffice it to say that it did the work. Antonine had the stigma of all crimes imputed to his memory ; and Alexander the good arose superior to all human frailties. Then and not till then, Rome began to be shocked. Men whose fortunes Antonine had made by his liberality, the Senate, whom he had snubbed so unmercifully, the army to whose donatives he had not attended properly, all these found it advisable to adopt the views of the new administration ; their education in ingratitude was complete. Instead of the generous, fearless, affectionate boy whom the populace had known, there emerged the sceptred butcher ill with satyriasis; the taciturn tyrant, hideous and debauched, the unclean priest, devising in the crypts of a palace infamies so monstrous that to describe them new words had to be coined. It was Mamaea's work, and for 1800 years no one has had the audacity to look below the surface and unmask the deception.

Antonine's Government from 221 to 222 a.d.

The events of the years 221 and until March 222 are mainly a record of internecine fights and struggles ; the Emperor was trying to retain his position in the state, the women leaving no stone unturned to possess themselves of power in Alexander's name. We have traced the events which led to the adoption of Alexander, and noticed the small amount of power which his position as heir to the Empire actually put into the hands of Maesa and Mamaea. We have seen further how the repudiation of the adoption by Antonine lessened even this modicum of power, and how the successful attempt to make Alexander Consul gained for their puppet the official position from which the terms of his adoption had excluded him. Once that position was secured, we have watched the successful plot against the Emperor's life, which placed Maesa and Mamaea in actual command of the state under the merely nominal headship of Alexander. It only remains for us to follow the governmental acts of these last months of Antonine's life, as far as the authorities will allow.

The first recorded action after the adoption of Alexander was one of religion. The ostensible object of the ceremony on 10th July, or rather earlier, had been to free the chief priest of Elagabal from his secular duties, in order that he might further the worship of the Great God. To this end, Antonine instituted a magnificent religious procession through the city, taking his God from the temple on the Palatine to that in the suburbs. Herodian, with his usual inaccuracy, announces that this ceremony took place each year at midsummer. Now, the temple on the Palatine was not finished by midsummer of the year 220, judging from the coins which celebrate the expansion of the cult, and that near the Porta Praenestina was even later in its completion. The inference is, therefore, that the procession could not possibly have taken place in the year 220 at midsummer. Further evidence is, however, forthcoming; Cohen mentions certain Roman coins struck in honour of the procession ; they show the God on a car, and date from the latter part of the year 221, by which time the suburban temple was finished and the procession certainly took place.

Before midsummer in the year 222, according to .Dion, Antonine was dead. He did not therefore conduct the Elagabal procession, and as the authors inform us that Alexander sent the God back to Emesa with considerable expedition, after reconsecrating the temple to Jupiter, it is very unlikely that Alexander continued the public parade of an unpopular worship, even though the God was still in Rome at the time mentioned.

Despite Herodian's statement that Alexander, as well as Antonine, was a priest of the Sun, it is fairly-certain that the former was never actually associated with his cousin in that priesthood, and was not in the least likely to begin the worship after Antonine's death. The obvious inference is that, as usual, Herodian was speaking without his book; *each* year meant that there was one procession, and one only, namely at midsummer in the year 221.

The correct interpretation of this function belongs to specialists in Semitic mythology. There are points about it, however, which incline one to the idea that its institution in Rome was due to the marriage of Elagabal and Juno Coelestis. Its real significance lies in the fact that it took place at midsummer. Ramsay tells us of many such processions in the East, notably those held during the month Tammuz, which (owing to the variations of the local Syrian calendars) fell in various places at different times between June and September. Now, these processions celebrated the nuptials of the divine pair Ishtar-Tammuz or Aphrodite-Adonis. The worship of this pair centred at Bylus, not 100 miles from Emesa, and from this shrine, in all probability, Antonine got his idea of the great procession, made memorable by the coins struck during the year 221, and also by the inscription to Hercules, erected either in the latter part of the year 221 or early in 222 (Domaszewski) by the Centurion Masculinus Valens, the standard-bearer Aurelius Fabianus, and the adjutant Valerius Ferminus, all of the Tenth Antonine Cohort of the Praetorian Guard. This inscription records their having taken part in the sacred procession, which seems to have been of a military as well as of a religious character. The magnificence was extraordinary. The chariot on which the God was transported was richly covered with gold and precious stones; great umbrellas were at each corner. It was drawn by six white horses (the coins give them all abreast), and the reins were so arranged as to make it appear that the God himself was driving, while the horses were actually guided by the Emperor, running backwards, and supported on either side by guards lest anything untoward should happen. Statues of the Gods, costly offerings, and the insignia of imperial power were carried, while the Equestrian order and the Praetorian Guards followed.

The streets were strewn thick with yellow sand, powdered with gold dust, and the whole route was lined by the populace, carrying torches and strewing flowers in the path of God. Precisely the same thing may be seen to-day following the same route and at the same time of the year. The procession of the Corpus Domini is still a popular function even in modern Rome, though its termination is no longer the occasion for temporal blessings such as Antonine's liberality provided. Herodian mentions this liberality, and condemns it as a sort of diabolical plot for the extermination of the citizens. He says that when the festival was over, Antonine used to mount on towers especially-constructed for the purpose, and distribute to the crowd vases of gold and silver, clothes and stuffs of all sorts, fat oxen and other animals, clean and unclean, except pigs, which were forbidden to him by his Phoenician (not Jewish) custom. Presumably the distribution was by tickets, exchangeable for these gifts, of which he says each was at liberty to take what he could seize. In the scramble, many citizens perished either by crushing one another, or by throwing themselves, in their eagerness, on the lances of the soldiers. The consequence was that the festival became a misfortune to many families. But surely to make Antonine responsible for the greediness of the crowd is as absurd as to record the fiction that he smothered people with flowers, or took luncheon in the circus when he was interested in the games, and then evince such harmless amusements as proofs of cruelty.

As we recorded in the last chapter, it was certainly not long before Antonine discovered that he had made a vital mistake in adopting his cousin. We are led to infer that the boys had not seen much of one another for some time previously, as Mamaea had kept them apart, fearing her son's contamination. Now that Alexander was actually in the palace and in daily contact with the Emperor, incompatibility of temper was the natural result, though in several places we are informed that Antonine loved his cousin at least up to 1st January, which interesting fact may be doubted on psychological as well as on the historical grounds already recorded. His second mistake had been in marrying his grandmother's elderly friend Annia Faustina.

By the autumn of 221 the Emperor had resolved (as we have already pointed out) to rid himself of both encumbrances at once. For Antonine, divorces, like marriages, were made in heaven, an opinion which he had no desire to hide from men. He therefore divorced Annia Faustina without intending to live a single life, even for a time, because he had grown weary, was tired of this struggle with his relations. Moreover, he wanted friends; the *coup d'état* by which he had freed himself from the irksomeness of Alexander's sonship, or had at least tried to do so, and by which he had at the same time got rid of his third wife, had naturally caused a break with his family; after which the Emperor seems to have considered himself at perfect liberty to make any appointments he chose, and to mismanage the state much as a Claudius or a Macrinus might have done. It was a period, according to Lampridius, when Antonine was specially drawn to members of the theatrical profession. Now such persons are admirable in their proper place, but are not much sought after in governmental positions. Unfortu-nately, the Emperor did not know this fact, and, . considering himself emancipated, did as Nero, Titus, Domitian, or Caracalla would have done ; he appointed his friends everywhere. The biographers, of course, assume that the men appointed were of loose character, as well as of base origin, without supplying a tittle of evidence either as to who the men were or what they did when in responsible positions. The supposition is that they were appointed on account of abnormalities ; the result, as chronicled, is that the state did not suffer from their mismanagement.

We can quite see the point of view of a boy feverishly anxious to regain the power and authority which he had lost, and imagining that the one way to do this was to put his own friends into office, whether they were barbers, runners, cooks, or locksmiths. Lampridius tells us that men from each of these trades were appointed as procurators of the 20th, though how many such appointments Antonine made it is impossible to discover. In the autumn of this year (221) the soldiers asked for the dismissal of four such favourites, of whom the Chariot-Driver Gordius, Praefect of the Night Watch, was one; Claudius Censor, Praefect of the Sustenances, another. In the same passage Lampridius reiterates the old lie about Eutychianus Comazon, who had been reappointed Praefect of the Praetorian Guard about January 222. He again calls Eutychianus an actor, who changed his offices as quickly as he would have changed his parts on the stage, and records that it was the height of folly to put him in command of the guards. In all probability it was annoying to Mamaea, as she might not be able to bribe the guards as freely as heretofore. Now, we have already seen that Eutychianus Comazon was a soldier as far back as the year 182 ; that he had held this same office (Praefect of the Praetorium) in 218; that he had been Praefect of the City in 219, Consul in 220; again Praefect of the City in 221, and that, when in the murders and proscriptions which followed that of Antonine, the then Praefect of Rome Fulvius Diogenianus had met his end, Comazon was reappointed to the city praefecture for the third time, and now by Maesa and Mamaea. It is, therefore, pure stupidity to condemn Antonine for appointing this actor (!) to a post in 222 which he had already held with honour, and which he was to hold again with renown. If none of Antonine's appointments were worse than this of Eutychianus Comazon, it is small wonder that the state suffered in no wise from the mismanagement. A further charge brought against the administration is, that the Emperor appointed freedmen to the posts of Governors of Provinces, Ambassadors, Proconsuls, and military leaders, thus debasing all these offices by conferring them upon the ignoble and dissolute.

Here is another wilful bit of misrepresentation. A short perusal of Petronius on the position of freedmen will disabuse any one's mind of the idea that they were either ignoble or essentially dis-solute. Patricians they were not, though they aped the manners and extravagances of that class, much as the plutocracy of to-day ape the aristocracy of yesterday, both in their wealth and their exclusiveness. Money in Old Rome carried much the same kudos as it carries in England to-day. The democracy could and did rise when they had acquired wealth; they were then just as vulgar, just as ostentatious, just as snobbish as their successors the plutocrats of this latter-day world; they had the privileges that wealth confers and none of the responsibilities which aristocracy involves, and were, equally with the modern plutocrats, without traditions or heredity to guide them. But this was their misfortune, not their fault. On the other hand, there was, as a general rule, plenty of ability amongst the men who had risen. They were clear-headed, far-sighted politicians; men who, being free from traditions, were best able to cut away the overgrowth of centuries, because their respect for archaeological institutions had not degenerated them into mere fossilized curiosities of an antediluvian age. Cer-tainly they were not all ignoble, if they were plebeian in origin, and it is mere supposition to say that they were all dissolute; so indecent a suggestion could only emanate from those who hoped to gain in comparison.

There was one obvious reason why Maesa and her party should object to any and every appoint-ment made by Antonine. Men thus appointed would not be her nominees, and she could not therefore demand the fees payable on such occa-sions. This mention of fees brings one to the second part of the charge against the Emperor, namely, that he sold offices either himself or through his favourites. It would certainly be more satisfactory if we knew something as to what he sold, to whom he sold it, or for how much he sold it. Lampridius is careful not to mention such trivial and minor details, he just brings the accusa-tion, without either proof or real likelihood to support it. The main contention seems to be that the prac-tice is immoral; if so, immorality is as rife to-day as in third-century Rome. Sovereigns, ministers, cabinets, universities, churches, in fact every species of authority confers its own offices, decorations, titles, and sinecures, for all of which fees are still charge-able, even exacted. This practice of royalties may account for the charge, as it is unlikely, psychologically speaking, that Antonine would ever have sought to profit pecuniarily from his friends, and certainly he would not have appointed enemies, even for money's sake; he had learnt too much about the ways of such people in the bosom of his own family. We have remarked in other places on Antonine's penchant for giving, and can well believe that the boy bestowed favours broadcast; that he sought to fill offices as they fell vacant, by the appointment of friends, especially with men who had endeared themselves to him, men from whom he expected loyalty in return for his devotion and generosity. Poor child, he had yet to learn that sycophants are ever to be bought by the highest bidder. Lampridius relates the trouble and increase of difficulty which, by their disloyalty, venality, and unbridled gossip, these men brought upon their benefactor in return for his trust. Fortunately for all parties concerned, they met their deaths (doubtless unwilling victims) along with the master whom they had betrayed. They thought they had secured themselves, but found they would have done better to secure him, which is not an unusual position with traitors.

Amongst the number of appointments made for his own pleasure during this period we must include the return of Aquilia Severa to the position of wife and Empress. Dion relates that, between the divorce of Annia Faustina and the return of the nun to connubial felicity, Antonine took two women to wife ; but adds sapiently that even he does not know who they were, or when the marriages took place. Now, as the time between the divorce of Annia and the Emperor's death cannot greatly have exceeded three months, and as he was obviously desirous of returning to Aquilia Severa from the first, the story of the two odd wives may be dismissed as not proven, another of those terminological inexactitudes which seem to be inseparable from the political amenities of every age; added to which we must remember that Antonine was still so passionately devoted to Hierocles that he would willingly have died rather than be parted from him.

The return of the nun was the crowning point in Antonine's folly. Undoubtedly he was getting more and more worried, was feverishly anxious to repair the damage to his shattered power, was ready to catch at any straw that would give him encouragement and help. In his extremity he turned to the one woman for whom he had ever cared,—if we except his mother, who, poor woman, was of an artfulness so bovine that her support was a much more useful asset in his enemies' game than to his own position. For Antonine, unfortunately, Aquilia Severa was also worse than useless; she may have cared for him, but her return spelt his ruin and destruction.

Not that Antonine was by any means at the end' of his resources as yet. If he hesitated, no one knew it. Like Caligula, he must have spent nearly £400,000,000 of our money, and was radiant because he had achieved the impossible. But he was worried, and, again like Caligula, in the nick of time he remembered the sure and certain way to glory. As an Antonine at the head of a conquering army he would again advance against the Marcomanni, the men inhabiting Bavaria and Bohemia, whom Commodus had reduced.

Now, the oracles had predicted that an Antonine should finish this war, a circumstance which commended itself to the Emperor from more points of view than one. Like every religious person in the Empire Antonine was superstitious. Zonaras recounts that the boy wore 600 amulets; but, as he was not there to see, and the contemporary authors do not mention the fact, we can dismiss this with similarly exaggerated stories. Not that the use of these aids to piety or tickets to heaven is even now extinct; the idea may still be found set forth, with both precision and logic, in any manual of prayers under the heading "Brown Scapular," or " St. Simon Stock." More ridiculous and more wicked were the figments of imagination, by means of which men tried to dissuade Antonine from undertaking this war. They told him that these Marcomanni had been conquered by means of enchantments and magic ceremonies, the sole property of Chaldeans and other soothsayers. Remove these enchantments, and those same enemies of the Empire would break out into open rebellion once more. Antonine, therefore, sought to know the enchantments and how to destroy them, so that a pretext might be found for recommencing the war, which he, as an Antonine, was eager to finish, lest that honour should fall to another. Here even Lampridius is sympathetic ; he says that a war would have enabled the Emperor to merit the name of Antonine, which he, along with nearly all the others, had sullied; but the opportunity was not given him ; death came too soon to enable him to make the preparations.

Lampridius now enters upon a few more pious reflections, and in the course of his argument a few more terminological inexactitudes concerning the Emperor's name and family history. He states that Antonine had not only usurped that august name, but had profaned it, until it became a name of public ridicule; that he was called nothing but Varius and Heliogabalus. These remarks are both unnecessary and untrue. The Emperor was never called either Varius or Heliogabalus. The name of his God, which he assumed at Nicomedia, was never in any sort of way an official title ; neither does Varius appear on any known coin, inscription, or document. This Emperor is frequently cited as Priest of Elagabal, Priest of the Most High God, which title was, by the way, often obliterated on the monuments instead of the name Antonine, when Alexander defaced, or partly defaced, these after his cousin's death.

Like the name Jahwe, the El of the Hebrews, this name Elagabal, the El of the Emesans, was in all probability considered too holy for common use, at least during the Emperor's lifetime. After his death, it was applied to him as a sort of nickname, just as Caligula or Caracalla had been applied to former Emperors, or even like the term "Romanist" was applied more recently to the last Stuart King of this country.[58]

To this latter period of the reign we may ascribe a certain amount of Antonine's activity in building. Lampridius mentions at least two monuments of importance, the first a gigantic column which he purposed to erect, a staircase inside, round which should be engraved or chiselled, not the history of the Emperor's deeds, not even the history of the family exploits, but a record of the miracles which God had wrought, and for which men gave thanks. Antonine was murdered before the project could be fulfilled, and Rome lost the finest of those most beautiful relics of antiquity—the columns which still grace her forums and market-places. The second was a high tower which he built in accord-ance with the prophecy of certain Syrian priests, that his death as well as his life should be violent. All traces of this tower and its location have disap-peared ; so have the sheets of gold covered with jewels, with which he paved the court below, in pursuance of his desire to perish magnificently. The idea of this extravagance was that of a splendid suicide, to be accomplished by throwing himself from the-summit of the tower on to the sparkling beauty beneath, thus finding sensuousness even in death. Antonine had read Iambulus; he knew the history of the men in the Fortunate Isles, who, when they were overtaken by the ennui of sheer happiness, lay-on perfumed grass which had the faculty of producing a voluptuous death. His conception was not so easy, but what it lost in ease it gained in splendour.

In addition to these works, mention must be made of the completion of the Antonine baths, now known as those of Caracalla, the Thermae Varianae on the Aventine, which are variously named by Pauly as Thermae Syrae or Surae, and the hall built for the Senaculum on the Quirinal. These are authentic works, and there are many other instances cited by Lampridius of this Emperor's passion for building. We hear of houses, baths, huge salt-water lakes, built in the mountains and fastnesses of the country districts. All these were erected, so the story goes, but for a moment, as temporary shelters for the monarch when travelling, and were destroyed when once he had reached his next habitation. Even Lampridius states that such records are obviously

---

[58] **The change of the name to its Greek and commonly received form is 100 years later than Elagabalus, in fact it occurs first in Lampridius, and was seemingly born of the necessity, which had been suggested to Constantine, of connecting the old worship of the only God with that of Mithra the Persian Sun deity.**

false, the inventions of those who wished to malign Antonine, once Alexander was possessed of the supreme power, sycophants Lampridius calls them, who makes such a poor show himself when occupying that unenviable position at Constantine's bidding.

There is yet another point which must be examined in connection with the murder of this Emperor, namely the so-called disaffection of the soldiers. Time and again, throughout the history of the reign, we learn from coins and inscriptions that Antonine was popular with all ranks of the army. On the other hand, we have the repeated assurance of all authors, both Greek and Latin, that the Emperor was continually losing his popularity.

More reliance could be placed on the written testimony if the authors agreed as to when this popularity was lost. As a matter of fact, Lampridius ascribes the beginning, progress, and culmination of this dislike to each separate year; on the later occasions, seemingly, because he had forgotten that he had already stated definitely that the affection for the Emperor was a thing of the past. Neverthe-less, the story cannot be entirely dismissed as a mere fable, since there were two military risings or disturbances, in the second of which the Emperor lost his life.

The question must occur as to whether these are traceable to actual disaffection or to some conspiracy. The side-lights which all authors throw on the progress of events leave no doubt in our minds that the two risings were definite conspiracies, worked up by interested persons,—such wholly un-successful plots as those of Seius Carus and Pomponius Bassus may be left out of consideration here, as they were at once discovered and as easily frustrated. The fact remains, however, that Antonine was killed, most probably in the Prae-torian camp, and that his body, having been dragged about the city, was thrown into the Tiber, near the Aemilian Bridge, or else cast down a drain which ran into the river, in order to show contempt for his sacred person. Again, there was no effort made to punish the wrong-doers. The Praetorians themselves, when they knew of the murder, made no outcry, which circumstances tend to show a certain amount of acquiescence on the part of the soldiers and people. How, then, had Antonine alienated in 222 the men who in 220 testified such devotion to his person and rule ?

A considerable amount of disaffection can be traced to the foolish neglect which the Emperor showed towards his troops. He was their nominee ; to them he owed his throne. He had promised them the money, privileges, and affection which had been his father's special care. Once in sure possession of the Empire, this policy was changed. The first congiary in 218 was undoubtedly accompanied by a donative of satisfying amplitude. At the second (on the occasion of his first marriage) we are told that the Emperor gave more to the humblest citizen of Rome, more to the wives of the Senators, than he bestowed on the men who had placed him on the throne a year previously. There is no record of any other liberality until the early part of the year 221, on the occasion of the dual marriage, his own with Aquilia Severa and that of his God with

Vesta, the Madonna of Old Rome. On this occasion no mention is made of any money distributed to the military forces. The same may be said for the fourth liberality, given in July 221, to celebrate the adoption of Alexander.

These official liberalities were by no means the only distributions by which Antonine endeared himself to the civilian populace. On the occasion of his taking the Consulate, he went out of his way to bestow magnificent gifts on the populace. After the great summer procession in 221 he distributed a vast number of costly presents amongst the crowd. He instituted two lotteries, one for the comedians, one for the citizens. He gave to his friends and to the poor more than they could carry away, but on all of these occasions we are expressly told that he limited his generosity to the civil population.

Obviously Antonine was tired of the army. And, being Emperor, he decided to give to whomsoever he pleased, to neglect whom he would. It was not immoral, at least in our judgment, it was stupid, which is far worse, and, as everyone has discovered for himself, stupidity brings greater penalties than immorality.

Of the fourth and fifth congiaries, concerning which Mediobarbus speaks, we can say nothing, as in the opinion of competent numismatists (Cohen and Eckhel) they do not belong to this reign at all ; there certainly are coins bearing the inscription " Marcus Aurelius Antoninus," and on the obverse " Liberalitas V. VI." ; but science and discrimination now assign these to the reign of Caracalla, not to that of the Emperor under discussion.

There is certainly one point of view from which this neglect of the soldiers appeared immoral, namely, the military. Promises had been made and, as is usual with promises, they had been broken.

Mamaea took advantage of this circumstance, and small wonder if, her secret, though regular, distributions aiding, the lords of Rome felt that their position was ignominious when they saw others, actors, sycophants, loafers, procurers, strumpets, and the like, receiving what they felt was theirs by right; small wonder if they listened to and profited' by her promises of the substantial gratitude which would follow the substitution of Alexander for the un-grateful civilian who now held the purse-strings.

It must be confessed that Mamaea's money and promises were of little effect while Antonine lived. The Emperor was certainly well served. Each plot was easily frustrated ; never would sufficient men turn out in rebellion. When he died, those whom she had paid most liberally convinced the rest of their proper attitude, and the first liberality of Alexander's reign was a sufficient *pourboire* to close most mouths. Those who created disturbances followed their master to the grave, or rather the cloaca.

The exact time of Antonine's murder is, as we have said, most uncertain. Dion ascribes to him a tenure of power lasting 3 years 9 months and 4 days from the day of the battle in which he gained supreme command—8th June 218. This fixes the day of his death as 11th March 222. It is a statement with which the editors of the *Prosopographia,* Groebe, Salzer, and Rubensohn, all agree. The *Liber generationes*[59] gives 6 years 8 months and 28 days, and is supported by the *Chronicle* of 354, which gives equally explicitly 6 years 8 months and 18 days. The discrepancy is at first sight most disconcerting, especially as the two latter statements are both—at least nominally—official. The coins limit the reign to four years at the outside, in con-sequence of which some explanation has to be found for the extraordinary addition of three years in both the *Chronicle* and the *Liber generationis*. Mommsen has suggested that a deflection of the two first strokes of III in the number of the years has created the error in both these documents. Later writers have accounted for the difference between Dion's VIIII months and the VIII of the Latin sources, as due to the omission of one stroke in the latter, the confusion in the number of days by the fact that an X has been omitted in the *Chronicle*. Mommsen's emendation seems perfectly plausible, but the absurd quibbles used to bring into agreement what was in all probability for some time a moot point can be passed over without much mention.

Rubensohn has a much more reasonable conclusion, namely, that the times given in the *Chronicle* and *Liber generationis* refer not to the date of the battle at all, but to the date of the proclamation or to the date of Julianus' defeat, sometime during the early days of May 218. Lampridius, of course, chips in with another discordant note, namely, that " a.d. pridie nonas Martias " the Senate received their new Emperor Alexander, with acclamations, but for present purposes he may be left out of count, as we have no confirmation of this very late statement. Eutropius' statement of **2** years and 8 months refers only to the residence in Rome, and Victor's 30 months is utterly out of the question, as is also Lampridius' statement that this monster occupied the throne for nearly three years. Still more disconcerting than the wild statements of the biographers is the fact that right up to 8th December 222 certain rescripts are dated with the names of both Antonine and Alexander, " Conss."; two only, one in March and one in October, appear with Alexander as sole Consul, and this inscription occurs on a rescript dated "III non. Febr.," when, if any other evidence is to be accepted, Antonine was still alive. It was on this count that Stobbe based his assertion that Antonine was killed, or at least put out of the government, as early as 5th or 6th January, and that Mamaea used her new power as soon as ever Alexander was officially recognised as Consul. It is certainly a theory for which something may be said, but would entirely dispose of the circumstantial accounts which the historians have left of the boy's murder. If this supposition is true, then Mamaea possessed herself of the Emperor's person by means of a riot in the camp, immediately after Alexander became Consul, deprived him of his friends and support, and thus gradually accustomed the populace to his absence, before she killed him. This would certainly account for the placidity with which Rome received news of his death at some later period, but would not account for the

---

⁵⁹ **The number of years in the *Liber generationis* is, however, debatable, since Rubensohn gives three years in his edition.**

discrepancy of the coins and rescripts, the first of which make Alexander sole Emperor by the early summer, the second, which call Antonine Consul, presume that he was still alive as late as December in the same year (222).

From a numismatic point of view there have been further difficulties raised as to the length of the reign, on account of Antonine having reached his fourth Consulate and fifth tribunician year, but these have been raised by persons who have neglected Eckhel and have not always verified their references. The regular coins tell us that Antonine had reached his fourth Consulate and fifth year of tribunician power when he died. Certain writers, notably Valsecchius and Pagi, have postulated that the Emperors always renewed the tribunician powers on the anniversary of their succession, others, such as Stobbe, that the date of the tribunician power would always be put on each coin when that of the Consulship was given. Neither of these contentions can be ad-mitted for an instant, as Eckhel has proved most conclusively, and as can be further demonstrated from the very coins these writers cite as proofs of their several contentions. Valsecchius' theory was that Antonine thought he began to reign on the murder of his father Caracalla, and dated his tribun-ician year in consequence from 8th April 217. This would make him in his second tribunician year by 8th June 218, and the coins should appear as "T.P. II Cos." Unfortunately for the theory, there is not . a single example of this aberration, as Turre pointed out some centuries ago. Pagi, on the other hand, thought that Antonine dated his reign from 16th March 218, and renewed his tribunician powers every year on that date; he accepted Dion's date, II th March, for Antonine's decease, and, in consequence, postulated that coins struck .with the legend "T PV Cos 1111 " were struck in anticipation of the event of 16th March 222. Against this Eckhel urges that the whole theory is utterly un-necessary, because it throws all the rest of the coins out of date in order to make a setting for nine, which are in reality perfectly regular.

The truth obviously lies in Eckhel's theory, which has been rejected by Stobbe because it is so simple and obvious, namely, that Antonine renewed both consular and tribunician powers on the same day, ıst January, a contention which the Fasti Romani amply corroborate. Naturally, as we know from Dion, the first year began on 8th June, when Antonine's name was substituted for that of Macri-nus. On 1st January 219 Antonine took his second Consulship and second tribunician powers. On 1st January 220 the Emperor became Consul for the third time, Tribune of the People third time. On 1 st January 221 Gratus and Seleucus were Consuls, Antonine Tribune of the People fourth time; 1st January 222 Antonine and Alexander Coss. IIII and I, Antonine Tribune of the People fifth time. All is duly set out on the coins in regular order.

The basis for other theories was found by fertile brains when Cohen listed a few irregularities in the dating, notably three coins dated T.P. Cos. II, which just inverted Valsecchius' theory, and, said Stobbe, showed that the Emperor had renewed his Consulate on 1st January, and had not yet renewed his powers as Tribune of the

People. It was undoubtedly plausible, but Stobbe omitted to notice another coin whose date is T.P. Cos. IIII, which, on his own theory of the number invariably affixed to T.P. as well as to Cos., would signify that the Emperor had never renewed his tribunician powers at all, or else had renewed his consular powers four times in one year, both of which ideas are demonstrably absurd. Along with his supposition that the number would always be affixed to T.P. whenever it also followed Cos., Stobbe formulated another theory partly based on the idea which had been enunciated by Pagi concerning the date of the coins marked T.P. V Cos. IIII, and supported his contention from an example listed by Cohen as T.P. IIII, Cos. IIII. It was to the effect that as the Emperors Septimius Severus, Caracalla, Geta, and Alexander Severus had renewed their tribunician powers about the middle of January, Antonine had done the same, and that the paucity of the coins marked T.P. V Cos. IIII is due to the fact that he was murdered very shortly after, if not before the issue was completed, and the tribunicial renewal had taken place. Stobbe's proof lay in the fact that Cohen had listed these three coins as above (T.P. IIII Cos. IIII), which, this critic affirmed, were issued after January ist and before the tribunicial renewal, — about the middle of the month.

But it was mere theory on both counts. As Egbert showed later, the tribunicial renewal in the case of Septimius, Caracalla, and Geta was not early in January at all; it was on the 10th of December.

Macrinus' renewal was early in January, so was Alexander's, but this was not conclusive evidence that Antonine renewed his powers on the same date. There certainly are coins, three of them, listed by Cohen, two in France at the Bib. Nat., and one in the British Museum marked T.P. IIII Cos. IIII. This was clear proof, said Stobbe, that the tribunician powers were renewed after the consular powers, and that T.P. V Cos. IIII were later in the same year (222) than T.P. IIII Cos. IIII. The French coins I have not seen, but I have had the privilege of examining that in the British Museum (Cohen, vol. iv. p. 342, No. 197), and find that Cohen has misread the number affixed to the Cos.; it is listed as T.P. IIII Cos. IIII, but is in reality T.P. IIII Cos. III P.P. (i.e. the year 221). The first P has been read into the number,—which same inscription is most probably on the French coins as well as on that in the British Museum, since it appears gratuitous to impute a mistake to contemporaries by way of making copy for later critics. I have noted yet another mistake, namely, two coins listed by Cohen as irregularities; they are dated, T.P. III Cos. IIII (p. 344, Nos. 210,211). On these another admirable theory has been based, namely, that Antonine was going to take the Con-sulate, had his coins struck, and then backed out at the beginning of 221, thus before he had renewed his powers as tribune. Again very pretty, but the British Museum has the coins, and they are not dated T.P. III Cos. IIII at all; they are quite ordinary—T.P. 111 Cos. II I, or of the year 220, and there is no need to transpose the numbers, which is an alternative theory to that stated above.

The evidence from the coins is quite conclusive. The Emperor renewed his dual powers either on the same day, 1st January, or on a day immediately succeeding. As Eckhel pointed out in 1792 there is no coin which, if the date be correctly read, gives any countenance to any other theory, while all such are unnecessary and at variance with known facts.

Lampridius gives us a certain amount of evidence that the Emperor took an interest in the affairs of state all through his life, both by his account of Antonine's sagacity as a judge, and his desire to appoint fourteen praefects of the city, under the headship of the Imperial Praefectus Urbis or Urbi. Naturally, the desire is attributed to base motives, namely, in order to benefit unworthy persons. The scheme, Lampridius tells us, was actually carried into operation during Alexander's reign, and is then applauded as useful and necessary, an obvious bit of special pleading on one side or the other.

It is with a singularly unanimous voice that the authors announce the general execration against the memory of Antonine, and the joy shown by the populace in dragging his dead body about the city. All are certain that the Senate made a general order to deface the name of Antonine on all monuments and documents through the Empire, as soon as that dishonoured Emperor was safely out of the way.

The unanimity is wonderful; all the more wonderful because so utterly unusual. Unfortunately, it is in no way borne out by the inscriptions. We have mentioned the rescripts which for the most part bear Antonine's name throughout the whole year 222. This circumstance is hardly in consonance with the senatorial action in ordering all mention of the dishonoured Emperor to be expunged (*i.e.* while they themselves continue to use his name publicly and officially). Again, there is an inscription C.I.L. VI. 3015, set up in July 222, which commemorates both Consuls as though alive; and another, though probably a forgery of Ligorius, No. 570, in which the two names appear on 13th April of the same year. Surely this would have been impossible if Antonine were dead and the Senate had ordered his name to be erased everywhere. This order, however, cannot be taken literally; an examination of the existing inscriptions gives quite other results.

The name of Antonine is erased, but only in 40 known cases, while in certain places the name Alexander is substituted for that of Antonine, which, if usual, is rather a cheap way of getting the honour and renown belonging to another. A few African inscriptions blot out the Emperor's claim to be grandson of Severus, and a few in different parts of the Empire blot out the title Priest of Elagabal, witness the inscription at Walwick Chesters. In 52 cases the names, styles, and titles of Antonine are left intact, which makes it improbable that there was any great campaign against his memory, such as Lampridius would have us believe that everyone in the Empire was only too anxious to institute.

Dion and Lampridius both tell us that Antonine was called Tiberinus and Tractitius after his death, in reference to the shameful treatment which his .body was supposed to have met with after his murder, and the final act of throwing it into the river in order that it should never be buried. Sardanapalus is another epithet applied to him by Dion and his copier Zonaras, who also call him Pseudo-Antonine, in reference to his grandmother's state-ment made "through hatred" in 221, that not he but Alexander was the only legitimate bastard; such and the like were the taunting adjectives by means of which the biographers sought to defame the boy's memory.

Here, for all practical purposes, Lampridius' account of the Emperor's life ceases. There are still seventeen chapters of mere biographical scandal, some of it illuminating, some hypocritically obscene. Nevertheless, it has been possible to abstract from these sections a certain amount of information descriptive of the boy's extravagances and their setting, his psychology and its result, his religious ambitions, and with them the reasons for his downfall.

These are all obvious traits in Antonine's character, and can be discerned despite the mass of exag-gerations and hostility with which the pages abound. To criticise these statements in any sort of detail is, however, obviously impossible on the information at present available, and furthermore, we are scarcely competent to judge the period from our modern standpoint of prejudice.

There is no period of history which fully corresponds to these last years of imperial greatness; few men who embody the spirit which breathed life into all that splendour, and even fewer in the modern world who understand the revived paganism of the Renaissance. Here too there was a difference. In old Rome it has been said that a sin was a prayer ; under Leo X. it was, rather, a taxable luxury. Sinning is still a luxury, but no longer taxable; the Reformation has set us free from such extortion and restraint, and supplied us with hypocrisy and cant to take its place.

From Suetonius we gather that the Roman world sinned and sparkled; we still sin, but are perforce to yawn in the process. The world of Suetonius was the world *où on s'en fichait.* Our world is the world *où on s'ennuie.* Hence our inability to grasp the spirit of philosophical paganism, a spirit whose morality does not consist in improper thoughts about other people, but in a mind set free from terror of the Gods, not very much caring what other people do so long as they do not interfere with us.

It is thus that we must view Elagabalus. To look at him through any other spectacles is to examine the restless, frivolous, perhaps debased dragonfly as though he were a vampire, and then, imagination aiding, describe him as a stampeding unicorn with a taste for *marrons glacés.*

It is absurd, purely grotesque, this caricature we have of Antonine ; perhaps that is why the world has left him alone, that they may gaze the longer on a mask that allures. If these criticisms have done anything to remove part of the accretions with which the world has daubed his figure at the bidding of his relations, the trouble is amply repaid. Naturally, this monograph is not the last word; it is, on the other hand, the first, put forward in the hope that it may at least commend itself as a point of view. Neither is it a compromise with the proprieties, which are, after all, in the modern world, little else save a compromise with either our neigh-bours or the police; what one expects from them, certainly not how much they may expect from oneself, or even from Elagabalus.

CHAPTER VIII. THE WIVES OF THE EMPEROR

This Antonine has been accused of building the Cloaca Maxima, into which, a century later, all Rome rolled, largely on the grounds that he divorced at least three wives, and was himself wife of the Chariot Driver Hierocles, amongst others of his unusually numerous acquaintance.

The imputation of excavating in Rome cannot be attributed to Elagabalus alone. Augustus had done a little digging there, but hypocritically, as he did everything else, devising ethical laws as a cloak for turpitudes of his own; Caligula had done the same, so had Nero, Hadrian, and Caracalla. Maecenas divorced himself and remarried twenty times, as both ceremonies were less expensive than they are to-day. Suetonius said of Caligula that it was uncertain which was the vilest, the unions he contracted, their brevity, or their cause. With such examples, it was inevitable that ordinary people should unite but to part, and that insensibly the law should annul as a caprice, a clause that denned marriage as the inseparable life.

Under the Caesars, marriage became a temporary arrangement abandoned and re-established at will. Seneca said that women of rank counted their years by their husbands; Juvenal, that it was in such fashion they counted their days. Paul, in a letter whose verbosity apes philosophical phraseology, regarded the privileges of divorce as inherent in the patriarchal theories of family life. Tertullian added, somewhat sapiently, that divorce was the result of matrimony.

Divorce, however, was never obligatory, matrimony was. According to the Lex Papia Poppoea, whoso at twenty - five was unmarried; whoso, divorced or widowed, did not remarry; whoso, though married, was childless became *ipso facto* a public enemy.

To this law, as was obviously necessary, only a technical attention was paid. Men married just enough to gain a position or inherit a legacy ; the next day they got a divorce. At the moment of need a child was adopted; the moment passed, the child was disowned. As with men, so with women. The Univira became the many-husbanded wife, occasionally a matron with no husband at all ; one who, to escape the consequences of the Lex Papia Poppoea, hired a man to lend her his name, and who, with an establishment of her own, was free to do as she liked ; to imitate men at their worst; to fight like them and with them for power; to dabble in the bloody drama of state; to climb on the throne and kill there or be killed. The Empire had liberated women from domestic tyranny, just as it had liberated men from that of the state.

Such was the position of matrimony when, early in July 219, the Emperor Marcus Aurelius Antoninus took to wife the Lady Julia Cornelia Paula, of the well-known though by no means patrician family of Cornelia. Her father was Julius Paulus, probably one of the most famous juris consults and lawyers Rome has ever known. As father-in-law to an Emperor, his position was doubt-less, like that of Sylla, the father-in-law of Caesar, somewhat heady. Unfortunately it impaired his usefulness to a considerable degree. We learn from the editors of the *Prosopographia* that there are only five decrees on subjects of jurisprudence which can be definitely assigned to this reign, and from Lampridius that Paulus was appointed to the pre-sumably lucrative, though certainly uninspiring office of usher to the young Alexander, on whose bovine intelligence he could unfortunately make no impression. It is doubtless wrong to promote relations to Court sinecures when they can be better and more usefully employed in arduous work for the state, but it is a position to which even the best of us aspire when fatigued with either a misspent or a full-spent life.

According to Barrachinus, the family of Cornelia came from Padua; Bertrand says they were from Tyro; and in Pignorius' estimation they may even have seen light in Rome. Julius and his daughter are the only two of the family who have come into prominence. Unfortunately, we do not know the date of the birth or death of either, nor the year in which Julius began to climb ; suffice it to say, that he had published many volumes before the death of Septimius Severus, in whose council, according to Digest xxix., he had a place. His first office seems to have been that of Praetor, and thence by regular stages he climbed to that of Praefect of Rome, finishing with the height of all ambition, the Praefecture of the Praetorium, and as such he was a Senator of the Empire. Tristran—who knew about as much of the lady personally as you or I can—has remarked that Julia was beautiful. His taste is certainly not a modern one, as her effigy represents her with a sharp beaky face, and a long scraggy neck. This author, with some show of fairness, attempts to justify his statement by a truism, namely, that the Emperor was such a connoisseur of beauty that he would never have chosen a lady who had not this necessary qualification. Precisely, but did Antonine choose the lady at all ? The probabilities are that she was well over thirty at the time of the marriage, and that the Emperor had neither seen nor heard of her before she was presented to him by his relations, on his arrival in Rome; in fact, that this marriage was a political move by means of which the official classes were closely allied with the imperial house.

We have already described the pomp and circum-stance with which this wedding was celebrated, the games, with their lavish waste of animal life, amongst the rarest of known beasts, the congiary and donative. As this is the sole mention of such splendour on the occasion of Antonine's committing matrimony, which holy estate he is said to have attempted six times in two and a half years, it inclines us to the opinion that this was his first experiment in that direction, especially as the evidence of coins and medals is perfectly conclusive on this point. Tristran and Serviez, however, place Annia Faustina as first wife, on Dion's faulty arrangement of the events at Nicomedia.

Cornelia Paula was, as we have said, a lady of some renown and position. Serviez tells us that it was generally believed she had been married before; was already, in fact, a mother of children ; and Tristran adds, enceinte by someone else at the time of the marriage. The Emperor's pretext for marrying her seems to lend support to this contention. It was that he wished the sooner to provide an heir for the Empire, though, as Dion says, he was not as yet a man himself. Since Cornelia had no children by Antonine, and the reason of her divorce, as given publicly, was a secret blemish in her body, which was only discovered after about eighteen months of married concord, the presumptive evidence is against Serviez' theory; in fact, it presupposes sterility rather than some corporal deformity, or even over-fruitfulness ; and it, of course, gives the lie to the gratuitous assumption of Tristran that the lady was enceinte when Antonine married her. What amount of genuine feeling existed between Julia Paula and her husband we cannot even surmise. From a psychological point of view, one would be inclined to predicate very little. The Emperor was too much wedded to his friends, was too feminine in character to appreciate a wife, other than, as Lampridius says, " a strumpet who could increase his knowledge of her art." The family of Julius Paulus rose to the height of power as soon as a daughter of his house became Empress. Lampridius is not by any means definite as to the date of Julius Paulus' domination in the state ; though it seems natural to suppose that, when Eutychianus Comazon vacated the Praefectship of the Praetorium in order to become Praefect of Rome (July 219), the Emperor's father-in-law was appointed in his room, and vacated this office either at the time of his daughter's divorce, or more probably at an earlier date, *i.e.* when his official year expired in July 220.

The precise date of the divorce is unknown. As we have said, there are coins struck at Alexandria with Julia's effigy and inscription, after 29th August 220, and others at Tripolis in Phoenicia, after October in that year. The most likely supposition is that Antonine divorced her somewhere in the beginning of 221, after he had made up his mind to take to wife the Vestal, Aquilia Severa, in accordance with his religious scheme or ideal.

Julia Cornelia Paula is the only wife of Antonine mentioned in inscriptions, and, as we hear nothing of her in any other way, it is improbable that she had much importance at Court. Possibly she was found to be of no use either to Antonine, Maesa, Soaemias, or Mamaea, each in their separate ways, and as such was relegated to unimportant obscurity, neglected as a cypher. Her coin types are equally unimportant. They make reference to the Concordia which was supposed to exist between the pair, and introduce the deities protective of matrimony. Her portraits vary from those of a woman of sixty-odd years to the representation of a woman about thirty years old, which latter age is almost confirmed by her so-called bust in the Borghese collection at the Louvre; but no known author can really do more than guess at what this lady was as careful to conceal as her less fortunate sisters.

Lampridius tries to leave one with the impression, that on the divorce of this Augusta (the Senate had accorded the title at the time of the marriage) Julius Paulus was banished. Unfortunately, he mentions him a little later on as being tutor to Alexander (in the beginning of the year 222). The inference is, of course, that Lampridius took the two impressions from conflicting sources. In all probability the great jurisconsult, having exchanged his position as Praefect of the Praetorium for a Court sinecure as Alexander's tutor, did not re-emerge into public life until his thick-headed pupil was safely seated on the throne. Quite what office he then occupied Pauly has not determined. It may have been once again the Praefecture of the Praetorium, a position second only to that of the Emperor himself, and one which carried with it practical sovereignty, in the Tudor sense, only excepting the one element which went to solidify Elizabethan greatness, the assumption of the powers, dignities, and privileges of the ecclesiastical headship.

Julia Cornelia Paula, shorn of her title and position some time during the winter of 220-221, retired into opulent privacy. No sane person would, at that time, have pitied Julia's lot, unless it were because she was no longer enjoying the position of Empress. Even in mediaeval times, when divorce was an ecclesiastical privilege, and in consequence most costly, it was not regarded as an unmixed evil. Of course, it was rare, and, being ecclesiastical, carried a certain stigma with it. Furthermore, as we have said, it was a privilege for which there was not the same need as in times of women's greater freedom. No one who, like the mediaeval husband, had canonical permission to beat his wife when she annoyed him, stood in vital need of dissolving the bond, *(vide* Beaumanoir, lvii. : " Tout mari peut battre sa femme pourvu que ce soit modérément, et sans que mort s'ensuive "). During the epoch in question, it was the most usual and ordinary circumstance of daily life. It was continued interest in, not satiety with, the charms of your spouse that created wonder in old Rome; suffice it to say, that Julia retired, a woman with a past, and the knowledge, that if she had her wits about her, there was a considerable future to look forward to. No one expressed regret at her going, so in all probability Maesa was agreeable, though we can scarcely think that the old lady knew of the scheme which her grandson was concocting when she allowed the mistake to be made without an effort to stop his headlong swoop to ruin; a flight which would certainly involve the whole family on its way, unless they could dissociate themselves from the new religious policy which dictated it.

Probably along with predilection Antonine had seen and admired a lady, whom Dion describes, or makes Antonine describe, as Chief Priestess of Vesta. With this designation Preuner emphatically disagrees, accounting for the *ἀρχιέρεια* on the grounds that she officiated in the chief worship of Rome, not that she herself was the chief priestess. It was in the early months of the year 221 that Antonine, having seconded Julia Paula, took from her nunnery the Vestal Aquilia Severa, thereby thoroughly shocking the susceptible. We have already discussed the reasons for this act of folly. From a religious point of view there was much to be said by the Emperor, and undoubtedly he said it. From an aesthetic standpoint it was a mistake. There are still in existence a certain number of coins and medals which bear her effigy; these give her the appearance of a sinister and rather evil-looking woman, utterly unlike the helpless Neophyte, young and beautiful, whom various writers have depicted in their efforts to excite our pity for the poor nun forcibly ravished by an unattractive and debauched Emperor.

The whole modern opinion of the community of Vesta is founded on a mistaken view of their position and usefulness. Our ideas of Vestals are largely derived from the conceptions which Egyptian anchorites bequeathed to the esoteric religious communities which flourished during the middle ages. The truth lies in the fact that the Roman Vestals have but one point of contact with the successors of the anchorites, namely, their reputa-tion for chastity, which was, however, grafted on to an entirely different religious foundation. The Vestals were a community of high-born Roman ladies, whose duty it was to tend and preserve the sacred fire which symbolised Rome's existence, and, while they worshipped the Phallus, to keep them-selves unspotted from the world, not otherwise from its contact. In the performance of their public functions they were admirable and most punctilious, but they were not cloistered virgins, as we know the race to-day. They were women of the world, with a value enhanced by an often (according to Suetonius) supposititious virginity; women who, clad in the white linen garments of a blameless life, their hair arranged in the six braids which symbolised chastity, were the chief figures at all public functions, the leaders of feeling at the games and gladiatorial shows, and the arbiters of public opinion in all that touched religion and morals, at a time when religion and morals meant courage, bravery, patriotism, and hardihood.

It would be as absurd to impute to these women Christian ideas of religion and morals as it would be to transfer the same neuroticism to the Spartan communities of a still earlier age. The ideal was not then suffering for suffering's sake, not even suffering to appease an offended deity, but suffering for the sake of virility, patriotism, and strength.

As we have said, Roman religion was in the third century what it always had been, purely politi-cal. It was the prosperity of the Empire, its peace and immortality, for which sacrifices were made; with the individual, his happiness and prosperity, it concerned itself not at all. The antique virtues were civic, not personal. It was the State which had a soul, not the individual. Man was ephemeral. It was the nation that endured, and to secure that permanence each citizen laboured. As for the citizen, death was near, and so he hastened to live ; before the roses could fade, he wreathed himself with them; immortality was, for him, in his descendants, the continuation of his name, the respect for his ashes. Any other form of futurity was a specula-tion. In anterior epochs, fright had peopled Tar-tarus, but fright had gone; the Elysian fields were too vague, too wearisome to contemplate. "After death," said Cicero, "there is nothing"; and philo-sophy agreed with him. Of such and kindred religious theories the Roman statesmanship—realis-ing the danger of independent religions—had constituted her

Emperor supreme governor. As Pontifex Maximus he held much the same position as that which our Tudor Sovereigns created for themselves as heads of the Church in England. The Emperor was supreme over religious dogma and practice, whenever occasion necessitated control.

The old faiths were crumbling, but none the less Rome was the abridgment of every superstition. The Gods of the conquered had always formed part of her spoils; to please them was easy—from Jehovah to the unknown Gods beyond the Rhine their worship was gore. That the upper classes had no faith goes without saying, but of the philoso-phical atheism of the upper classes the people knew nothing ; they clung piously to a faith which had a

theological justification for every sin ; and turned with equal avidity to the Mithraic, Egyptian, and even to the Nazarene religion with which Constantine finally replaced the ancient worship, as long as they were all the same thing under a different name ; the religion of the Empire with local or foreign mysteries thrown in ; the accustomed traditions, miracles, feasts, and nature worship, unfortunately, as men found after Constantine, grown contentious and continually more expensive to maintain.

The Vestals were still the guardians and types of the older theories they professed ; they were the link between philosophy and superstition, and as such they played their part admirably : in private much the same as other women, in public exact. Occasion-ally there was a public scandal, but very rarely. Domitian had recalled the archaic law and had buried one defaulter alive. Claudius, referring to Messalina, had told them that the fate which made him the husband of impure women had destined him to punish such. The lady whom Caracalla buried alive protested, not against the imputation of a broken vow, but because the vow had not been broken satisfactorily enough for her liking.

Apparently Antonine was quite without Roman prejudice in this, or indeed in any other matter. He liked the lady; whether from a religious or an aesthetic point of view is uncertain. If it were the latter, and her portraits do her justice, Antonine's reputation as a judge of female beauty is irretrievably gone. She was frankly old and ugly. Nevertheless he wanted to marry her, and what he wanted he usually got. Whether or not Aquilia Severa wanted him is unknown, at any rate she was perfectly willing to exchange supposititious virginity for the imperial marriage bed on more than one occasion. Rome, as we have pointed out, was shocked, frankly dis-gusted. The Emperor had the report, probably through the Senate, and thereupon pointed out to that august body the essential piety of the proceeding : a Vestal and the Chief Priest of the Holy God were bound to produce children entirely divine.

It was a veritably Tudor argument, than which nothing more specious, for the allaying of prejudice, could have been produced by Henry, the Eighth of that name. Unfortunately, Rome in the third century enjoyed considerably more of that Tory virtue, and was less bored with a religion which affected no one personally, than England was in the sixteenth century. Rome continued to object to the Emperor shocking her prejudices. England changed her mind, and with it her prejudices, at the bidding of her sovereigns, and, sacerdotal extermination aiding, she forgot in a generation what it had taken her a thousand years to learn.

Needless to say, this union of the Emperor was productive of nothing either human or divine, concerning which, or as a sort of mild reflection thereupon, Lampridius utters his psychologically illuminating remark concerning the use this Emperor had for wives and women generally.

The history of Severa's family is obscure. Her father was the notable jurist Aquilius Sabinus, who had been Praefect of Rome both in 214 and 216.

He was the firm friend of Silius Messala, the king-maker, and possibly as a Senator, was one of that gentleman's judges when he was condemned for treason against his sovereign. We hear further of a son, one Fabius Sabinus, who, on account of his wisdom and learning, has come down to history as the Cato of his age. The daughter must have partaken of the family ability. Her father's senatorial rank would, in all probability, have opened to her the doors of that most exclusive of corporations to which she belonged, but his position could scarcely have raised her eyes to the imperial purple.

We can form no absolute judgment from the records at our disposal, as to the precise date at which this lady exchanged the practices of open celibacy for those of problematical matrimony. The most likely suggestion is that it was early in the spring of the year 221, at a time contemporaneous with the alliance celebrated between Elagabal and Minerva. The Alexandrian coins bearing her name are dated L$^\Delta$, or subsequent to 29th August 220, while the coins " Aequitas Publica "—which also bear her name—were issued early in 221, obviously for the third distribution of money which was held in honour of the double marriage. No games or excitements such as celebrated Antonine's first alliance were at this time attempted; the Emperor had quite enough to do in allaying the trouble caused by the marriage itself, and in con-sidering projects for the furthering of his religious schemes. Of the lady's position and influence we know nothing, though we can quite believe that she was no friend of the elderly Maesa, or the cross-grained mother of Alexianus, both of whom wished her so ill. Serviez is by no means complimentary to Severa, on account of the avidity with which she changed her position. He calls her ambition unbounded, though it is very doubtful whether, placed in a similar position, any one of us would have refused the flattery, and undoubted compliment made to our superlative worth.

The title of Augusta, of which Julia Cornelia Paula had been relieved, was conferred on Aquilia, and doubtless the Emperor looked forward to some considerable degree of felicity in the company of a woman of whose marriage every one disapproved.

As we know, Antonine found out quite soon that he had made a vital mistake; that he had attacked the one superstition that Rome would not allow to be touched, and, with extreme reluctance, he sent both the Goddess and her Vestal back to their appropriate dwellings. Antonine has been censured right royally both for his marriage and for the con-sequent divorce. Now, if the marriage were wrong, as all the authors say, surely the divorce was right; certainly Rome thought so, since his compliance with national wishes seems to have won men over, and appeased their minds, thus restoring the Emperor to his popularity. Why then did he further alienate them by remarrying Severa in the early part of the next year, as Dion and the coins relate? It is a mystery.

Antonine does not seem to have done anything at all for the family of this wife; there is no record of any offices held by them, or official appoint-ments given, taken, or received by men of their name. Of course, they may have got jobs which came under the generic term of "appointment of unfit persons "; if so, we have no record of what they got, while the duration of the marriage was so abbreviated that there was scarcely time for any scandal to develop. The date of the divorce, like all the dates of the reign, can only be fixed approximately. It was not before the early spring and not later than the end of June, by which time Julia Maesa had regained her power (what she had of it) over the mind of Antonine, that she persuaded him to return both Minerva and her personification to their respective homes, to send for Astarte, for Elagabal, to marry Annia Faustina himself, and, above all, to adopt Alexianus; which latter ceremony took place sometime before 10th July 221. We can well imagine the boy's disgust at the failure of his plans and at the early loss of a friend in Aquilia, who, as both Dion and Herodian tell us, was Empress for only a little time.

One of the greatest obstacles which the imperial family had met with was their lack of connection with the Roman nobility. No doubt this could easily have been remedied. Maesa might have tried to make her first alliance in this direction ; she seems to have imagined, however, that such persons were extinct. They had died twice, we are told, at Pharsalus and Philippi, and those who had not died then had suffered for real or imaginary crimes under succeeding Emperors. The absolutely necessary step, therefore, which Maesa had to take in this policy of alliance was to find the most influential marriageable woman in Rome and put her into the place that Aquilia Severa was holding to the jeopardy of all concerned. The lady appeared as if by a miracle. Amongst other persons who disapproved of Antonine's proceedings were the two Senators Silius Messala and Pomponius Bassus, of whom mention has already been made, as having been concerned in a plot for dethroning the Emperor. Both had been men of importance for years. Pomponius Bassus had been Consul under Septimius Severus and Governor of Mysia under Caracalla. In fact, so important were they in their own estimation, that nothing set bounds to their ambition. Already between them they had contrived the deposition of the Emperor Julian us, and the election of Septimius, and, like the great Earl of Warwick of fifteenth-century fame, they were by no means averse to putting their heads together once again, in order to rid the state of whomsoever they thought *incapax imperii.*

Now, this was just the work that Mamaea wanted. For other reasons, Maesa was not averse to the plot. The gentlemen held a secret court to examine into the Emperor's actions, and presumably they found him *iticapax,* so set to work to corrupt the guards in the usual fashion.

Unfortunately for Antonine, that infamous system of informers which had flourished and been of such vital use under former Emperors (under his father Caracalla, to go no further back for an example) was considered by his own government as harsh and objectionable, an utterly intolerable practice in a good and settled state. Antonine had, therefore, refused to allow delators to assist the government. This being the case, he ought to have apprehended all known traitors himself. Messala and Bassus were known for such; they had always been dangerous persons. Nevertheless, Antonine left them at large. True, as Lampridius tells us, he did send for Silius Messala and probably also Pomponius Bassus to come to him at Nicomedia, because he considered it safer to keep these gentlemen with him in the East than to allow their tongues to wag freely in Rome, before such time as he had dictated his own terms of government to the Senate and people. When they returned to Rome, these men obviously plotted freely in the accustomed way until they approached too many soldiers, after which time they were condemned by the Senate, and sent to other spheres of usefulness, or, as they themselves would have put it, to an endless nothingness, where an absence of all energy could do neither good nor evil. It is quite impossible to fix the exact date of this execution. There is a tendency to assign it to the early part of the reign, *i.e.,* about the beginning of the year 219, whilst the Court resided at Nicomedia; this, on the very frail evidence that their names appear amongst Dion's list of those who were executed during the reign, which list was published amongst the acts of the first winter. No cause has been shown, however, for any plot to dethrone and murder the Emperor at that date; indeed, until the religious mistake in 221, any such plot would have been utterly impossible, though there is plenty of evidence concerning the various attempts of the years 221 and 222, of which almost certainly this conspiracy was one. The execution was obviously connected, in Dion's mind, with Antonine's third marriage. He says that the real reason, as everyone knew, was because the Emperor wanted to play David to Bassus' Uriah, with Annia Faustina taking the hackneyed part of Bathsheba.

But it is a stupid story. Antonine was married to a woman of his own choosing, and certainly did not want the friend of his grandmother, even though to please that relation he did take Annia almost as soon as her husband was dead. This is again the only possible explanation of Dion's phrase that " This inhuman monster *(i.e.* Antonine) would not allow Annia Faustina to spoil her beauty by weeping for her departed husband," a story either adapted from the similar lie related of Caracalla and his mother, or designed to do honour to the work of the unconscionable traitor Pomponius. It is quite true that Maesa found ample means of drying any tears that the usual decencies extracted from the Lady Annia; but, as things turned out, no one seemed more anxious than this scion of the imperial house of Commodus to marry the present Antonine, despite all his relations' epithets, and, through these, what later commentators have found to say against the boy.

Annia Faustina was the only wife of Antonine who did not assume the title of Julia; this, presumably, because she was the only lady who had a name of her own by birth. Her gene-alogy is obscure, at least on her mother's side. Everybody is agreed that she was great-granddaughter of the Emperor Marcus Aurelius through his fourth daughter Arria Fadilla. This lady married a certain Cn. Claudius Severus, whose son Ti. Claudius Severus was Annia's father. Authorities disagree as to the wife of Titus. Pauly does not mention any marriage, presumably on the grounds that all are conjectural ; Ramsay, from an inscription found in Phrygia, postulates that he married a second cousin, one of the Cornificia family. Tristran asserts that it was yet another cousin, Aurelia Sabina. Eckhel's genealogy is too obscure to be of much use, though he also traces the descent of Titus' wife to Lucilla, yet another relation. The main contention is, however, the same in all cases : Annia was descended on both sides from the imperial house of Commodus, unless the amours of the younger wife of the Emperor Marcus Aurelius made it more probable that some lusty soldier or gladiator, rather than her philo-sophical husband, had been responsible for the accidents of her children's birth. Be that as it may, Arria Fadilla had passed with the rest of the family as an imperial child, and her descendants enjoyed her worship and renown.

As usual, we are told that Annia was young and beautiful, neither of which statements is borne out by the coins extant; to judge from these one would postulate that she was between forty and forty-five years of age at the time of her marriage with Antonine. Eckhel states definitely that she was thirty-eight years old at that period. Pauly ventures on neither the date of her birth nor death. It is, therefore, most unwise to assert, as the biographers do, what neither portraits nor authorities will in any way corroborate.

As with her age, so with her life : Annia's words, deeds and political aspirations are quite unknown to us. Obviously, coming at the political juncture of Antonine's mistake, and bringing the alliance with the old nobility that Maesa wanted by way of support, Annia was the friend of the Alexander party in the state. As such, she must have been an extraordinary annoyance to the Emperor and his friends. Certainly, from Lampridius' accounts, the boy-husband was moody, distrustful, and generally miserable during the whole of this period, which does not presuppose connubial felicity.

There is no mention of Annia having taken any special part either for or against her husband in the network of treasonable attempts which his family were continually trying. We do not even know how the marriage was dissolved. The natural presumption is that he divorced Annia, as he had divorced Cornelia and Aquilia, though it is allowable in the absence of the usual gibe at his inconstancy, or any suggestion of foul play, to suppose that she died—allowable, but not very probable. Antonine obviously took her as part of his grandmother's scheme, and got rid of her when he tried to get rid of Alexander, by repudiating the adoption. Dion relates that he then took two nameless women to wife, finally returning to Aquilia Severa. The first part of the statement is obviously a fiction. All Antonine, or any one of his temperament, wanted from a wife was friendship and affection; this he certainly had in Aquilia, whom he' only divorced as a precautionary measure, and whom he certainly took back just as soon as he could get rid of Annia.

Of course, to divorce Annia, a really important imperial lady, was a disagreeable step; it would alienate the whole of the upper classes, unless he could show reason for the change. Annia, by the extreme eagerness with which she had jumped at the chance of being Empress, was certainly not going to be party to the divorce—not that her con-sent was necessary in such times of freedom, when divorce was of daily occurrence, even in the best-regulated families. Cicero divorced his wife, we are told, because she did not idolise him ; Caesar his, on the pretext that she ought to be above suspicion. Certainly no actual misconduct was necessary, unless the whim of the moment be regarded as such. Antonine exercised this right to act on his whim, or rather on his knowledge that the lady was an unneces-sary burden, but it cost him dear, the lady was not born to take such snubs in a chastened spirit, even if her imperial relations liked to adopt that attitude, which is, to say the least of it, an unlikely supposition.

The odd ladies may be ignored. Dion says they were wives, not concubines.   But time did not permit of so many weddings and divorces ; while the Emperor's inclination, continually veering back to Aquilia, would not have let him try so many others. Dion tells us that Antonine remarried this Vestal before the last and fatal plot was set on foot; a statement which is corroborated by certain Alexandrian coins struck after 29th August 221. It was a proceeding, as far as we can judge, more mad than his first mistake. Admitting that Antonine knew that his first error, in taking the nun to wife, had angered the people, it is impossible for us to imagine why he took her again, thus once more upsetting the city. It was the most unaccountable blunder, and one which would finally alienate those whom he had so lately tried to propitiate. There may have been goodness in the act, kindness towards the woman, who had given up so much for his sake. There is goodness everywhere, often the basis of evil is in that virtue ; certainly much madness may be traced to it.

In reading the account of this epoch, one feels as though one were assisting at the spectacle of a gigantic asylum where the inmates were omnipotent. From this disease of madness Rome might have recovered, had not her delirium, which was fine, turned to softening of the brain. Until a century later, there was hope, because the guilt was conscious ; it was only when guilt became ignorance, that Rome disappeared.

CHAPTER IX. THE PSYCHOLOGY OF THE EMPEROR ELAGABALUS

" I would never have written the life of Antoninus Impurissimus," said Lampridius, "were it not that he had predecessors." Even in Latin the task was difficult. In English it would be impossible, at least Lampridius' life. There are subjects that permit of a hint, particularly if it be masked to the teeth, but there are others that no art can drape, not even the free use of Latin substantives. Our task therefore is to deal, rather with their sins of omission, than with the biographers' offences against all canons of good taste in recording the inexpressible. In his work on the Caesars, Suetonius displayed the eccentricities simply, without adding any descriptive placards ; therein lay Suetonius' advantage ; he was able to describe; nowadays a writer may not, at least not the character we possess of Elagabalus. It is not that he was depraved, for all his house was ; it is, that, like many moderns, he made depravity a pursuit, and the aegis of the purple has carried the stories   beyond the limits of the imaginable, let alone beyond the limits of the real. Were we to accept unexamined, the testimony of his traducers of the Christian era, we would gather that "at the feet of that painted boy Elephantis and Parrhasius could have sat and learned a lesson," that "apart from that phase of his sovereignty, he was a little Sardanapalus, an Asiatic Mignon, who found himself great." Of course it would have been curious to see him in that wonderful palace, clothed like a Persian queen, insisting that he should be addressed as Imperatrix, and quite living up to the title. It would not only have been interesting, it would have given one an insight into how much Rome saw and how much she could stand.

   Lampridius himself drew breath once, to remark that he could not vouch for the truth of the stories he was committing to paper, but he was employed to show the contrast between Constantine's "execrable superstition," as Tacitus describes it, and those of the ancient world, so went on to record things even more impossible. Perhaps his remark was unnecessary. His record has defeated its own end. He has come down to posterity as the biographer whose contradictory collection of scandalous enumerations becomes monotonous rather than amusing as he gets deeper into the mire. For ages the world has secretly revelled over these records, making no sort of effort to get at the truth, perhaps because, in secret, men like to believe that their predecessors were more inhumanly wicked than they are themselves.   Not that, in the light of modern science, any physician would consider Elagabalus inhumanly wicked, any more than he would be inclined to apply the term to a man born blind, or with the taint of leprosy in his system ; in fact even wickedness itself has been described as " a myth invented by good people to account for the curious attractiveness of those whom they dislike." The greater part of the dislike which men have exhibited towards this Emperor and his faults comes from the fact that he was psycho-sexually abnormal, and was possessed of a genius for the aesthetic and the religious that his historians wished to decry. He was evidently abnormal, even in an age that produced abnormalities like Nero, Tiberius, Commodus, and Hadrian ; further, he was frankly abnormal, and to-day we know better than to be frank about anything.

Since the world began, no one has been wholly wicked, no one wholly good. The truth about Elagabalus must lie between the two extremes, admitting, however, a congenital twist towards the evil tendencies of his age. He had habits which are regarded by scientists less as vices than as perversions, but which, at the time, were accepted as a matter of course. Men were then regarded as virtuous when they were brave, when they were honest, when they were just; and this boy did, despite his hereditary taint, show more than flashes of these virtues. The idea of using the expression " virtuous" in its later sense, occurred, if at all, in jest merely, as a synonym for a eunuch. It was the matron and the vestal who were supposed to be virtuous, and their virtue was often supposititious.

The ceremonies connected with the Phallus, and those observed in the rituals of the city were of a nature that only the infirm could withstand. Indeed, the symbol of human life was then omnipresent. Iamblichus, the philosopher, has much to say on the subject ; so have Arnobius and Lactantius. If Juvenal, Martial, and Petronius are more reticent, it is because they are not Fathers of the Church nor yet antiquarians. The symbol was on the coins, over the bakers' ovens; as a preservative against envy it hung from the necks of children ; the vestals worshipped it; at weddings it was used in a manner which need not be described. It was a religious emblem, and as such formed the chief symbol in the training of the boy who was now ruler of the world. By birth a Syrian, by profession High Priest of the Sun, whose devotees worshipped the Phallus as his symbol, was it likely that he, the chief exponent, should remain cold, should take no interest in what was an all-absorbing topic? Besides which, the family was corrupted by the presence of a living fire in their veins, engendered by the perpetual heat of the sun. Consider the history of his rela-tions, and no one will wonder that he was by nature voluptuous. But it was not his voluptuousness that the world objected to; it was the abnormal condition of his mind ; because in the body of the man resided the soul with all the natural passions of a woman. He was what the world knew as a Psycho-sexual Hermaphrodite.

In form he was attractive and exceedingly graceful ; his hair, which was very fair, glistened like gold in the sun ; he was slender and possessed of glorious blue eyes, which in turn were endowed with the power of attracting all beholders to his worship ; and he knew his power over men ; he had first realised it when the legionaries flocked to the temple at Emesa attracted by the reports of this Prince Charming. He was then just at the age of inci-pient manhood, and his woman's instinct taught him, as no outside force could have done, that virility and strength were the finest things in the world ; his religion, surroundings, and education told him nothing about the restraint of, what was to him, a perfectly natural, perhaps even an hereditary passion, the exercise of which so endeared him to the soldiers that they forthwith placed him upon the throne of the world. As Emperor he had every desire, and was under no compulsion to abstain from gratifying the craving to study and exag-gerate that swift, vivid, violent age, when what Mill in his Essay on Liberty desired was enjoyed by the Augustitudes, "There was no check on the growth of personality, no grinding down of men to meet the average." Not that anyone has ever accused Elagabalus of being average. In no particular can he be considered mediocre. Perhaps his life and habits were not those to which the virile Roman world was addicted, despite the fact that Hadrian had deified, in Antinous, not a lad, but a lust, whose worship, a half-century later, Tertullian noted was still popular; since which time Christian diatribes of all kinds have been levelled against the pagans of the decadence, merely because their atriums dropped, not blood, but metaphysics.

Were it permitted to examine Elagabalus' extravagances in print, we should at once realise that they are those common (in a greater or less degree) to all animals at the age of puberty, where instinct has not associated the developing powers with any one special person or thing, but that they are, in this instance, exaggerated by the traits of his heredity and surroundings. What character should we expect to-day from a child of nature if he were free with an unbounded liberty, and rich beyond the efforts of imagination, to say nothing of the pos-session of a congenitally perverted instinct ? The more one sifts the records, the clearer it appears that Elagabalus' actions are those of an incredibly generous person, instinctively trusting, open-hearted and affectionate, a mighty contrast, both in his pleasures and his punishments, to the persons who preceded him, and to his successors, who mistook new superstitions for progress in the development of the world. The example he set in tolerance of opinions not his own, and his reluctance to punish those who opposed him, must have led men to expect great things from his manhood. Alone of all the Emperors he stands out with the proud boast that no murder for political or avaricious purposes can be laid to his charge. There were a few executions, amongst the adherents of Macrinus, rendered neces-sary by attempts to take the crown from the new Emperor; but despite the fact of serious provocation, his amnesty to the Senate and to Rome, for their participation in the usurpation of Macrinus and his son, was scrupulously kept. In religious matters—his special domain—no one can say that he was apathetic, and yet there is no instance of perse-cution recorded, even by Fathers of the Church. His whole life was devoted to the introduction of a fantastic eastern monotheism, designed to extin-guish the polytheistic atheism which permeated Roman society. Undoubtedly opposition and bitter-ness would have been raised if the Emperor had not shown a moderation foreign to his years, unless he had exercised a restraining influence over a mob which was still thirsting for the blood of the Judaisers, as later records demonstrate. In one particular, however, we are told that Elagabalus was fierce, namely, in the contradiction of his pleasures, none of which can in fairness be said to have affected the outside world. He might have been led ; certainly he could not be driven; what Antonine could ? His tutor Gannys found this out too late, and suffered for his mistake.

With a singular lack of consistency, Lampridius ascribes all Elagabalus' moderation to his grand-mother Maesa, all his excesses to his own fault, whereas psychologists can demonstrate from a mass of similar cases that both his virtues and excesses are those usually exhibited by one of his tempera-ment, and at any rate his relations were responsible for his lack of early training and non-association with sane, healthy-minded persons.

Undoubtedly Maesa's influence, in the executive government, was an aggravating factor; but considering the state of autonomy which the machine had then reached, and the large influence exerted by favourites, it cannot be said that she was supreme ; indeed, on more than one occasion, we see the boy of fourteen years opposing her influence most strenuously, especially after she had hoodwinked him into appointing Alexianus as his coadjutor in the Empire. It was pitiable, then, to see the old lady's efforts to retain her position ; this, however, she only managed to do by persuading the troops to mutiny and slay her grandson. There is not much to be said for either party, but Elagabalus obviously found relations a tedious pack of people, and their influence, like drugs, best taken in small quantities.

Quite a cursory study of authorities on psychology, such as Krafft-Ebing, Bloch, Forel, Moll, etc., will show us that characters like Elagabalus have occasionally appeared, and are still known in history. They are almost curiosities of nature, and are rarely if ever responsible for their own instincts, neither are they cruel nor evil by nature.

To-day we are inclined to regard the romantic friendships exhibited in the stories of David and Jonathan, Herakles and Hylas, Apollo and Hyacinth, to mention no others, as the outcome of somewhat similar natures, and we decry some of the noblest patriots, tyrannicides, lawgivers, and heroes, in the early ages of Greece, because they regarded the bond of male friendship as higher and nobler than what they called the sensual love for women, or because they received friends and comrades with peculiar honour on account of their staunchness in friendship. Nevertheless, psychologists have noted that this tendency towards the more elevated forms of homo-sexual feeling is still to be found, more or less developed, amongst religious leaders and other persons with strong ethical instincts. It is only therefore when this tendency occurs in slightly abnormal minds that we excite our passions against men whom our imagination alone has branded as debased criminals, men for whom the only fitting reward is an application of the stake and faggot, without further inquiry.

To the vulgar-minded, all persons who present deformities, whether physical or mental, are subjects of derision and hatred ; to those who realise something of the disabilities under which these unfortunates are labouring, they are the objects of either active or passive sympathy, — in the abstract, of course ; should the insane, the leprous, or even the man of genius get in our way we, as normal persons, feel ourselves justified in ridding the world of its nuisance. It is thus that the instinct of fear, rather than that of justice, spurs us on to use the collective strength of the average, to exaggerate the abnormal-ities of the few ; but it is not a high or noble instinct, this fear which has led men for many centuries through a mire of cruelty, superstition, and deceit; and it is under this lack of justice that the memory of Elagabalus has long suffered. No credit has been given him for the quality of mercy which he displayed, though an absurd charge of cruelty has been preferred, on the ground that he occasionally took luncheon in the circus during the progress of the games; his biographer gratuitously assuming that it was only done when there were criminals to be executed. Another absurd charge of cruelty has been raised on account of Antonine's passion for flowers, of which, says Lampridius, such masses fell from panels in the ceiling that many were smothered; an obvious exaggeration, unless the guests were paralytics or suicidal lunatics, and, as even the author's account mentions no compulsion put on these gentlemen thus to die, he would seem to invite a verdict of death by misadventure, rather than by design, however aesthetic.

There was nothing sinister about Elagabalus' feasts, nothing after the style of Domitian's little supper parties, where all was melanic, walls, ceilings, linen, slaves; parties to which everyone worth knowing was ultimately bidden, and, as usual in state functions, every one that was bidden came, only to find a broken column inscribed with a too familiar name behind his allotted couch, and Domitian talking very wittily about the proscriptions and headsmen he had arranged for each.

Caligula and Vitellius had been famous as hosts, but the feasts that Elagabalus gave outranked theirs for sheer splendour. His guests certainly suffered from his passion for teasing, and to dine with the Emperor in such a mood was no sybaritic enjoyment. He might serve you with wax game and sweets of crystal, the counterparts of what he was eating himself, and expect evident signs of enjoyment as you endeavoured to masticate the repre-sentation ; he would seat you on air cushions, and have them deflated surreptitiously, thoroughly enjoying your discomfort; but when that was over you would be served with camels' heels, platters of nightingales' tongues, ostriches' brains (six hundred at a time), prepared with that garum sauce which the Sybarites invented, and of which the secret is lost. Therewith were peas and grains of gold, beans and amber, quail powdered with pearl dust, lentils and rubies, spiders in jelly, fig-peckers served in pastry. The guests that wine overcame were carried to bedrooms ; when they awoke, there, staring at them, were tigers and leopards—tame, of course, but some of the guests were stupid enough not to know it, and died of fright. It might not be pleasant to be promised adorable sirens, and to find oneself shut up for the night with an elderly Ethiopian, but it was not essentially cruel or debased, at least not from the humorist point of view, as was proved by the laughter of the Emperor at the sight of your dis-gusted face when he let you out in the morning. Unless you were fond of the water, it could not have been a pleasant experience to take the part of a water Ixion—tied to a revolving wheel—for the Emperor's lust of the eye ; but if you submitted to these things, you were sure of a reward more liberal than any you had expected. Lampridius reports that no guests left the Emperor's presence with empty hands. After dinner he would give you the gold and silver plate from which you had eaten, or cause you to draw lots for prizes which varied from a dead dog to the half of his daily revenue. Elagabalus saw no virtue in sending men away in the style of Domitian with their heads under their arms,— it was too con-ventionally the pose of the Christian martyr.

The description applied to Caesar's sexual condition can with equal justice be applied to this youth of seventeen. He was a woman for all men, and a man for all women, at least if one can judge by the number of wives he married during his short reign of less than four years. The number was six, according to Dion Cassius. Three of them were well-known women, one a Vestal, by whom he designed to produce a demi-god. The others are only referred to, their names are quite unknown. By none of them, however, had he any issue, which perhaps is as well, since he frequently remarked that should he have children, he would bring them up to his way of living, in his outlook on life, and the world could scarcely have stood a successor of his abnormal temperament. How far his marriages were true matrimony we do not know, but the fact of his going through the ceremony presupposes that the statements of Lampridius and Zonaras to the effect that he was initiated a priest of Cybele (in the full sense) are exaggerations, and also that the operation which would have made him a woman to outward appearance as well as in sentiment and affections, never took place; indeed, this is im-possible on both physiological and psychological grounds.

Despite these marriages, the one romance of this boy's life was with the fair-haired chariot-driver Hierocles. His identity is somewhat involved, though Dion Cassius states that he was a Carian slave, by profession a chariot-driver. This lad found his fortune by a mere accident. One day he was thrown from his chariot, right against the imperial pulvinar, and lost his helmet, Elagabalus was there and at once noted the perfect profile and curly hair of the athlete. He had him transferred to the palace, where on account of a similarity of taste the intimacy soon ripened into love, and that again, according to Xiphilinus, into a contract of marriage.

Hierocles must have been the best, and certainly was the most powerful, of that army of sycophants and courtesans which had always thronged the Roman Court. We have no complaints against his exercise of authority, though Lampridius says that his power exceeded that of the Emperor himself. His banish-ment was demanded, with that of others, in the first mutiny, but he was immediately allowed to return, despite the fact that Elagabalus meditated conferring the imperial title upon him. He was a good son, and in his prosperity was in no way ashamed of his mother. He openly pur-chased her from her owners, and sent a company of the Praetorian Guard to bring her to Rome, there placing her amongst the women whose husbands had been Consuls. He appears to have been proud not only of his position, but also of the Emperor's love for him, as the story of the Smyrnian Zoticus related by Xiphilinus and Zonaras well illustrates. They relate how he gave the youth a drug which made him useless to the Emperor during the first night, and thus procured his expulsion from the palace, though probably the story of Zoticus' disgrace, on account of his treachery and venality (Lampridius' version) contains as much truth as any other. Certainly Hierocles had no just cause for fear; Elagabalus' affection was too feminine, too deep-rooted, to do more than tease the man from whose hands, like many another woman in history, he was more than willing to take ill-usage and stripes, if only they were signs of jealousy or proofs of affection.

Of course there were others. The Elagabalus of whom Lampridius treats was a second Messalina in the variety of his tastes, and in the frequency of his visits to the various lupanars of the city, and like this Empress he measured his attractiveness by the amount of gold he could carry home after such expeditions. He cultivated the class of person who could discourse on the spintries with which Tiberius had refreshed his jaded mind and en-feebled frame, and made much of the man who could invent new sauces or other species of Sybaritic enjoyment. All such he treated with consideration, teased them and excited them, it is true, but pampered and fed them (sometimes, exclusively on their own inventions, till they could produce something more palatable), and loaded them with gifts, honours, offices, dignities, until they learnt that the condition of perfection is idleness, the aim of perfection is youth. We can well imagine the fury of the legitimate office seekers when they saw these children of pleasure preferred before them.

In a discussion on his psychology mention must be made of Elagabalus' love of colour. To the Roman, white in its cleanliness and simplicity was the acme of an aesthetic taste, though the profusion of purple borderings, the mingling of scarlet and gold, showed his kinship with the children of the south. Syria, and the East generally, loved that mass of brilliancy which relieves the aridity of the land; Elagabalus, posing as the aesthete of his time, annoyed the Roman world by his love of purple and shaded silk garments, by his passion for green, in all its known shades, and for feasts in which everything was in the deep azure of a cloudless sky. To-day we still cultivate colour schemes without much hostile comment, as it takes the philosopher to discover their puerility, the prurient-minded their wickedness and degeneracy.

We are told that the blatant discussions of his amusements made right-minded men blush, causing ultimate nausea for his tastes and opinions. But it could only have been the few he had the opportunity of disgusting; the majority had heard the same before and showed no desire to be shocked. Other Emperors had been as outspoken, be it said to their reprobation as well as to his, but other Emperors had not been so good-hearted, so filled with the charity that thinketh no wrong. When they had scented opposition they had removed the cause forthwith ; Elagabalus let it grow and strengthen till it swallowed him up.

It may be that, as Lampridius says, his effemin-acy disgusted the virile Roman world. It was a vice as reprehensible then as now. The genius of the Greek and Roman friendships was all against the weak softness of the Semitic races. Greek love had been regulated "to strengthen hardihood, to breed a contempt for death, to overcome the sweet desire for life, to humanise cruelty, to which powers almost as much veneration is due as to the cult of the Immortal Gods," says Valerius Maximus, in his treatise *De amicitiae vinculo.* It would have been small wonder if the whole mass of healthy - minded individuals had turned from Lampridius' picture of this little painted quean of seventeen years, who never showed in himself any traits of manliness, except when he was on the seat of judgment. If he had been portrayed as wholly woman, or wholly man, we could have understood him, but for this strange admixture even the physicians are at a loss to account, almost to understand. He had his good qualities and had them in plenty, but overshadowing them all, like a terrible blight, there was this organic affliction of the senses, passions, and general outlook. Unfortunately, this blight of femininity still exists in the world to a certain extent, especially amongst religious persons. Gulick holds that the reason why only 7 per cent of young men attend the Christian churches is because the qualities demanded are feminine not virile, such as passive love, passive suffering, rest, prayer, trust ; whereas Confucianism and Mahommedanism attract men because the demand is for virile qualities, and the place for women is small. Such faiths make even more than individual demands on the virtues of courage, endurance, self-control, bravery, loyalty, and enthusiasm. Gulick says also, that the able- bodied boy who lacks the courage to fight is generally a milksop, or a sneak, without any high sense of honour.

In this epitome of the qualities demanded of men we see the true grounds on which the world has instinctively condemned Elagabalus, though probably without quite knowing why they did so. It is because they have been told that he pos-sessed the virtues, along with the mind, of the woman, and a voluptuous woman at that, and had nothing of what the world expects to find in the male animal. His reign was short, so he left no traces of his mind on the Empire, and what little he did effect was reversed by his successor. His reign of prodigal extravagance caused not one single new impost; his government of the city and provinces alike was one of peace and harmony. That in-famous system of informers under which the aristo-cracy and plutocracy of Rome had suffered so direly up to the death of Caracalla was never re-estab-lished by Elagabalus; despite the fact that his rule had been subverted, on more than one occasion, by the existing aristocrats. The people was sovereign, and it was important that that sovereign should be amused, nattered, and fed. All was done that had been done before by the demi-gods, and all was done with an exaggeration unparalleled. His games in the circus were such that even Lampridius admits the people considered him a worthy Emperor, because he was endowed with a sense of the grandeur of the imperial position, and expressed it by his marvel-lous prodigalities. They made him what he was, and has ever remained in history, the Emperor of extravagance. In him the glow of the purple reached its apogee. Rome had been watching a crescendo that had mounted with the ages. Its culmination was in this hermaphrodite. But the tension had been too great, even for the solidarity of Imperial Rome ; it was as though, the mainspring had snapped, and the age of anarchy, both military and religious, did the rest: undermining the State, till the Emperors, whose sceptre had lashed both gods and sky, became little better than a procession of bandits, coloured and ornate it is true, but utterly lacking in that strength and virility which is the essential of real government throughout the world.

Thus did Rome make way for Attila, the scourge whom God sent for the final extinction of art and philosophy, and incidentally for the refurbishing of the world under its mediaeval guise.

CHAPTER X. THE EXTRAVAGANCES OF THE EMPEROR ELAGABALUS

The Rome of Elagabalus was a dream aflame with gold, "a city of triumphal arches, enchanted temples, royal dwellings, vast porticoes, and wide, hospitable streets; a Rome purely Greek in conception and design. On its heart, from the Circus Maximus to the Forum's edge, the remains of the gigantic Palace of Nero still shone, fronted by a stretch of columns a mile in length; a palace so wonderful that even the cellars were frescoed. In the baths of porphyry and verd-antique you had waters cold or sulphurous at will, and these Elagabalus threw open to all whose forms pleased him, men and women alike " (a custom of mixed bathing which had been abolished by Hadrian and was again proscribed by Alexander Severus). " The dining-halls had ivory ceilings, from which flowers fell, and wainscots that changed at every service. The walls were alive with the glisten of gems, with marbles rarer than jewels. In one hall was a dome of sapphire, a floor of malachite, crystal columns and red gold walls; about the palace were green savannahs, forest reaches, the call of the bird and deer ; before it was a lake, eight acres of which Vespasian had drained and replaced by an amphitheatre, which is still the wonder of the world."

Into this profusion of aesthetic loveliness the youth of fourteen summers stepped proudly, realising how fitting a background it made to his glorious beauty. It was Nero's creation, and here was a young Nero (in face and manner) suddenly re-appeared to enjoy what he had been prematurely forced to leave.

In spite of everything, Nero was still the idol of the masses. For years fresh roses had lain on his tomb, the memory of his festivals was unforgettable, regret for him refused to be stilled; he was more than a god, he was a tradition, and his second advent was confidently expected. The Egyptians had proclaimed that the soul has its avatars; the Romans had sneered in their philosophical fashion at all ideas of soul migration till Elagabalus saun-tered from that distant Emesa, an Antonine at the head of an adoring army ; then they began to think that the Egyptians were wiser than they looked, for in the blue eyes of the young Emperor the spirit of Nero's magnificence shone.

All men were charmed ; the Senate with their Aurelius, the people with their Nero, the army with their Antonine. Certainly in profusion Elagabalus was destined to rival his prototype. His prodigal-ities were more excessive, his mignons more blatant, his wives more numerous, and his processions more splendid. Only in cruelty (at which none can cavil) did the resemblance fail. Nero had regretted his ability to write when first a death-warrant was pre-sented for his signature ; he appended his name and soon found the taste for blood. Elagabalus wept at the sight of suffering, poverty and misery to the end of his life; and as he never avoided seeing it, he must have wept often. In fact, a favourite pastime, according to Herodian, was wandering disguised through the purlieus of the city; sometimes he would serve as potboy in the taverns, or as barber's assistant in the slums, as itinerant vendor of vegetables and perfumes about the streets ; which antics assume a most reprehensible flavour in the mouth of the historians after the Emperor had conceived the notion of taking the world into his confidence and had ordered paintings of himself in the plebeian garbs above mentioned. Anyway, Elagabalus tried to alleviate distress, which was more practical than tears, though an unusual extravagance amongst the Emperors of the decadence.

From his infancy the boy had gloried in extravagance. Even as a private citizen we are told that he refused to stir without a procession of sixty chariots following, a foible which had caused Maesa to gnash her teeth instead of adopting measures which would prevent the recurrence of such ostentation. He had never even thought of austerity, simplicity, and poverty as necessary evils, let alone as Christian virtues, to be borne with fortitude and temperance. Once when a friend asked him whether he was not afraid that his prodigalities would land him in ultimate necessity, he replied with an astounding self-com-placency, " What can be better for me than to be heir to myself." Like many a modern child, he objected to woollen garments, and his parents were foolish enough to give way to his whimsies; he disliked the feel of wool, he said. Another prejudice was against linen that had been washed. So dainty was he that he never used the same garments, the same jewels, the same woman twice (unless it were his wife), says Lampridius. But in Rome wool was necessary ; Rome was never healthy. Maesa knew it by experience, but was more than willing to tempt providence by returning thither. The Tramontana visited it then as now ; fever too, and sudden death. Wool was certainly necessary; besides, it was the accustomed dress of the country, and Rome was intensely conservative, she would not endure an Emperor who came dressed as an Eastern barbarian ; the boy of thirteen years must adopt the clothes, habits, and customs of his adopted country, of his reputed father; thus the grandmother argued till Elagabalus was bored with the discussion, and told the lady so. He was devising, moreover, he an-nounced, garments more splendid and more bizarre than any Rome had found outside the temple at Jerusalem. His fancy was a frail tunic of purple silk diapered with gold, or that even more resplen-dent vestment which was woven throughout of fine gold and encrusted with gems. Alone of the garments he had seen, this enhanced his beauty and gave dignity to his movements. The sleeves were long and full, reaching to his heels, open to show the rounded softness of his girlish arms; gilded leather covered his feet and reached to his thighs ; it was softer than wool and certainly showed his form to better advantage. Sometimes after supper he would appear in public dressed in the stiff dalmatic of a young deacon, calling himself Fabius Gurgis, and Scipio, because the parents of these youths had formerly shown them to the people in this costume in order to correct their bad manners.

Encircling his curls (but in the palace only) was a diadem of heavy gold, studded with jewels; not the simple golden circlet known to the Roman world, but one after a Persian design, first introduced by Caracalla, rich, splendid, and brilliant with the numbers of rubies, sapphires, and emeralds which he thought became him. Unfortunately, his taste for precious stones did not stop here. Lampridius and Herodian pour deserved scorn on the numerous bracelets, rings and necklaces, all as rich and costly as could be made, with which he decked his person ; but, perhaps unnecessarily, on his shoe-buckles, whose stones, engraved cameo and intaglio, were the wonder of the beholder, and their cry has been increased to a howl by later commentators, who seem to consider it a species of indecency that the Emperor's shoes should be of fine leather, his stones priceless, while theirs were of ill-dressed cowhide, held together with buckles of paste.

Of course, it is not a pleasant taste, this overlaying of the body with an inordinate display of wealth, even when done merely for the honour of one's God, as Elagabalus protested. Unfortunately, it is still known both in the Plutocratic and Sacerdotal worlds. Certain minds still revolt, still see its snobbery, vanity and degeneracy, are even foolish enough to imagine that the personal vanity of such functionaries will one day renounce what is their main means of attraction.

Elagabalus' love of extravagance comes out most strongly in his ritual of worship. Never in the history of Rome had such daily waste of life and liquor, such profusion of colour and gold, flowers, music, and movement displayed the honour of God or man. The Emperor's one idea was to eclipse all that his predecessors had imagined. It was a stupendous task to surpass Nero in fantasy, Otho and Vitellius in greediness; but he had read Sue-tonius, and not an eccentricity of the Caesars had escaped his notice. He knew, too, where to exceed them, and still lives on the reputation of a work accomplished.

The hecatombs of oxen and innumerable quantities of sheep which came daily to the temple of the Only God required a perfect army of butchers that their slaughter might do homage to the Deity while day-light lasted. These, with the spices, wine, and flowers, were but part payment of the interest which the high priest felt his family owed to Elagabal for the past and present successes of his house, while his most beloved title was that which styled him Invictus Sacerdos, Dei Soli." There is a great variety in his medals, both in those coined by "the Senate and in those struck by himself, whereon this priesthood of his is described. Chief Priest and Invincible Priest of Elagabal, or the Sun, are commonly to be met with round his image, which stands in a sacrificing posture, with a censer in his hand, over an altar. It was in this supreme ineffable spirit that the Emperor put his trust, to him he ascribed his health, wealth, and security, together with that of his whole catholic church militant here on earth.

On his arrival in Rome in the year a.d. 219, Elagabalus thought well to carry through the laud-able custom (for the poor) of bestowing the usual congiary on the people. If Mediobarbus were to be trusted, he gave six such during his short reign of approximately four years, besides the soldiers' donatives (which to his cost and undoing be foolishly neglected as time went on). To-day such liberalities on the part of a sovereign take the form of free meals and a limited supply of beer, but are amiable and satisfying methods of spending the public money in an ingratiating fashion. What Elagabalus gave was from the private funds of his house, and was given in a manner quite his own. Formerly it had been usual to distribute gold and silver (Nero had added eccentric gifts, of course) on such occasions, but Elagabalus signalised his assumption of the Consulship by the distribution of fat oxen, camels, eunuchs, slaves, caparisoned saddle-horses, closed sedans and carriages, hoping, as he remarked, that all men would remember these were the gifts of the Emperor; as though any were likely to forget when they found themselves saddled with a dromedary, and expected to conduct it safely to their own back-yard through the crowded lanes of the city. Such gifts were often more trouble than they were worth, and the scramble at the distribution much what it would be now, at least, according to Lampridius' description of those yearly distributions which followed the translation of the Great God to his temple in the suburbs.

At times Elagabalus gave money; witness the congiary and donative to celebrate his marriage with Cornelia Paula, when, as Herodian tells us, not only the people, but also the Senators, Equites, and even the Senators' wives partook of the liberality, receiving 150 denares each, the soldiers 250, on account, presumably, of their superior usefulness.

Had this boy's megalomania stopped short at donatives and congiaries, we should know little but good of him; unfortunately, he considered that to love oneself is the beginning of a lifelong romance, and spent his money as best pleased his fancy at the moment, which was always with a taste for resplendency.

We can imagine the beauty of his reclining couches, solid silver, richly chased, the cushions upholstered in purple woven with pure gold. Entire services in silver for table use, very massive; even the saucepans were in the same metal, and elegantly fashioned vases or cups containing 100 lbs. weight of precious metal apiece, with the most obvious indecencies engraved or repoussed on the sides; the strange part of it all being that he took delight, not so much in the possession of all this splendour as in the giving of it to his friends, so much so that the silversmiths could scarce keep pace with his generosity. It is a good feeling that of giving generously, better to give than to receive, and what Elagabalus got in return cost the giver so little pain.

To food and drink the Emperor was as much addicted as the traditional city alderman, though his imagination certainly surpassed that of the retired tradesman, at least in quality and design. His chief authority was Apicius, the renowned author of a book entitled *De re coquinaria,* but he had other models almost as famous, if not as long-lived, in the Emperors Otho and Vitellius, and managed to outdo them all in extravagance. Lampridius states that no feast cost Elagabalus less than 100,000 sesterces, and often reached the stupendous figure of 300,000, *tout compris.* The number of dishes has been reached, if not surpassed, by modern luxury, but to Lampridius twenty-two courses sounded absurd; not so, however, the ablutions and courtesans who always attended and utilised the intervals in an unbecoming manner. Occasionally these intervals were of some length, caused by the removal of whole services of plate to the possession of some guest who had said the right thing at the psycho-logical moment. Another means of delay was found in the practice, which Elagabalus instituted, of taking each course in the house of a different friend, an arrangement which necessitated the transference of the whole party in their gold and ivory chariots from the Capitol to the Palatine, thence to the Coelian Hill, and again to another friend who might live beyond the walls, or yet to another in Trastevere. This, with the usual impedimenta, arriving at the house of each, for the dishes in their order, took time, and in such a fashion we can well believe the chronicler who states that a single feast was scarce finished in the daytime, especially as the intervals for customary enjoyments were arranged with due regard for the utmost desires of the guests.

It is charming to imagine a feast such as is recorded of Maecenas, where "in ungirdled tunics the guests lay on silver beds, the head and neck encircled with amaranthe— whose perfume, in opening the pores, neutralises the fumes of wine—fanned by boys, whose curly hair they used as napkins. Under the supervision of butlers the courses were served on silver platters, so large that they covered the tables. Sows' breasts with Lybian truffles ; dormice baked in poppies and honey; peacocks' tongues flavoured with cinnamon ; oysters stewed in garum —a sort of anchovy sauce made of the intestines of fish—flamingoes' and ostriches' brains, followed by the brains of thrushes, parroquets, pheasants, and peacocks, also a yellow pig cooked after the Trojan fashion, from which, when carved, hot sausages fell and live thrushes flew; sea-wolves from the Baltic, sturgeons from Rhodes, fig-peckers from Samos, African snails and the rest." A full list of the dainties set forth would weary the amateur, might even make him envious of the times that are now long dead, times when the ceaseless round of beef and mutton would have been considered monotonous or bad art, and year in year out plain boiled greens were unknown; times when the Emperor served, as we have recorded, grains of gold with his peas, rubies with lentils, beans and amber, for the mere pleasure of sight; though his salads of mullets' fins with cress, balm mint, and fenugreek, we should probably have found no greater delicacy than the undercooked vegetables of this twentieth century of our salvation and discomfort.

As with food, so with wine, Elagabalus was a glutton. Mulsum, that cup composed of white wine, roses, nard, absinthe and honey, was *vieux jeu*. The delicate wines of Greece were always palatable ; so was the crusty Falernian of the year 632 a.u.c., to those who were of an age to appreciate its worth. The young gourmet thought otherwise, and rendered them noisome by the addition of crushed pine kernels and fir cones. It was a youthful taste, such as we still distrust, but scarcely immoral in the generally accepted sense of the term. As regards a tendency to over-indulgence in good liquor, we have no data; there is a passage in Lampridius (though evidently faulty) which asserts that the Emperor used to mix wine with the baths and then invite the guests to drink, the basin from which he had drunk being easily distinguishable by the fall in its level; an utter impossibility, and not even clever as a bit of scandal. Another extravagance culled from the same biographer tells how this child realised the summer by feasts at which all was of one colour, food as well as fittings, and how he would order all the dishes of a certain day to be composed of a single sort of flesh : it might be pheasant under twenty different garbs, fowls served on the same scale, even fish, if the Court happened to be at a distance from the sea. At another time you would be served with a vegetarian diet, or occasionally with nothing but pork, which sounds inconsistent when we consider that the same author has sneered copiously at the Emperor's adoption of the Jewish superstition in this matter. He further tells us that it was not magnificent enough for this child's fancy to recline on silver beds, with covers fashioned in cloth of gold ; his cushions were of hare's fur, or down from under the partridge's wing, whilst the whole was strewn thick with flowers and perfumes, those of important guests with saffron and gold dust. Wherever he went were flowers strewing the way—lilies, violets, roses, and narcissus.

No mention of psychological extravagance would be complete without a certain disquisition on the use of perfumes. Here, as everywhere else, Lam-pridius tells us that Elagabalus contrived to outdo his predecessors. The use he made of unguents was little short of dissolute. As usual, the biogra-pher would have us believe that the failing was an idiosyncrasy peculiar to the Emperor, whose life he was decrying. He had obviously not heard of the soporific nastiness of Solomon's beloved, a lady who is represented to us by the writer of the Canticles as a cluster of camphire, a mountain of myrrh, a hill of frankincense, spikenard and cinnamon, additions which would not only have made her sticky, but noisome to boot. Mahommed and his pavement ' of musk was beyond Lampridius' ken, but he had certainly heard of the perfumes which scented the temple at Jerusalem, and it would have been no new sight for him to have watched Elaga-balus pour tons of aromatics upon the new altars erected to the ancient gods.

Even to-day we know something about the odour of sanctity and occasionally inhale its delights by stealth, because, despite undoubted legal pro-hibition, the clergy have persuaded us that the Gods still love the smell of incense. Our point is, however, that everything sacred and profane stank horribly at the period. Thank heaven, the personal use of *mille fleurs* which then obsessed the world has now given place to a smell of the open. But there was nothing unusual during the third century in the fact that Elagabalus burnt Indian aromatics instead of coal in his dining-rooms, balm instead of petroleum in his lamps, and heated his stoves and bathrooms with odours instead of the more com-monplace materials. What is repulsive is the depraved use which the world made of perfume. The tunics of men, their baths, beds, horses, rooms, streets, servants, even their food smelt. Caligula had wasted a fortune on perfumes. Nero had waded in them.

Myrrh, aloes, and cassia, saffron and cinnamon, not to mention others equally objection-able and even more costly; these all made life heavy and cloying, turned conceptions of wrong into right, made the unholy adorable, stained the thoughts and depraved the mind, just as M. Huysmans (in *À Rebours)* describes what he succeeded in doing during his stay at Fontenay.

Not that Rome was as objectionable as Athens. There, we are told that both men and women painted their faces with white lead, their eyelids with kohl, and their nails with henna ; and in order to draw attention to the depravity, they perfumed their hair with marjoram, rubbed their arms with mint, their legs with ivy, and the soles of their feet with baccaris. In Greece this idea of attention to personal beauty was a perfect cult — the latest recipes for artificial adornments were engraved on tablets and exhibited in the temples of Aesculapius, and, this done, the state imposed a fine for a slatternly appearance ; but for all that it was decadent and nasty. People, of course, still spend money on their personal appearance, but patchouli, thank heaven ! has gone, even from Piccadilly.

The Emperor's fondness for fish was tempered by its rarity. He would never eat of its living things whilst he sojourned near the sea ; he would have them transported to the immense salt-water tanks he had constructed amongst the mountains and in the interior of the country, both for their preservation and his own amusement. We are told that he invented a method of fishing in which oxen figured, a conceit which later years has not revived.

First in history he conceived of sausages made from lampreys' roes, soft-shelled oysters, lobsters, and crayfish, and fed the country peasants on the same. Indeed, his generosity here, as in Rome, was unbounded, the chroniclers relating how he would throw from the windows as many dishes as he offered to his own guests then at table. There was nothing of our niggardly idea of charity here, no notion that any crusts were good enough for the hungry. His dogs were fed on foie-gras, his horses on grapes, his lions on pheasants and parroquets— an unnecessary and unpleasant waste when one knows how much these beasts would have preferred a more ordinary fare.

His fish sauce was a triumph of the culinary art, which is utterly lost. It was a transparent bluish-green, the counterpart of sea water, in which the fish looked alive and natural, utterly unlike the ragged ugliness which is now presented for our con-sumption. So famous were his dishes that the pastrycooks and dairymen of the day were wont to reproduce them in their own particular wares, selling the same as imperial affectations.

The menus also were his own conception, embroidered on the tablecloth—not the mere list of dishes, but pictures drawn with the needle of the dishes themselves—which, of course, necessitated a change of cloth with each service. He first, we are told, made the public feasts, as well as private dinners, great and magnificent. Formerly these feasts had been of a military simplicity. Elagabalus could not see why even political guests should not enjoy themselves when they came to dine with him, and served them with hydrogarum, the then last word in Sybaritic enjoyment. His successor Alexander thought differently, and reverted to the old order, a proceeding which pleased no one save the flatulent.

Elagabalus was, unfortunately, tainted with what is perhaps natural in young people, though in elderly plutocrats is an acquired vice, that of overt snobbery. It is recorded by more than one of his guests that he would often ask them to price his dishes, in order to hear an excessive value suggested, remarking that great cost gave a good appetite, especially when one knew that dishes were scarce and out of season. Of course, it was bad form, even in a boy, but how much else that happens is the same ? There are other things in plenty to cavil at.

It was not by food alone that Elagabalus drained the treasury; he had other ways of nattering the sovereign people of Rome. The spectacles which he gave in the amphitheatre were unique. Fancy 80,000 people on ascending galleries, protected from the sun by a canopy of spangled silk, an arena three acres in extent, carpeted with sand, vermilion, and borax, in that arena were naval displays on lakes of wine, and the death of whole menageries of Egyp-tian beasts (in one show, Herodian tells us, fifty-one tigers alone were killed). There were chariot races, in which not only horses, but also stags, lions, tigers, dogs, and even women figured, till the spectators showed a colossal delight. The magnificence of the spectacle almost surpasses belief: from below came the blare of a thousand brass instruments, and from above the caresses of flutes, while the air, sweet with flowers and perfume (for the Emperor had provided saffron even for the cloaks of the crowd), was alive with multicoloured motes. The terraces were parterres of blending hues, when into that splendour a hundred lions, their tasselled tails sweeping the sand, entered obliquely, and anon a rush of wild elephants, attacked on either side ; another moment of sheer delight, in which the hunters were tossed upon the terraces, tossed back again by the spectators, and trampled to death. By way of interlude, the ring was peopled with acrobats, who flew up in the air like birds, and formed pyramids together, much in the fashion that we know them to-day. There was a troop of tamed lions, their manes gilded, that walked on tight-ropes, wrote obscenities in Greek, and danced to cymbals, which one of them played ; a chase of ostriches and feats of horsemanship on zebras from Madagascar. The interlude at an end, the sand was re-raked. Then, preceded by the pomp of lictors, interminable files of gladiators entered, while the eyes of the women lighted and glowed ; artistic death was their chiefest joy, for there was no cowardice in the arena. The gladiators fought for applause, for liberty, for death —fought manfully, skilfully, terribly too, and received the point of the sword or the palm of victory with an equally unmoved expression, an unchanged face. It was a magnificent conception on which the Romans, or, more exactly, the Etrus-cans, their predecessors, had devised to train their children for war and allay the fear of blood. It had been serviceable indeed, and though the need of it had gone, the spectacle endured, and, enduring, con-stituted the chief delight of the Vestals and of Rome. By its means a bankrupt became Consul, an Emperor beloved. It had stayed revolutions, because it was felt to be the tax of the proletariat on the rich. Silver and bread were for the individual, but these things were for the crowd. When evening descended, so did torches and the Emperor to take chief part in the ballet which he considered as the culminating point in the performance.

In a robe, immaterial as a moonbeam, his eyelids darkened with antimony, his face painted in imitation of the courtesans who sat on high chairs and ogled passers-by in the Suburra, he entered the arena, and there, to the incitement of crotals, he danced with his Syrians before the multitude, a protecting claque of 80,000 persons toasting the performer with the magnificent cry, " Io Triumphe ! " whatever they thought of its indecency. Lampridius tells us of his importing from Egypt those little serpents, known under the name of " good genius," and letting them loose amongst the audience, among whom many were bitten, many killed, in the stam-pede. It was quite a likely prank to play—is even heard of to-day — but one cannot imagine that Elagabalus wanted to disperse the audience, as his biographer suggests, before they had witnessed the magnificence which he had prepared for their delectation. It would have been too foolish, especially if he wanted an appreciative reception for his own turn.

So much for his public appearances. Many of his private pleasures are quite repeatable, though all are extravagant, such as his chariot races in the palace and in the Gardens of Hope, his teams of great dogs to draw him from place to place, his naked women for the same purpose, or when he himself, in the attributes and customary undress of Bacchus, was drawn by lions, tigers, and the female sex. In driving, Elagabalus had a splendid nerve, as we learn from the record of his chariot races with camels and elephants even over the Vatican and its tombs. He seems to have imagined that others were possessed of the same daring and hardihood. Witness his requests to guests that they should drive chariots, to which were harnessed four wild stags, through the porticoes in front of his dining-rooms, which porticoes were strewn thick with gold and silver dust, because he could not get electrum. Many found the task most unpleasant, especially if they were portly, or Senators whose pomposity ought to have put such antics out of the question; but Elagabalus was no respecter of persons, unless, of course, they were young, beautiful, and full of lust; to such he was ever considerate, whether they were men or women. One day, because they pleased him, he presented to the courtesans and procurers of the city the whole supply of corn for a year's provision, and promised a like amount to those dwelling outside the walls. On another he collected the *cocottes* of the theatres and circuses, and, having harangued them as "companions in arms," presented them with a soldier's donative of three pieces of gold, saying, " Tell no one that Antonine has given you this."

Elagabalus is the originator of lotteries, which have since become a source of profit to European states. There was one for the people, one for the comedians. Of course, he provided the prizes, and there does not seem to have been any purchase of tickets. These were singular, as were all his other gifts, and varied from ı lb. of beef to 100 pieces of gold or 1000 of silver.

In summer he had the audacity to erect a snow mountain in his orchard, in order that cool airs might relieve the oppressiveness of Sol in Leone. Even in the relief of natural functions he was magnificent, using only vases of gold, onyx, and myrrhin. Whether this last is a metal or sort of agate has been disputed, but Pliny had no doubt as to its extreme worth. He tells us that a drinking cup was sold for 70,000 sesterces, and a sacrificial capis for 1,000,000, to his own knowledge.

The progresses of Elagabalus were a sight that made even the citizens of Rome stare open-mouthed. Nero had taken a train of 500 carriages, and the boy Emperor was not to be outdone. He ordered a following of 600 at a time, saying that the King of Persia had a train of 10,000 camels, and for himself, his numerous courtesans, procurers, and the rest, whom he had bought and freed, all richly habited, could not be accommodated with less, wherein he showed a certain chivalry, as also in the case of the very famous *cocotte,* whom he had bought for 100,000 sesterces, and then relegated to perpetual virginity.

The Syrian astrologers had told Elagabalus that he would meet with a violent death, which information seems in no way to have disturbed his equanimity; it merely added to his extravagances, in that he built a tower, from which he designed to throw himself, when his hour was come, on to a pavement of gold encrusted with gems, in order that men might say, " qualis artifex periit." To make assurance doubly sure, he carried with him little cases fashioned in emeralds and rubies, containing deadly poisons, also cords of purple silk, with which he might strangle himself if he were in any real trouble, though the adulation of the people made it doubtful if such could ever happen. Was it a wonderful thing that the people loved him — the originator of lotteries where no one but the Emperor was the loser, the distributor of an incessant shower of tickets that were exchangeable, not for bread or trivial sums, but for gems, pictures, slaves, fortunes, ships, villas, and estates ? Such a one was bound to be adored ; indeed, his lavishness deified him in the eyes of the sovereign people of Rome.

There is one record of wanton waste which Lampridius has laid to his charge, namely, that of sinking laden ships in the harbours in order to show men at what a price he valued his wealth, that it could pay any compensation, could stand any strain. It is a foolish and criminal fault for a statesman to squander the wealth of his country, but an accusation which is still levelled against the statesmen of our own time, and that not infrequently. They may not attempt to realise the greatness of their country by collecting cobwebs by the ton, as Elagabalus once managed to do, saying that he wished thus to realise the greatness of Rome, but they are perfectly capable of ordering equally unproductive labour and paying for it at an enormous price, which is, ethically speaking, much the same thing. The psychology of extravagance has not yet been examined, so we are still free to condemn what we do not fully understand. Megalomania we all know something about and can all condemn as experts. It was Elagabalus' success, as it has tended to the progress of other equally well-known persons.

CHAPTER XI. THE RELIGION OF THE EMPEROR ELAGABALUS

One of the main causes of complaint against the Emperor Marcus Aurelius Antoninus was his religion. Lampridius and Xiphilinus are unani-mous in their condemnation of its tendencies and beliefs. Into these it is unnecessary to enter at greater length than has been done in preceding chapters. If there is one point on which all his biographers are fully agreed, it is that the Emperor was pre-eminently religious. God took the first place in his calculations and designs.

Had he been a private person, no one could have objected to this tendency. In general, piety towards the Gods has been commended throughout the world's history. It is only when a man occupies a public position and subordinates his civil to his religious duties that the world is apt to look askance at the latter. This is the position of Elagabalus, at least in part; he is accused of neglecting the business of the state for the sake of his conscience. Other sovereigns have been likewise accused, and have likewise suffered at the hands of a world even more vitally religious than were the Senate and people of third-century Rome. Similar instances may be found not far from home which have perhaps even less justification, when we consider that the cause of offence here was ceremonies, not vital creeds.

A word may also be said concerning the objects which Antonine's biographers had in view when they condemned what we should—at first sight— have expected them to have praised in the Emperor's life.

As we have already pointed out, Constantine's determination to impose Christianity on the empire led to grave opposition, chiefly from the adherents of the similarly monotheistic cult of Mithra, a cult which was certainly identified with that of Elagabal, the only God. It was—if on that account alone— obviously necessary that, not only the opposing religion, but also the chief exponent of that worship, should come in for severe censure at the hands of the fourth-century monotheism.

As one reads the story of Antonine's life, one is struck not so much by the record of his perverse sexualities, about which no one can have known anything definite, and which, even if the reports be true, we are bound to regard as congenital, in the light of modern research, as we are by the record of his religious fanaticism. This trait is, and in all pro-bability justly, considered to be reprehensible. It is not, however, restricted to the Emperor in question; probably everybody has come across it, in one form or another, during the course of his life; some have even suffered under its potency.

Antonine was, as we have said, in a peculiar position ; he was young, powerful, and extremely religious ; he ascribed the success of his house to the favour of his God, and desired to make some return in the shape of coercing men to that God's worship. To this Emperor the possession of supreme power meant limitless possibilities for the effecting of his scheme. Further, as we have seen, he came of a religious stock, or rather of a family whose traditions were bound up with a very definite form of religious worship, which is generally considered as the same thing.

The origin of religion is a much-disputed point. Some men have considered that the source of all religion is fright; others prefer love ; both of which appeal to the superstitious instinct inherent in man. It may be that these instincts breed reverence, fear, or love for forces outside man's control, and incomprehensible to him; in any case, these forces were the first things to be deified in the history of religions, and took their precedence in the natural order of their mystery or usefulness, becoming a sort of aristocracy of talent, with a supreme head, the God of Gods.

In process of time the older religions of Greece and Rome gave way to philosophies; and the thinkers having reasoned away the potency of their deities, fought against what they considered a decadent and sentimental, not to say a baseless tradition, with all the aids that experience gave them. Then it was that the signs, portents, and miracles which had bolstered up the faith of the ignorant, which had kept fright and superstition alive, even the very prophecies and revelations which were the sacerdotal proofs of inherent genuineness became either natural phenomena or debasing charlatanry, amongst men who knew their origin and history, or had learned from Archimedes the principles of mathematics.

Nevertheless, in imperial Rome the atmosphere was charged with the marvellous, very much as it was in Northern Europe until the time of the Renaissance. The world was filled with prodigies, strange Gods, and credulous crowds. The occult sciences, astrology, magic and divinations, all had their adepts, and commanded the respect which kindred practices command amongst the credulous to-day.

But the philosophy of the older religions was undoubtedly hard and cold. Courage, moderation, and honour were qualities that enforced the permanence of the state, not of the individual. Men laboured not for hope of reward, but for the sake of duty ; they knew that vice was part of the universal order of things, perhaps an error of the understanding, certainly an error which it was idle to blame, yet righteous to rectify. But the older religions as they had developed during the latter days of the republic were far from satisfying the whole aspira-tions of man.

The mind of man is not his only function, he has physical parts and passions as well, such as fright, superstition, attractions, antipathies, and sex. Some men were incapable of thought, few were single in aim, and there was a craving, it may be quite irrational, but still human, which longed to create, or at least to imagine, something higher than self, something mightier than mind, something to which the irrational and traditional side of man could appeal; and so, as one God died, a newer and more mystical personage took his place. Jupiter had ceased to dominate the world with a visible potency, Mithra, more mystical, more sentimental, took his place as a power, so intimately connected with man's physical parts and passions, that the world of philosophy, which dealt with the body through the mind, could scarcely touch the fringes of his garment.

There was, therefore, in Rome at the beginning of the third century a.d. a party of men strongly attached, for sentimental or neurotic reasons, to one or other of the recently imported Eastern creeds ; but there was also a large party of conservatives whose atheism was as cool and detached as that of Horace ; and a still larger party of ordinary people whose attachment to the old practices of Roman Polytheism expressed all that they considered either necessary or expedient, from the point of view of ordinary piety. But in each case the religion was subordinated to a paramount political, not to an essen-tially religious life, which life was evolving, as we learn from nearly all authors, towards degenera-tion, despite the fact that culture and literature was still based upon the philosophy of intellectual freedom.

Unfortunately, the very rule which had made for political greatness was now robbing men of every liberating interest, was leaving society sterile and empty. As a consequence of this, each generation was becoming less wishful to think, and less capable of thought; not that the intellect of Rome had by any means descended to that ultimate plane of intelligence from which it was ready to enslave itself under the retrograde tendencies of Eastern theistic beliefs. Rome, the mistress of the world, had seen good in all Gods ; she had acknowledged and included in her worship the philosophies and deities of all nations, tribes, and tongues ; every force, natural, physical, and political, was represented at her altars. Rome was comprehensively, sceptically Polytheist, when to her palaces flocked the engineers, astronomers, and philosophers of that vast empire. It was only to the common people, possessed as they were by beliefs in non-human powers, in beings that beset life with malignity, that the restoration of cults and ritual commended itself, and even they were eclectic in their tastes and fancies.

Despite pulpit learning, we know that Rome was no more attracted by those doctrines of the universal socialistic brotherhood which had emanated from Nazareth, than she was by the system of the ecstatic visionary from Tarsus, who was destined—by a more systematic and regular development of his revelations—to capture the freedom of the earlier intellectual religions, as soon as the world's hoary wisdom, having lost its virility, was involved in the dotage of an unreasoning antiquity.

In the long run we know that the mob triumphed, and that every religion of the West was orientalised, every superstition and neurotic tendency developed, and philosophy was brought to its knees utterly debased, until its function was merely to be the apologist of all that superstition taught or did. For the present, rational thinking men were alive. When they died, exclusive monotheism came, carrying before it, like a flood, the greatness of the former world. But the issue was still uncertain. Had Elagabalus lived ; had the beauty and impressive-ness of his Semitic ritual made its way ; had time been given for men to grasp his idea of one vast, beneficent, divine power, into the empire of whose central authority men might escape from the thousand and one petty marauders of the spirit world, they might have been attracted to the worship of life and light instead of enmeshed by the seductive force of obscure and impossible dogmas, tempted by the bait of an elusive socialism and a problematical futurity.

It was not that Rome, atheist or religious, ob-jected to the worship of Baal. She had her own and a round dozen other Jupiters, as men conceived him to be, and was quite ready to include him amongst the number. The trouble was that rational thinking men could not bring their minds to conceive of any supreme potency in the world, outside man himself; while religious persons had each his own particular conceit in the way of deities, all of which the new Emperor, with more zeal than discretion, proceeded to make subject to his own Lord's will.

But there was obviously more than mere amalga-mation in Antonine's scheme. We have already pointed out the Emperor's position of supremacy over the old cults, and discussed the disintegrating tendency of the mystical and independent monotheisms, which was already apparent even in the city itself. The danger which these new religions imported into political life lay in the establishment of an imperium over the souls of men, which, based on superstitious terrors rather than on any appeal to reason or logic, claimed an authority over the mind equal to that of the State over the persons of its subjects.

The main attraction of these forms of faith lay in their ability to supply men with a personal and spiritual religion, which, being free from State intervention, was able to incite its adherents to rebellion, against any policy of which its priesthood disapproved, on spiritual or even on financial grounds. Statesmen had long recognised the danger, and were obviously attempting to cope with the new forces. Antonine's proposal was one for the extension of his jurisdiction (as Pontifex Maximus) to the new monotheisms, by the amalga-mation of these with the older worships over which his authority as Pontifex Maximus was unchallenged. If he had succeeded he would have exerted his, headship of religion in much the same fashion as Elizabeth Tudor—claiming a similar headship— exerted hers in the sixteenth century. This policy meant the appointment of State officials endowed with the wealth, titles, and a portion of the vesture of those old prelates, who had by their traditions and claims to magical powers, coerced, and indeed still coerce the minds of the credulous to the disintegration of the State. Antonine fore-shadowed what Tudor greatness effected ; namely, the erection of a State church, whose business it was to replace an independent priesthood which fostered fanaticism, by a race of civil servants who would restrain and modify superstition, turning all dangerous and harmful elements in the religious life into useful and philanthropic energies, concerning whose profit it would take an anchorite to disagree.

We have traced the steps by which Antonine proceeded to carry out his policy of amalgamation. The erection of that superb and gigantic temple in the XIth region; the summer residence for his God near the Porta Praenestina ; and the proces-sion, in which all men and most of the Gods took part, have been catalogued already. It was, how-ever, this very amalgamation to which Rome, atheist and religious, objected. Antonine could have done what pleased him in the way of introducing a new worship ; he might have caused all men to assist at his ceremonies, and no one would have objected ; but to desecrate the older religions, and deprive them of their treasured possessions, was an offence against all canons of Roman taste.

There can be little doubt that one by one the temples were despoiled of their chief objects of veneration in order that these might contribute to Baal's glory, and attract more worshippers to his shrine.   It was in this way that the Emperor designed to extinguish all the other cults in the city, and so leave his God supreme ; but persecution would have been preferable to contempt. Elagabal's temple was indeed a perfect museum of ecclesiastical relics, all *ad majorem dei gloriam* ; still it did not attract, because it was contrary to the whole spirit of the time ; no one demanded a monotheistic creed, and, though all the worships of the city should be comprehended in that of Elagabal, men could not raise devotion towards an amalgamation which, they felt, was neither good deity nor good philosophy.

Undoubtedly the Emperor was most eager. Why he did not persecute in order to attain his end was a mystery, until men understood something of his psychology. He would go (according to Lampridius) to any lengths of personal inconvenience in order that he might further his plan, but would put no one else to unnecessary discomfort or loss. We are told that his desire to obtain the sacred objects from the temple of Cybele led him to sacrifice fat bulls to that Goddess, with his own hands, and, when that was not enough (as the priests proved difficult), that he submitted himself to their ordination (a ceremony which included cas-tration) in order that he might possess himself of their sacred stone.

Lampridius has been understood to assert this castration, using the words " *genitalia devinxit"* but, as Professor Robinson Ellis has pointed out to me, *devinxit* usually means no more than " tied up." Aurelius Victor, being later, is naturally more explicit. He says "*abscissis genitalibus"* but despite his fourth-century statement, there is considerable ground for doubt as to whether the operation actually took place, chiefly on account of the records which his biographers have left concerning the Emperor's later proclivities— matrimony and the like—in which he is supposed to have indulged until the last moment of his life. And it would certainly have been a miserable ending to a life of pleasure, as he under-stood the meaning of the word. If it is true, it certainly proves a zeal for the Kingdom of Heaven's sake which we are scarcely capable of understanding.

Towards idols made with hands Antonine had no attraction. It was the acquisition of stones with a claim to divinity on which he had set his mind, even (according to a most faulty passage in Lampridius) to the Laodicean statue of Diana, which Orestes with his own hands had placed in its proper sanctuary. These he made, one and all, servants of the only God—some chamberlains, some domestics. Early Christianity had much the same idea as Antonine concerning the position of the older Gods, but, with a singular lack of perspicacity, it turned them into demons, — where they did not become saints,— and by so doing created a power of evil out of what had formerly been a powerful beneficence.

Undoubtedly, one of the Emperor's chief mistakes was his attempt to amalgamate the kindred worship of Jerusalem, in its various forms, with that of the Roman deities, and even though his circumcision almost certainly belongs to the period when he became High Priest of Elagabal (the period when he attained to puberty), the connection of this ceremony with the kindred Jewish observance was sufficient, in the Roman mind, to brand Antonine as a Hebrew innovator. The same odium would not, however, have been attached to him when it was reported that he had submitted to the triune baptism practised by various of the Christian sects ; since this practice was well known to the Romans on account of its inclusion amongst the ceremonies at the Mithraic initiations. The ceremony, therefore, would only become unpopular when men realised that it was an outward and visible sign of their Emperor's inclusion of the Nazarene sect in his grand reunion of churches.

Much has been said by persons, whose business it was to find causes of complaint, against the foolish and blasphemous proposal of the marriage for his God. To our modern notions it was a scheme quite unworthy of the great work the Emperor was inaugurating. In the third century modern notions of religion were as yet unborn. There was at the time many a divine pair, both in Rome and in the provinces, who attracted attention. The proposal was, therefore, neither unusual nor sacrilegious. It was certainly inadvisable to subordinate the chief cult of Rome in the drastic fashion which Antonine employed, and the Emperor paid for his temerity; but when he proposed Urania as consort, no one objected, and it was only the return of the Vestal to connubial felicity that re-aroused the annoyance which his compliance with Roman sentiment had pacified. The idea of matrimony amongst the Gods was quite usual, so much so, that the expressions of the biographers betray wilful ignorance, not only of contemporary religion, but also of the Emperor's scheme and purpose.

Concerning the magnificence of the worship all authorities tell us something, and from them we can gather that, accustomed as the Romans were to a severe and simple ritual, the Syrian worship, whether on the Palatine or in the temple at Jerusa-lem, was a thing for fools to gaze at and wise men to scorn. A few grains of incense, a few drops of wine in libation, a perfect pentameter verse, and the dignified Roman passed on. Here there was one long succession of butchery, hecatombs of oxen, and runlets of the finest wines, which, together with clouds of incense, served to increase the feeling of nausea caused by the smell of the victims. Nor was this all. Round and round the countless altars the wonderful painted boy, in whose eyes fanaticism and mystery glowed, led men and women through the latest and most approved terpsichorean measures, to the accompaniment of a band whose noise recalls that of Nebuchadnezzar ; if there be any truth in either record, as we have it. The psalms and hymns which formed part of the worship were equally unusual in the city of the Caesars ; their only place was in the Eastern religions which gave them birth, because such a display of barbaric worship had long been superseded amongst the intellectual and progressive peoples of the West. Such useless waste of life, such prodigality of movement, music, and colour, was but little in accord with the Western philosophy of religion, and it was with a sigh for his sanity that wise men escaped from the orgy in which their Emperor was taking chief part.

It was all so freakish that men might have looked and listened quietly, if the High Priest—in accordance with his scheme of reform—had not desired the assistance of his great **officers** of state ; naturally, these men objected all the more strongly because they were perforce to profess interest in their new duties, and joyfully spread disaffection, once they were amongst the conspirators and out of the Emperor's hearing.

Lampridius' legend of Antonine's human sacrifices must be dealt with as another calumny. He says that the Emperor used to sacrifice young boys of the best families, preferring those whose parents were alive, and, being present, would be most grieved at the deed. In this case the refutation is scarcely needed, since the author asserts that such was the custom of the Syrian worship, whereas it is now certain that Rome had caused the cessation of human sacrifices long before the second century amongst all Semitic peoples. It is in all probability the same legend which was attached to the early Christian mysteries, and with even less reason, for while the Christian worship was in secret, and so might lend itself to the supposition of nefarious practices, that of the Sun God was public and blatantly open before the world, following a well-known and approved ritual.

No, Antonine may have been mad, but there was a certain method in his madness, and this form of lunacy would only have alienated the very people he was striving so hard to win. It was in the method he failed, not in the conception, for monotheism was continually gaining ground; Paganism was obviously falling asleep quite gently; Isis was giving way to Mary, apo-theosis to canonisation, and saints succeeding divinities. Antonine, with the true Eastern conception of religion, strove to impress men with his vivid monotheism by means of the magnificence of the worship, the prodigal expenditure of a gorgeous pageant. This he gave the world right royally, but it was precisely this that the austere Roman could not understand was meant to be connected with the simple philosophy of his Western religion. Antonine thought to make his God great by means of a pom-pous show. He succeeded in presenting him as a low comedian in the last act of a puerile melodrama; unfortunately not the first, or last, deity who has been thus presented before the eyes of an astonished world.

It had long been a Roman custom to commemorate the greatest of her victories by the erection of gigantic columns in the forums of the city; Antonine proposed to build the most magnificent that had yet greeted human eyes. It was to be a memorial to the triumph of the Lord over the deities of chance and circumstance. Its summit, which he designed should be reached by a stairway inside, was to support the great meteorite. Death intervened to spoil the plan and to deprive Rome of a monument surpassing in grandeur any that the city should ever see. Such were the methods by which the boy strove to win acceptance for Elagabal, and through him for the great monotheistic prin-ciple in religion. It must be clearly understood that the religion of Emesa was in no sense idola-trous. It is true that the city possessed a huge black meteorite, which it venerated exceedingly, because it was a portion of the being of its God. In shape, we are told, it was a Phallus, and as such was the symbol of fecund life, typifying the great force of light, joy, and fruitfulness, which men regarded as the be-all and end-all of their existence.

Of this theory in religion Marcus Aurelius An-toninus was high priest and chief exponent, and even his boy's mind could see the superiority of life to death, of the supreme beneficent being to the lesser deities who oppressed other peoples. Certainly he was so impressed, and resolved to spread that worship and knowledge by means of the vast power which resided in his childish hands from the year of grace 218.

Little, when the young Emperor undertook the task of unifying churches, could he have imagined the magnitude of the task, or the reason of the opposition. As we have said, this opposition came from the fact that an entirely different system of religion held sway. To-day we would call the Roman system natural 'religion and Antonine's conception dogmatic truth. He ascribed too much to his God, which is no uncommon failing amongst the credulous ; probably he claimed a revelation from on high, and was inclined to consign those who disagreed with him to that special limbo which the ignorant have reserved for all those who make them look foolish, for all that spells truth contrary to their own limited imaginings ; if so, he would not have been unusual. The genius of natural religion is that it is comprehensive, tolerant, righteous and just. It has no dogma save the individual experience of each. The genius of dogmatic religion lies in the assumption to itself of absolute exclusiveness; it alone contains truth, and in its later editions, finality as well. Whether Antonine's form included this latter pretension we do not know, certainly it claimed what no Roman thinker could accord to any faith under the sun—the proposition that God was one and God was supreme. The Roman had been bred on Pyrrho, Epicurus, Lucretius, and Cicero, and was more inclined to postulate that God was the cosmic entity of spirit, something as potent as, if not analogous to, the entity of electricity in modern science. He had no relations with the older deities who had made life terrible by their persecutions of the human race, and had no desire to submit himself again to a system which would erect fright into yet another national deity. He had long since grown weary of trying to propitiate infinity, and now understood that he might as well sacrifice to the animals in the Zoological Gardens, in the hope of staying their hunger, as make oblation to the deities in the expectation of a return in kind.

This was no new struggle that Antonine proposed to inaugurate in the city of Rome. It is the contest between rationalism and dogma when pushed to its logical conclusion. Doubtless there is much to be said on both sides; certainly much has been written and more has been said during the history of civilisation. The rationalists have set it forth as the struggle between ignor-ance and reason; the dogmatists as that between good and evil; certainly it was not a struggle on which Antonine was either old enough or wise enough to lay down any definite line of truth for the future guidance of the world. Unfortun-ately, this was just what he attempted to do. He knew that the national deity of every nation under heaven was fright, and forgot that its anti-thesis was truth. He knew that fright was bound to predominate ; that men would continue to pay their worship as they paid their taxes, lest a worse thing should happen to them. It had been the same in Homer's day. Men had been brought up to fright, and as one God died they demanded another. The Prophets had given men Gods, laughing the while at the divinities they created, because they believed as little in the sacerdotal fables as Tennyson did in the phantom idylls of Arthurian romance.

The point is, that what the mass of men demand they will get. It is the usual law of supply and demand, where the man who can increase' the 'demand and satisfy it to any extent is the successful founder of a new religion. This is undoubtedly the business of the sacerdotal caste in every generation, and their success is assured as long as they are capable of increasing the supply, while they whet the demand. They fail when someone else appeals to popular imagination as more mysterious, or more spiritual.

Now, Antonine seemed to think that mere dictation of what was to himself obvious should be enough to give his God a start, and, that done, all men would discover the vital attraction for them-selves. Perhaps he was right; stranger things had happened before his day, and were to happen not long afterwards; we can never know, as the system had no more time for a fair trial than had that of Constantine's successor Julian.

For the moment Rome was bored with all Gods; they had found them so cruel, vindictive, and malignant that the citizens had got irritated and sceptical, had left their deities feeling that already for too long time had blood and treasure been spent without avail. Now at last, men said, "dread has vanished and in its place is the ideal." Evemerus had asserted that the Gods were just ordinary bullies who would cringe if men stood up to them, and even the lower classes had agreed with him.

This, Antonine felt, was a deplorable state of affairs—rank atheism if not something worse. He knew the potency of his God, and desired, by gentle means, to set it forth to others that they too might believe. Unfortunately, no one desired belief, and he had to fight against rationalism as well as convention. The Romans were not yet tired of their chase after impossible delights; when they were, another dogma presented itself, and as often as not it was accepted, as being the line of least resistance.

If Antonine had given them what Julian did, his success would have been assured. Such was philo-sophy, freedom, and beauty under the guise of a God whose existence he admitted, but whose intervention he denied. Antonine was not Julian; he was an

Eastern monotheist, far nearer to the worship and doctrines of Jehovah than to those of any Western mode of thought. He could not understand the deification of attributes, because he wanted something more tangible, real, and superstitious, something that appealed to his neurotic nature and erotic passions.

Thus it is that his vain efforts to unite all worship, all religions in that dedicated to Deus Solus are derided, as well by the monotheistic Hebrew as by the tritheistic Christian. His fault lay in the fact that he was too young for the work, too unaccustomed to the circuitous and mole-like burrowings by which a religion captures society. But the scheme in itself showed purpose and a pre-cocious propensity for the mysterious, unnatural and unhealthy in a child of his age.

Had Antonine been born in the twentieth instead of the third century of this era, had he enjoyed the advantages of a modern education, he would have learned that religion and unusual propensities are the last things a gentleman is expected to parade before the world. Further, he would have certainly emerged from the training—which though drastic is certainly   most   salutary—with his waywardness curbed, his mind and will strengthened, his lithe and graceful body healthy and fit to bear the fatigues and responsibilities which life was going to lay upon his splendid shoulders. Unfortunately for him, he was a Syrian with wonderful eyes and a mystical temperament, and was born at a time when the monarch's wayward will was a law unto himself and all the world besides ; yet despite these draw-backs, with so many of the elements of success to hand, he might have triumphed, if the usual conspirators had not been at work. "Rome was still mistress of the world though she was growing very old. A few more years and the Earth's new children fell upon her; then the universe was startled by the uproar of her agony. Then and not till then, where the thunderbolt had gleamed did the emaciated figure of the crucifix appear, and upon the shoulders of a prelate descended the purple which had dazzled the world."

BIBLIOGRAPHY

Accursius (Bonus). Vitae Caesarum. 1475.

Arnold (W. T.). Roman Provincial Administration. Oxford, 1906.

Audollent (A.).

1. Carthage romaine. 1901. École françhaise a Athènes.
2. Mission épigraphique en Algérie. 1890. École françhaise a Rome. Aurelius Victor.

Historia Romana. 1819.

De vita et moribus imperatorum Romanorum. 1533.

Breviarium. Antwerp, 1579.

Baumeister (A.). Denkmäler des klassischen Altertums. München and Leipzig, 1884.

Bayle (P.). Dictionnaire historique et critique. Paris, 1820. Beaumanoir (Jean de). Variétés historiques et littéraires. (Reprint) 1855. Becker (U.).

Observationes in S.H.A.[60] Breslau, 1S38. Bernhardy (G.).

Proemii de S.H.A. Halle, 1845-6.

Bibliotheca scrip. Lat. Halle, 1838-47. Bernouilli (J. J.). Römische Iconographie. Stuttgart, 1882-94.

Bibliothèque des Écoles françaises d'Athènes et de Rome. Paris, 1877.

BINET Sanglé. Bibliothèque de l'École de Psychologie. Paris, 1905.

Bloch (Iwan). Sexual Life of our Times. Rebman and Sons, 1910.

Blount (Chas.). Two first Books of Philostratus' Life of Apollonius of Tyana. London, 1680.

Boehme. Dexippi fragmenta. Leipzig, 1882.

Boissier (Gaston).

L'Opposition sous les Césars. Paris, 1905.

La Religion romaine d'Augustus aux Antonins. Paris, 1874.

La Fin du paganisme. Paris, 1891.

L'Afrique romaine. Paris, 1909.

Borghesi (Count Bartolommeo). (Euvres. Paris, 1862-97.

Bouché Leclercq (Aug.).

Les Pontifes de l'ancienne Rome. Paris, 1871.

Manuel des institutions romaines. Paris, 1886.

Leçons d'histoire romaine, République et Empire. Paris, 1909.

Boxhorn (M. Z.). Historiae Augustae scriptores. Leyden, 1632.

Brocks (Emil). Studien zu den S.H.A. Marienwerder, 1877.

[60] S.H.A. - Scriptores Historiae Augustae. 289

De quattuor prioribus S.H.A. Koenigsberg, 1869.

Bulletin de l'Éicole française a Athenes. Athens, 1868.

Bulletin de correspondance hellénique. Athens and Paris, 1877, etc.

Burton Brown (E.). Recent Excavations in the Roman Forum. 1904.

Bury (Prof. J. B.).

Gibbon's Decline and Fall. 1909.

Constitution of Later Empire. 1910.

History of Later Roman Empire. 1889. Bussell (F. W.).

Marcus Aurelius and the later Stoics. 1910.

The Roman Empire. London, 1910. Butler (O. F.). Heliogabalus. 1908.
University of Michigan Studies.

Cagnat (René).

L'Armée romaine d'Afrique. Paris, 1892.

Inscrip. Africae Proc. Lat. Eds. R. Cagnat et J. Schmidt. Soc. Reg. Sci. Berlin,
1891.

Callegari (E.). Quando abbia cominciato a regnare Alexandro Severo? 1876.

Carpenter (Edward). Iolaus. 1902.

Love's Coming of Age. 1906. Prisons, Police, and Punishment. 1905. Die
homogene Liebe, etc. Leipzig, 1895. Casaubon (Isaac). Hist. Aug. Script, vi.
1603.

Ceuleneer (Adolphe de). La Vie et règne de Septime Sévère. Liége, 1884.

Clinton (H. F.). Fasti Romani. Oxford, 1845-50.

Cohen (Henry). Description historique des monnaies frappées sous l'empire
romaine. Paris, 1884. Consularia Constantinopolitana. Monumenta Germ. Hist.,
Chronica minora, vol. ix. Berlin, 1892.

Conybeare (F. C). Myth, Magic, and Morals. London, 1910.

Corpus Inscriptionum Latinorum, vol. viii.

Coulanges (Fustel de).

La Cité antique. Strasbourg, 1864.

Histoire des insts. politiques de l'ancienne France. Paris, 1875. Cumont (F.).
The Mysteries of Mithra. 1903.

Les Religions orientales dans le paganisme romain. (Conférences),
3. Textes et monuments figurés relatifs aux mysteres de Mithra. 2 vols. Brux,
1899, 96.

Czwalina (C). De fide atque auctoritate epistularum auctorumque quae a S.H.A.
proferuntur. Bonn, 1870.

Daendliker (Karl). Die drei letzten Bücher Herodians. Buedinger Untersuch.
vol. iii. Leipzig, 1870.

Daremberg et Saglio. Dictionnaire des antiquités grecques et romaines. Paris,
1873 and fol. Dessau (Hermann).

Über die S.H.A. Hermes, vol. xxvii., 1892.

Prosopographia, Imper. Rom. vol. ii. Berlin, 1899, etc.

Die Uberlieferung der S.H.A. Hermes, vol. xxix., 1894.

Über Zeit und Persönlichkeit der S.H.A. Hermes, vol. xxiv., 1889.

Dieudonné (A.). Revue numismatique. Paris.

Dill (Sir Samuel).

ı. Roman Society from Nero to Marcus Aurelius. London, 1904. 2. Roman
Society in the Last Century of the Western Empire. London, 1898.

Dion Cassius. History of Rome. Teubner Classics. 1863. Dirksen (H. E.).

1. Die S.H.A. Leipzig, 1842.

2. Über Verfügungen der rom. Kaiser. Kön. Pr. Ak. Abhdl. 1846.

Domaszewski (Alfred von).

Geschichte der römischen Kaiser. Leipzig, 1909.

Abhandlungen zur römischen Religion. Leipzig and Berlin, 1909.

Die Rangordnung des römischen Heeres. Bonner Jahrbuch, vol. cxvii.,.
1898.

Religion des römischen Heeres. Trier, 1895.

Drake. Studies in the S.H.A. American Journal of Philology. 1899.

Dreinhoefer (A.). De fontibus et auctoribus vitarum quae feruntur Spartiani,
etc. Halle, 1875. Duruy (Victor).

ı. Histoire universelle. 1846.

2. Histoire des Romains. 1879.

Duviquet (Georges). Héliogabale. Paris, 1903.

Echkel (J. ll. von). Doctrina num. vet. vol. vii. Vienna, 1797.

Egbert (J. C). Introduction to the Study of Latin Inscriptions. New York, 1896.

Ellis (Professor Robinson).

Correspondence of Fronto and M. Aurelius. London, 1904.

Hermathena, vols. xiii. and xiv. Dublin, 1905-6.

Enmann (A.). Eine verlorene Geschichte der röm. Kaiser. Philologus, Supplt.
vol. ix. 1901.

Eusebius. Ecclesiastical History. Introduction by W. Bright. Oxford, 1872.

Eussner (Dr. A.). Bericht über die neueste Literatur zu den römischen
Historikern bis zum Schluss des Jahres 1877. Jahresbericht Forch. Class. Alt. vol.
xxii. 1882.

Eutropius (F.). Breviarium ab urbe condita. (Teubner Classics.) Leipzig, 1887.

Ferrero (G.).

The Greatness and Decline of Rome. London, 1907.

Characters and Events of Roman History from Caesar to Nero.
London, 1909. Forel (A.).

ı. The Sexual Question. New York, 1908. 2. Sexual Ethics. London, 1908.

Forquet de Dorxe (C). Les Césars africains et syriens, et Panarchie militaire. Angers, 1905. Foster (H. B.). Dion Cassius. Troy, New York, 1905. Frazer (J. G.). Adonis, Attis, Osiris. London, 1907.

Totemism and Exogamy. London, 1910.

Friedländer (Ludwig). Darstellung aus der Sittengeschichte Roms. Leipzig, 1888-90 and 1910.

Froelich (Franz). Die Mode im alten Rom. 1884.

Gemoll (Albrecht).

Die S.H.A.I. Leipzig, 1886.

Spicilegium criticum in S.H.A. Wohlau, 1876.

Giambelli (Carlo). Gli Scrittori della Storia Augusta. Rome, 1881.

GINZEL (F. K.). Spezieller Kanon der Sonnen - und Mondfinstemisse für das Ländergebiet der klassischen Altertumswissenschaften. Berlin, 1899. Glover (T. R).

Conflict of Religions under the Early Roman Empire. London, 1909.

Studies in the Fourth Century. Cambridge, 1901.

Gourmont (Remu de). Introduction to Duviquet's Héliogabale. Paris, 1903. Groebe (P.).

Pauly-Wissowa, R.E. vol. ii., article on Alexander Severus.

Die Obstruktion im röm. Senat. Beiträge zur alten Geschichte, vol. v. 1905.

Gulich (L. H.). The Efficient Life. New York, 1907.

Habel (Paul). De pont. Rom. inde ab Augusto usque ad Aurelium. Vrat., 1888.

Hall (Dr. G. Stanley). Psychology of Adolescence. New York, 1904.

Haupt (H.). Dio Cassius. Philologus, vol. xliv. Havelock-Ellis (H.). Sexual Psychology. 1897 and 1899.

Haverfield (F. J.). Translation of Mommsen's Provinces of Rom. Emp. from Caesar to Diocletian. 1909. Henzen (G.).

Acta fratrum Arvalium quae supersunt. 1874.

Inscriptiones urbis Romae Latinae. Henzen and De Rossi, Soc. Reg. Sci. Berlin, 1876-82.

Fasti consulares. Soc. Reg. Sci. Berlin, 1863.

Herodian. Herodiani ab excessu Divi Marci libri octo. (Bekker rec, Teubner Classics.) Leipzig, 1855. Herzog (Ernst). Geschichte und System der römischen Staatsverfassung. Leipzig, 1884.

Heer (J. M.). Der historische Wert der Vita Commodi. Leipzig, 1901.

And in Philologus Supplt. vol. iv., 1883. Hieronymus. Letters and Select Works. Eds. Wace and Shaff. Oxford, 1893.

Hirschfeld (H. O.). Die Rangtitel der röm. Kaiserzeit. Sitzungsber. Der Berlin. Acad. 1901.

Hirschfeld (M.). Sappho und Sokrates. Leipzig, 1902. Hitchcock (A. W.). Psychology of Jesus. Boston, 191 o. Hopkins (R. V. N.). Life of Alexander Severus. Cambridge. 1889.

Huelsen (c).

Die Ausgrabungen auf dem Forum Romanum. Mitt. Deutsch. Inst., Rom. Abt., vols. xvi. and xvii. 1891-2.

Vierter Jahresbericht über neue Funde und Forschungen zur Topographic der Stadt Rom. 1892-94. Hydatius. Migne, Pat. Lat. vol. li. col. 904.

Imperial Chronicle. Mommsen, Monumenta Germ. Hist., Chronica minora, vol. ix. Berlin, 1892.

Jastrow (M.). The Religion of Babylonia and Assyria. 1898. John of Antioch. Edition Mueller, Fragmenta Hist. Graec. 1S41. Jordan (ll.). Die Resultate der Ausgrabungen auf dem Forum zu Rom.

Hermes, vol. vii., 1873. Jornandes. Chronica Magistri Jordanis. Monumenta Germ. Hist.

Julianus. Convivium. (Hertlein, Editor, Teubner Classics.) 1875.

Klebs (Kumar).

Die Vita des Avidius Cassius. Rhein. Mus. vol. xliii., 1888.

Die Sammlung der S.H.A. Rhein. Mus. vols. xlv. and xlvii., 1890-92.

Das dynastische Element in der Geschichtsschreibung der röm. Kaiserzeit. Hist. Zeitschrift, N.F. vol. xxv., 1889.

Koerte (Alfred). Kleinasiatische Studien. Mitt, der deutsch. Arch. Inst., Athen Abt., vol. xiv.. 1899.

Kornemann (Ernst).

Kaiser Hadrian und der letztegrosse Historiker von Rom. Leipzig, 1905. , 2. De civibus Romanis in provinciis Imperii consistentibus. 1892 (Berliner Studien).

3. Die neuste Limesfoischung im Licht der röm. kai. Grenzpolitik. Klio. Beiträge zur alten Geschichte, vol. vii., 1907. Krafft-Ebing (R. von). Pyschopathia Sexualis. Stuttgart, 1886.

Krause (A.). De fontibus et auctoritate S.H.A. Neustettin, 1874.

Kreutzer. De Herodian. rer. Rom. scriptore. 1881. Kruger (Paul). Codex Justinianus. 1888.

Lampridius (Ae.). Vita Héliogabale (Edit. h. Peter, Teubner Classics). Leipzig, 1884.

Lanciani (R. A.).

l. Pagan and Christian Rome. London, 1892.

Topographia di Roma antica. Rome, 1880.

Lécrivain (C). Études sur l'histoire Auguste. 1904.

Leigh (E. and H.). Choice Observations on the Roman Emperors.

London, 1657. Lessing (C).

Studien zu den S.H.A. Berlin, 1889.

Lexikon der S.H.A. Leipzig, 1901-6.

Marcellinus (Ammianus). Rerum gestarum libri qui supersunt (Edit. V. Gardthausen, Teubner Classics). Leipzig, 1874.

Marolles (M. de). L'Histoire Auguste des six auteurs anciens. 1667.

Marquardt (G.). Staatsverwaltung, 1887. Mead (G. R. S.). Life of Apollonius of Tyana. London, 1901.

Mediobarbus (F.). Imperatorum Romanorum numismata. 1683.

Milne (J.). Hist, of Egypt under Roman Rule. 1898.

Moll (A.). Die conträre Sexualempfindung. Berlin, 1891.

Mommsen (Theodor).

Die S.H.A. Hermes, vol. xxv., i860.

Rom. Staatsrecht. 1876, Bande 1-3.

Monumenta Germ. Hist., Chronica minora, vol. ix. Berlin, 1892.

Römische Forschungen. Berlin, 1864-79.

Römische Geschichte. Berlin, 1856-57.

Moulines (G. de). Les Écrivains de l'histoire Auguste. Paris, 1806.

Movers (F. C). Die Phoenizier, 2 vols. Bonn, 1841.

Muche (Eugenius). De imperatore M. Aur. Sev. Alex. Vratislav., 1868.

Mueller (J. J.). Der Geschichtsschreiber Marius Maximus. Buedinger Untersuch. vol. iii., Leipzig, 1870.

Niebuhr (B. G.).

Rhein. Mus. fur Philol. und Gesch. Bonn, 1827, etc. (Ed. Niebuhr.)

Römische Geschichte. Jena, 1844-45.

1. Niehues (Bernard).

De Aclio Cordo rerum Augustarum scriptore commentatio. Muenster in Westfalen, 1885.

De Vulcacii Gallicani vita Avidii Cassii commentatio. Muenster, 1885-86.

Notizie degli scavi. 1885.

Oberdick (J.). Die Römerfeindlichen Bewegungen im Orient. Berlin, 1869.

Oppolzer. Canon der Finsternisse. Kaiserliche Akademie der Wissenschaften, Band 52. Wien, 1850. Orosius (Paulus). Adversum Paganos libri VII. historiarum. Leipzig, 1889. (Teubner Classics.)

Pagi (Ant.). Dissertatio hypatica. Lugduni, 1682.

Pasciucco (Giac). Elagabalo. Feltre, 1905. Pater (Walter II.).

Marius the Epicurean. London, 1885.

Greek Studies. London, 1895.

Miscellaneous Studies. London, 1895.

Paucker (C. von). De latinitate Scriptorum Historiae Augustae. Dorpat, 1872.

Pauly-Wissowa. Real-Encyclopädie. Stuttgart, 1894 fol.

Peter (Hermann). Historia critica. Leipzig, 1860.

Die Scriptores Historiae Augustae in den Tahren von 1865-82. Jahresbericht, Philologus, 1884.

Exercitationes criticae in S. H. A. Posen, 1863.

Die S.H.A. : sex literargeschichtliche Untersuchungen. Leipzig, 1892.

Bericht über die Literatur zu den S. II. A. in dem Jahrzhent 18S3-92.

Jahresbericht F.C.A. vol. lxxiii., 1894.

Bericht über die litteratur zu den S.H.A. in den Jahren 18593-1905.

Jahresbericht F.C.A. vol. cxxx., 1907.

Berliner Wochenschrift für Philologie, vol. xxii., 1902, and vol. xxv.,1905.

8.   Historicorum Romanorum Fragmenta. (Teubner.) Leipzig, 1883.

Petronius Arbiter.

Cena Trimalchionis. Lowe. 1905.

Satyricon. Bohn. 1883.

Philostratus. Life of Apollonius. (Teubner Classics.) Leipzig, 1870.

PIGNORIUS (Lorenz). Epistola I,. Pignorii qua l'aulum Romae patriae adversus Bertrandum asserit. 1718.

Plew (J.).

1. Kritische Beiträge zu den Scriptores Historiae Augustae. Strassburg, 1885.

2.   Marius Maximus als direkte und indirekte Quelle der S.H.A. Strassburg, 1878.

3.   De diversitate auctorum Hist. Aug. Scrip. Koenigsberg, 1869.

Preuner (August). Hestia Vesta. Tubingen, 1864.

Prosopographia Imp. Rom. Dessau and Klebs (Editors). Berlin, 1897.

Ramsay (Sir Wm. M.). Cities and Bishoprics of Phrygia. Oxford, 1895.

Renan (J. E.). Marc-Aurèle et la fin du monde antique. Paris, 1882.

Reville (J.). La Religion à Rome sous les Sévères. Paris, 1886.

Richter (Fr.). Über die VI. S.H.A. Rhein. Mus. vol. vii., 1850.

Richter (Otto Ludwig). Topographia der Stadt Rom. 1901.

Roscher (W. H.). Ausführliches Lexikon der griechischen und römischen Mythologie. Leipzig, 1884, etc.

Rubensohn (M.). Zur Chronologie des Kaisers Alexander Severus und ihrer literarischen Überlieferung. Hermes, vol. xxv., 1890.

Ruebel (C). De fontibus quatuor priorum S.H.A. Bonn, 1873 (Diss.). Rufus (Sextus). Opera. Bibliothèque Latine-Française. Paris, 1843.

Saltus (E. E.).

Imperial Purple. London, 1906.

The Anatomy of Negation. London, 1886.

Historia Amoris. London, 1906.

Saumaise (C). Historiae Augustae Scriptores. Paris, 1620.

Schiller (H.). Geschichte der römischen Kaiserzeit. Gotha, 1883-87.

Schulz (Otto).
Beiträge zur Kritik unserer literarischen Überlieferung für die Zeit von Commodus' Sturze bis auf den Tod Caracalla's. Leipzig, 1903.
Leben des Kaisers Hadrian. Leipzig, 1904.
Kaiserhaus der Antonin. Leipzig, 1907.

Serviez (Roergas de). Les Impératrices romaines. Paris, 1728.

Seyffert (O). Dictionary of Classical Antiquities. London, 1902.

Seeck (O.).
1. Die Entstehungszeit der S.H.A. Neue Jahrbücher Phil, und Pad. vol. cxli., 1890.
2. Zur Echtheitsfrage der S.H.A. Rhein. Mus. vol. xlix., 1894.

Smith (W. Robertson). Religion of the Semites. 1889-94.

Smits. De Héliogabale et Alexandro Severe Amsterdam, 1902.

Spon (J.). Recherches curieuses d'antiquité. Lyon, 1683.

Stobbe (J. E. O.). Tribunat der Kaiser. Philol. vol. xxxii., 1873.

Strabo. Geographica. (Ed. A. Meineke, Teubner Classics.) Leipzig,1852.

Studniczka (F. J.). Mitt. Deutsch. Arch. Inst., Röm. Abt., vol. xvi.

Suetonius Tranquillus. Quae supersunt omnia. (Ed. C. L. Roth, Teubner Classics.) Leipzig, 1908.

Symonds (J. A.).
ı. Sketches in Italy and Greece. London, 1874.
Studies of Greek Poets. London, 1893.
A Problem in Greek Ethics. 1901. Privately Printed.
Essays Speculative and Suggestive. London, 1907.
In the Key of Blue. London, 1893.

Teuffel und Schwabe. History of Roman Literature. London, 1900. Tristan (Jean), Sieur de St. Amant. Commentaires historiques contenants l'histoire générale des Empereurs et Impératrices de l'Empire romain. Paris, 1644.

Tropea (Giac). Studi sugli S.H.A. Messina, 1899.

Turre. Dissertatio apologetica de annis imperii Marci Aurelii Antonini Elagabali. Patav., 1713.

Valerius Maximus. Opera. (Ed. C. Kempf, Teubner Classics.) Leipzig, 1888.

Valsecchius. Dissertatio historica chronologica de Marci Aurelii Antonini Elagabali tribunitia potestate. Florence, 1711.

Wahle (F. J.). De imperatore Alexandra Severa quaestiones hist. 1867.

Weininger (Otto). Sex and Character. London, 1906.

Whittaker (Thos.). Apollonius of Tyana and other Essays. London, 1906.

Wirth (Albrecht). Quaestiones Severianae. Leipzig, 1888.

Woelfflin (Eduard). ı. Die S.H.A. 1892.

2. Sitzungsberichte der philos.-philol. Klasse der K. Bayer. Akad. 1891.

Wotton (W.). Roman History. London, 1701.

Ziedler. Universal Lexicon. Leipzig and Halle, 1740.

Zonaras.

1. Epitome historiarum. (Teubner Classics.) 1868.

2. Annales. (Ed. M. Pinderi.) Bonn, 1841-97.

Zosimus. Ex recognitione I. Bekkeri. Bonn, 1837.

THE END

Made in the USA
Monee, IL
22 March 2024

55518511R00095